Berkshire County Library.

This book must be returned to the Local Librarian within **14 days** from the latest date marked below.

YALE STUDIES IN ENGLISH
Benjamin Christie Nangle · Editor

VOLUME 122

THE OLD ENGLISH

𝕰𝖝𝖔𝖉𝖚𝖘

EDITED WITH INTRODUCTION, NOTES, AND GLOSSARY BY

EDWARD BURROUGHS IRVING, JR.

INSTRUCTOR IN ENGLISH, YALE UNIVERSITY

NEW HAVEN: YALE UNIVERSITY PRESS, 1953

LONDON: GEOFFREY CUMBERLEGE, OXFORD UNIVERSITY PRESS

999 9 022140

for M. K. I.

PREFACE

THE Old English poem *Exodus* has been frequently edited, as a whole and in part, and the first duty of a new editor is to justify his own undertaking. The reasons for the present edition will perhaps emerge most clearly in a brief review of the long history of the *Exodus* text at the hands of its various editors.

Nearly 300 years ago, in 1655, the Dutch scholar Franciscus Junius first published the Junius Manuscript as "Cædmon's Paraphrase," seeing as one long poem the collection which we now know contains at least five separate poems (*Genesis A, Genesis B, Exodus, Daniel,* and *Christ and Satan*). Benjamin Thorpe published the first readable text in 1832 together with a translation and a few notes. Karl Bouterwek's edition (1851–54) contained an elaborate commentary but suffered from excessive and often unnecessary emendation. C. W. M. Grein's edition of 1857 was sounder; he first formally distinguished the separate poems and consequently gave the poem we now know as *Exodus* its name.

Of more recent editions the best, in spite of its shortcomings, is that of F. A. Blackburn (1907), who edited the poem together with *Daniel*. He saw clearly the imperative necessity for more extensive explanatory notes and in his commentary provided much useful information, in particular by detecting a number of the many biblical allusions which the poet employs. Yet Blackburn's extremely conservative method of dealing with the text leaves much to be desired. He preserves MS readings where they are almost certainly meaningless and indefensible and too often disregards any metrical standard for judging the plausibility of a line.

W. J. Sedgefield included most of the poem in his *Anglo-Saxon Verse-Book* (1922), but the treatment of *Exodus* there is naturally not a complete one and is marred by some fairly insensitive and highhanded emendations. In 1927 Sir Israel Gollancz published a fine facsimile reproduction of the whole Junius MS. His introduction provides some interesting speculation on specific problems of interpretation and draws attention to the importance of the background of traditional biblical commentary.

The latest edition, that of George Philip Krapp (1931), shares the unavoidable defects of the *Anglo-Saxon Poetic Records* series as a whole in that sources and larger problems beyond the merely textual are treated summarily or not at all. Too narrow a basis for judging the worth of an emendation is furnished, since no background material is available either in the notes or in the brief introduction.

In addition to these editions there is a vast body of textual commentary scattered in notes in various periodicals. More important still, such basic studies as those of Samuel Moore and James A. Bright on the probable sources of both the poem as a whole and of individual passages have yet to be given proper attention in an actual edition of the poem, beside the text where they belong.

Exodus presents so many difficult problems of interpretation that the marshalling of all our knowledge is required for even partial understanding. I have tried to bring together the most useful elements of past scholarship and the results of my own investigations with the single aim of clarifying the text and making it as readable as possible. Many obscurities remain unsolved, but some are now provided with plausible explanations. I have made a special effort to define the unique qualities of the poem as precisely as possible—to point out, for example, that the poet was neither an ignorant primitive nor a religious sophisticate, to mention the two extreme views which have been proposed in the past.

In its original form this edition was submitted to the faculty of the Graduate School of Yale University as a dissertation for the degree of Doctor of Philosophy. I wish to acknowledge my heavy debt to the counsel and kindly encouragement given to me from the outset of my studies in Old English by the late Robert J. Menner. Benjamin C. Nangle has been of great assistance in the preparation of the manuscript. I owe thanks to my father, Edward B. Irving, and to William P. Hayes for substantial help. E. Talbot Donaldson has read the manuscript and offered some useful criticism. For his patience in criticizing the manuscript in all its stages and for the many improvements he has suggested, my greatest debt is to John C. Pope.

EDWARD B. IRVING, JR.

TABLE OF CONTENTS

INTRODUCTION

I. *The Manuscript*

THE MS in which the poem *Exodus* is included is in the Bodleian Library at Oxford and is known officially as MS Junius XI but is commonly referred to simply as the Junius Manuscript or the Cædmon Manuscript. A complete description of the MS as a whole may be found elsewhere; [1] here only a brief summary of the facts will be given.

The MS consists of 116 parchment folios, 12¾ inches by about 7¾ inches, in 17 gatherings, usually of 8 leaves, although some are missing. The pages are numbered from 1 to 229 by a modern hand. The MS was bound in the fifteenth century in vellum-covered oak boards. Four scribal hands are discernible in the handwriting. The first scribe wrote the poems *Genesis* (pp. 1–142), *Exodus* (pp. 143–71), and *Daniel* (pp. 173–212); the other three scribes wrote *Christ and Satan* (pp. 213–29). The first hand, with which we are here concerned, has been dated about the year 1000. [2] The other hands seem to be about a generation later. [3]

The portion of the MS which contains *Exodus* presents no difficulties so far as legibility goes; it is written in a clear hand with only a few erasures or corrections. There is no positive evidence that the scribe considered *Exodus* to be a separate poem. It begins on p. 143 following a page left two-thirds blank after the final lines of *Genesis* and ends on p. 171 where, after a blank page, the poem *Daniel* begins. So much blank space is to be found in this MS, however, that these occurrences mean little. The first letter of the poem, on the other hand, is an elaborately ornamented zoomorphic capital *H* resembling closely the capitals which appear in *Genesis* up to p. 68 and which no longer appear beyond that point. The isolated appearance of this one capital, which is the only decorative touch in the *Exodus* portion of the text, offers some evidence

1. F. H. Stoddard, "The Cædmon Poems in MS Junius XI," *Anglia, 10* (1888), 157–67; Sir Israel Gollancz, Introduction to *The Cædmon Manuscript* (a facsimile reproduction, Oxford, 1927); G. P. Krapp, *The Junius Manuscript, Anglo-Saxon Poetic Records, 1* (New York, 1931), ix–xxiv; B. J. Timmer, *The Later Genesis* (Oxford, 1948), pp. 3–10, on history of the MS; the illustrations are discussed by C. R. Morey in an article appended to C. W. Kennedy's translation, *The Cædmon Poems* (New York, 1916), pp. 177–95.

2. Wolfgang Keller, *Angelsächsische Palaeographie* (Berlin, 1906), p. 19, places it in the last decade of the tenth century.

3. Gollancz, p. xviii; M. D. Clubb, ed., *Christ and Satan*, Yale Studies in English, 70 (New Haven, 1925), pp. xi–xiii.

that the poem was regarded as a separate unit and that its beginning was to be specially indicated. Space has been left for capitals on pp. 146, 148, and 149; after this someone, possibly the scribe, proceeded to furnish rather simple capitals of his own for the rest of the poem.

The problem of capitals is only part of the problem of the illustrations (and lack of them) in this MS. The following table shows the occurrence of blank space in the *Exodus* portion:

Page
144	Top half of page blank.	11 written lines.
145	Bottom half blank.	13 written lines.
147	Bottom two-thirds blank.	9 written lines.
149	Bottom third blank.	17 written lines.
150	Completely blank.	
152	Completely blank.	
153	Bottom two-thirds blank.	9 written lines.
155	Bottom two-thirds blank.	8 written lines.
156	Bottom third blank.	18 written lines.
157	Top two-thirds blank.	9 written lines.
159	Completely blank.	
163	Some blank space at bottom.	20 written lines.
164	Completely blank except for the words "tribus annis transactis" in later hand.	
165	Completely blank.	
168	Completely blank.	
171	(Conclusion of poem) Bottom two-thirds blank.	10 written lines.
172	Completely blank.	
173	*Daniel* begins.	

The system of leaving blank space for illustrations is followed in a similar way throughout "Liber 1," the section of the MS containing the first three poems. Illustrations fill the spaces in *Genesis* up to p. 96, but none appear after that point. It is certain that the blank spaces were to have been filled with drawings eventually and that there must have been some elaborate planning and collaboration between scribe and artist (or editor) in the placing of blank spaces. In the margin of p. 98 are found the words *healf trymt* and on p. 100 *healf tm̃t;* as Krapp points out,[4] the abbreviated word is *tramet* 'page' and the notation is a direction to the scribe to leave a half page vacant for the illustrator.

The foregoing subject has been treated in some detail for the bearing it might have on possible rearrangements of the text or the reconstruction of missing sections of the text.

Other aspects of the general appearance of the MS are covered thor-

4. *The Junius Manuscript,* p. xviii.

oughly in Krapp's Introduction. There are a great number of accents in the MS, occurring seemingly without much system on both long and short syllables.[5] The most common form of punctuation is the dot, which sets off phrase units or metrical half-lines fairly regularly throughout. On the whole the scribe is quite accurate in following the meter, although he occasionally makes mistakes, usually where he may not have understood the meaning of the passage.[6] In addition to the dot there is a mark consisting of a dot with a check over it, very frequent in *Genesis* but quite rare in *Exodus*.[7] It may mean in this part of the text little more than the end of a page. Perhaps a heavier mark (or fuller stop) is intended by the mark consisting of two dots with a sign resembling the OE abbreviation for "and" beneath them. This is found on p. 163 at the bottom, after l. 446, where one would expect a full stop from the sense, and in a somewhat defaced or incomplete form, looking like a little triangle of dots, on p. 147 after l. 106.

Exodus, like the rest of the poems in this MS and like all sizable OE poems, is divided into sections. "Liber I," which includes the first three poems, is divided into 55 sections running continuously to the end of *Daniel*. These sections are clearly marked by spacing and capitalization and have been numbered by the scribe in a little more than half the cases. *Exodus* begins with Section XLII and runs through XLVIIII, *Daniel* commencing with Section L. The following table shows the divisions:

XLII: Pp. 143, 144, 145; ll. 1–62; 62 metrical lines.

[XLIII] (Not numbered but marked by a space for a capital): Pp. 146, 147; ll. 63–106; 44 lines.

[XLIIII] (Not numbered but marked by a space for a capital): It begins in the middle of a sentence and is incomplete, having lost two folios (see below, p. 6). P. 148; ll. 107–41; 35 lines.

[XLV] (Not numbered but marked by a space for a capital): Pp. 149, 150 (blank), 151, 152 (blank), 153, 154, 155; ll. 142-251; 110 lines.

XLVI: Pp. 156, 157, 158, 159 (blank); ll. 252-318; 67 lines.

XLVII: Pp. 160, 161, 162, 163; ll. 319–446; 128 lines. (Page 164 blank)

[XLVIII?]—Probably missing entirely: a folio has been cut out (see below, p. 10). (Page 165 blank)

---

5. See Krapp, *The Junius Manuscript*, pp. xxii–xxiv, and Timmer, *The Later Genesis*, pp. 1–3; a complete list of the accents in the Junius MS, which are not always visible in the facsimile, may be found in Krapp's edition of *The Vercelli Book, Anglo-Saxon Poetic Records, 2* (New York, 1932), lxv–lxxiv.

6. E.g., *mearc hofu · mór heald · moyses ofer þa* (61), or *þeod mearc tredan on hwæl · hwreopąn · here fugolas* (160 ff.).

7. It occurs, for example, at the end of p. 143 after l. 29, at the end of p. 158 after l. 318, and at the end of p. 167 after l. 510.

XLVIIII: Pp. 166, 167, 168 (blank), 169, 170, 171 (final word incomplete); ll. 447–590; 144 lines.

The significance of these sections is puzzling. Some of them (XLII, XLV, XLVI) may be regarded as passable rhetorical units; on the other hand, Section XLIIII seems to begin in mid-sentence. It is impossible to determine whether these sections originated with the poet or at any rate with the first man to commit the poem to writing. It seems likely, from the way that the scribe omits numbers constantly but rarely loses count of his sections, that the numbered sections existed in a previous copy. *Genesis B,* which was probably written in the late ninth century, a hundred years before the Junius MS was written, contains the same divisions; the numbering of the sections could hardly be older than that, at any rate. It may be observed that the average length of the sections in *Genesis* is about 80 lines, although the range is great. Further discussion of the sections in this MS may be found in Gollancz.[8]

II. Textual Problems

THE poem begins with the conventional *hwæt* formula and the usual praise of the hero, in this case celebrating Moses as lawgiver and emphasizing the value of the laws themselves (1–7). From this it proceeds to a somewhat confusing summary of the career of Moses up to the time of the plagues in Egypt, stressing the wisdom and military prowess of Moses and the great honors shown him by the Lord. There is also a glance forward at the wars of conquest in Canaan and the eventual winning of the Promised Land (8–32). An obscure transitional passage leads into a description of the grief of the Egyptians at the death of the first-born, an account which seems to be chiefly in the form of an elaborate metaphor and which is climaxed by a general statement on the fate of the Egyptian nation (33–53).

At this point the real action of the poem begins as Moses leads his people through mysterious lands to the first camping place and then on to Etham. Fear of the extreme heat of the Ethiopian regions forces the host northward, and God shields them from the heat by a pillar of cloud which is described at some length in startling metaphors (54–87).

In the following passage, several scholars have recommended a rearrangement of text (which Krapp does not incorporate into his text or indeed even mention). The chief difficulty which has led to such measures has been the sequence of events in the narrative in the MS as it stands. After the first appearance of the pillar of cloud is described in terms of a sail, the poet goes on to refer to the third camp and then immediately to the *two* pillars (of cloud and fire) which guide the host (*bēamas twēgen* 94). Then he describes the breaking up of camp and

8. *The Cædmon Manuscript,* pp. xxx–xxxii.

the setting out in the morning, and at that point he introduces the pillar of fire for the first time separately, telling us that it appears every evening. From one point of view, certainly this order of events might be considered confused and illogical; one would expect a separate description of each pillar as it first appears and then a mention of them together. Yet there is no false joint perceptible in the text, which makes sense from line to line as it stands.

A. S. Napier [1] proposed shifting the section from l. 108 to l. 124, which contains the description of the pillar of fire and its functions, to follow l. 85, the description of the sail-like pillar of cloud. Then would follow ll. 86–107 describing the two pillars and the departure at morning, joining easily enough to ll. 125 ff. Gollancz [2] suggested placing ll. 108–24 after l. 92, with ll. 93–107 following l. 124. Both these rearrangements assume that a loose page in a previous MS had been turned around by mistake.

It is doubtful whether such rearrangement is justified or entirely necessary. It would involve disturbing the sectional divisions of the MS to some extent, since a new section or fit seems to begin at l. 107. More important, if the passage in question is read carefully in its original form, the sequence of thought can be worked out tolerably well.

The encampment at Etham, which is described first in ll. 63–7, was traditionally considered to be the first place where the pillar or pillars of cloud and fire appeared (Exod. 13:20–2). The poet thus takes the opportunity to describe the two pillars as they will henceforth appear to the Israelites. In one sense the Israelites are at Etham throughout the passage until they move on to the *fēorðe wīc* in ll. 127–34. But the two pillars are described as they will appear by day and night for the rest of the long journey. Supplying the necessary logical connectives, then, the passage would be read as follows. In ll. 68–71a the predicament of the Israelites is described; they are forced northward because of the intolerable heat of the southern regions. At this point God sends them the pillar of cloud to protect them from such heat (ll. 71b–85). But, the poet seems to say, this was merely one of the beneficial functions of the pillars, for from that time forward (if we so translate *siððan* in l. 86), that is, from the time of the third camp, Etham, the *þridda wīc* of l. 87, God honored those loyal to him. For example, he measured out camping grounds for them by means of the pillar and also employed it to guide them by day and night. Consequently, returning to the immediate situation at Etham, when they awoke in the morning they saw the pillar of cloud leading them. And every evening (from that point on) the pillar of fire would rise and shine over the host, keeping away the terrors of darkness and serving as a threat to reinforce the authority of Moses.

1. "The Old English 'Exodus,' ll. 63–134," *MLR*, 6 (1911), 165–8.
2. *The Cædmon Manuscript*, p. lxx.

Ll. 125–9, in which a night scene is apparently described, suggests strongly that the poet imagined the Israelites as arriving at the fourth camp on the Red Sea by night. The gleaming of shields and the phrase *gesāwon randwigan rihte strǣte* suggest that their path was being illuminated for them. The Bible does not actually describe their arrival at the Red Sea.

It is by the Red Sea that news reaches the Israelites of the approach of the pursuing Egyptian army. An account of the previous relationship of the Israelites and Egyptians is begun but is interrupted by a break in the MS (135–41).

This is the first of two major gaps in the existing MS. In the 12th gathering (i.e., the first of the 3 gatherings which contain the poem *Exodus*) there are only 6 leaves, or 3 folded sheets of parchment, instead of the usual 8 leaves. Although there is no trace of removal, it seems clear that the 2 inner leaves of the gathering—4 sides altogether—between pp. 148 and 149 are missing. The break occurs after l. 141, the last written line being: *wǣre negymdon . ðeah þese yldra cyning . ær ge,* ending abruptly in the middle of a word after a full page of writing.

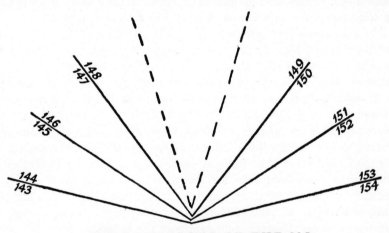

1 2 T H G A T H E R I N G O F T H E M S

P. 149 begins with a space for a capital, indicating a new section, even though the previous capital (and new section) appeared on p. 148. Editors have often tried to connect the last words on p. 148 with the first words of p. 149 by supplying the rest of the word beginning with *ge-;* Gollancz calls such attempts "altogether futile." [3]

Further discussion of the sense of the passage in question may be found in the Notes. From the MS evidence alone, however, it is clear that 4 sides are missing here and it is very probable that the missing sides

3. *The Cædmon Manuscript,* p. lxix.

contained some of the text. Just how much is missing is not easy to conjecture because of the custom in this MS of leaving blank space at irregular intervals for illustration. The amount of missing material might range from a few lines to as many as 120 verse-lines, if one assumed that no space had been left for illustration and the pages had been filled in with the average of 50 verse-lines apiece. The material which was lost probably included some account of Joseph—certainly at least the mention of his name—and the way he saved the Egyptians from famine. On literary grounds, it is also difficult to judge how far the poet might have seen fit to go in this direction. The reference to Joseph's treasure at the end of the poem perhaps indicates that some definite description of the treasure had appeared earlier, in this section now missing. The development of the hostility between Egyptians and Hebrews may have been as important in this poet's mind as the careful explanation of the political relationships of Danes, Swedes, and Geats was to the poet of *Beowulf*. Returning to the physical aspects, however, it seems very unlikely that more than two of the missing pages at the very most would have been completely blank; there was probably only one and perhaps parts of another. On the whole perhaps 50 lines is a fair guess at the amount of missing material.

The Egyptians are eager to avenge their brothers, for various reasons, and the Israelites are terrified as they watch the impressive advance of the enemy. The poet describes the advance in the conventional terms of battle; wolves and birds of prey gather in expectation of slaughter (142–69). The oncoming Egyptians are described at some length as they draw near, and the vast number of their host is vaguely suggested in an account of the manner in which the army had been raised (170–99). The Israelites are in despair until the mighty angel who is guarding them suddenly separates the two armies for the space of a night (200–7). The disheartened Israelites are summoned at dawn by Moses to an assembly and hasten to prepare for battle. The organization of their army is described in some detail (208–51). A herald introduces Moses to the assembled troops (252–8). In formal epic style Moses tells them to trust in the Lord and have no fear, rebuking them for their timidity and reminding them that the God of Abraham is protecting them. Then he himself describes the opening of the Red Sea as he strikes it with his wand. The ancient foundations of the sea appear and he urges them to hasten across the newly formed path (259–98).

The Israelites prepare to cross over (299–309). First goes the tribe of Judah. They carry the golden lion as their standard, and their courage and fighting ability are stressed (310–30). Next comes the tribe of Reuben, who because of his sins had lost the right of the first-born to Judah (331–9). The tribe of Simeon follows as the sun rises (340–6). After the first three come the rest of the tribes, aware of their proper order. There was one father of them all (presumably Abraham). Wise men have traced the genealogies skilfully (347–61).

The following passage, ll. 362–446, has often been treated as an interpolation. It begins with a brief account of Noah, who sailed over new floods and rescued the most precious treasure on earth. The transition from a discussion of the history of the Israelite race to the mention of Noah is at best rather abrupt and surprising. The poet then observes that Abraham's father was ninth in line from Noah (377–9). Abraham's career is touched on and the poet tells in some detail, as perhaps the most significant incident in it, the story of Abraham's attempted sacrifice of his son Isaac on the mountain where Solomon later built his temple. Stress is laid on the enormity of the deed and the meaning of Abraham's obedience. As he lifts his sword he is halted by a voice from heaven (380–418). The voice approves the way that Abraham has met the test and promises that the Lord will reward him by making his descendants infinitely numerous and prosperous in the land they will one day possess (419–46). At this point there is a break in the MS (a page cut out), and then the action resumes in the midst of a spirited description of the drowning of the Egyptians in the Red Sea.

Modern critics began very early to regard this passage as an interpolation. It was given a separate title in some of the standard histories; Alois Brandl, for example, listed it as an independent fragment under the name "Noah und andere Patriarchen," [4] and others have often referred to it as "Exodus B." Almost the only dissenting voice in the nineteenth century was that of Adolf Ebert, who regarded it as an integral part of the poem.[5] F. A. Blackburn defended its integrity in his edition but without very convincing reasons; W. J. Sedgefield omitted the passage entirely in his edition and later, in a review of Krapp's edition in 1931,[6] reproved Krapp for defending it. Gollancz's defense of the integrity of the passage, however, is decidedly convincing.[7]

In spite of all the difficulties involved, the present editor is convinced that "Exodus B" forms a part of the original poem. If nothing has been lost around the beginning of the passage, and there is no indication of loss, we must concede that the poet has made a rather awkward transition but not one which cannot be paralleled elsewhere in OE poetry (e.g., the introduction of the þrýð episode in *Beow.* 1931). The transition back to the main narrative, on the other hand, has been lost; at least something has been lost after l. 446. The proponents of the theory of interpolation argue that "Exodus B" may have been taken from another poem and

4. *Grundriss der germanischen Philologie,* hrsg. von H. Paul (2d ed., Strassburg, 1908), Bd. 2¹, p. 1029.
5. "Zum *Exodus,*" *Anglia,* 5 (1882), 409–10.
6. *MLR, 26* (1931), 353.
7. *The Cædmon Manuscript,* pp. lxxii f.

inserted here accidentally or even deliberately to fill a break in the MS.[8] They maintain that the passage has no real connection with the rest of the poem and point to the fact that the style of "Exodus B" is more temperate, quieter, and more conventional and so differs from the style of the rest of the poem.

In answer to these understandable objections it may be observed first of all that the mention of Noah and Abraham is by no means basically irrelevant to the poem. The covenant of God with man is certainly one of the central themes of the poem, and here we are shown two earlier covenants which God had made with the Hebrews. Abraham and the promise which God made him are mentioned elsewhere in the poem. This general question of the overall unity of *Exodus* will be discussed below in more detail.

It is true that the style of "Exodus B" is different in some ways from that of the rest of the poem, but the closest verbal study of "Exodus A" and "Exodus B" produces ultimately no evidence which could really stand up in court. The difference in tone and movement ("B" is characterized by shorter and simpler lines) may simply stem from the great difference in the subjects treated: "A" is concerned with massive actions and warlike activity; "B" is far more static and is focused largely on a moral problem. In vocabulary, certain resemblances may be noted in words and phrases which appear in both "A" and "B"; [9] one might of course say that an interpolator was deliberately imitating the style of "A." On the whole, however, it is more credible, if one assumes an interpolation here at all, that this was a ready-made bit of verse which found its way here somehow than that a scribe or editor wrote this passage to fit into this place. Krapp [1] suggests that the poet in "B" is consciously imitating the style of the older Cædmonian poetry as being appropriate to a story from Genesis. The differences between this Abraham episode and that in *Genesis A* (2846–936) are much more striking than the similarities, however. Both poets rely scrupulously on the facts as set forth in the Bible, but the poet of *Exodus* has rigorously selected and rejected details to make a version of the story which fits his purpose, while as usual the *Genesis* poet includes almost everything in his source.

At l. 446, Section XLVII seems to come to an end. The writing ends in the middle of a line at a point where the voice from heaven certainly seems to have concluded its speech, and there is a "colon," a dot and

---

8. For example, W. A. Craigie, "Interpolations and Omissions in Anglo-Saxon Poetic Texts," *Philologica*, 2 (1925), 9, calls it "a fragment from a lost Genesis poem containing accounts of Noah and Abraham," which the scribe had mechanically copied into the text without noting its irrelevance.

9. Cf., for example, the peculiar and probably related compounds *ingeðēode* 444: *ingefolc* 142, *ingēmen*[d] 190; the word *wǣr* for 'covenant' 387, 422: 140, 147; *be sǣm twēonum* 443: 530; *langsum* in the sense 'long-lasting' 405: 6; *lāstweard* 400: 138.

1. *The Junius Manuscript*, p. xxviii.

check-mark, after *sēlost,* the last word. This is on p. 163. Pp. 164 and 165 are blank; p. 166 begins in the middle of a description of the trapped Egyptian host. An examination of the MS shows that in the 13th gathering, the second of the 3 which contain *Exodus,* there are only 14 sides instead of 16; a leaf (2 sides) is missing between the two blank pages 164 and 165. Stoddard observes that "a folio has been cut out and the knife marks are visible." [2] Presumably the missing leaf contained a transitional passage of some sort, probably at least a description of the entrance of Pharaoh's army into the sea. It might be argued that the missing page may have been blank and that the loss may have occurred in a previous MS; but the scribal editor would scarcely have left four consecutive blank sides even if he suspected a loss. Elsewhere in the MS completely blank pages occur only singly, at least in the middle of poems. There is a strong likelihood therefore that the two sides of the missing leaf were fully covered with writing, since the leaf was flanked on each side by pages offering ample space for illustration. The lost material very probably comprised the missing Section XLVIII. P. 166 is clearly marked as the beginning of Section XLVIIII. An estimated 30 verse-lines on each side of the missing leaf would amount to about 60 missing verse-lines at the most—a plausible length for a section in this MS.

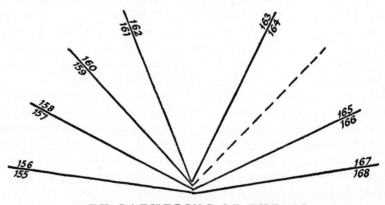

13TH GATHERING OF THE MS

The MS begins again on p. 166, l. 447, with a description of the Egyptians trapped and struggling in the waters of the Red Sea. This section of the poem is marked by striking metaphors and considerable confusion of the normal chronological order in the events recounted. Textual corruption, apparently due in large part to the difficulty of the style, is very frequent. The terrified Egyptians are overwhelmed by the bloodstained waves as God's ancient sword strikes from heaven. Pharaoh

2. "The Cædmon Poems in MS Junius XI," *Anglia, 10* (1888), 162, corroborated by Gollancz, *The Cædmon Manuscript,* p. lxxiii.

discovers at last the might of the Lord. None of all that host remains alive to carry the evil news to the cities and women of Egypt (441–515).

The text of the remaining portion of the poem has been rearranged in the present edition. As it stands in the MS, the passage from l. 516 to the end is confused to the point of incomprehensibility. The passage from l. 516 to l. 548 (MS numbering) may be summarized as follows. Moses gives eternal counsels to the Israelites on the seashore. These counsels are still to be found by scholars in scripture. Interpretation can unlock the mystery and teach us that we have hope of God's mercy. Even though we live in sorrow in this transitory life, after the Judgment Day the righteous may praise the Lord in heaven forever and ever. From l. 549 to l. 590 the poem may be paraphrased: Moses speaks to the attentive host of Israelites after the miracle, telling them of the promise of Canaan and the power of the Lord and of their future joy. The host rejoices at these words and at the fact that the Lord has saved them from their enemies. Both men and women begin to sing praises. The women are to be seen adorned with gold ornaments which they have picked up on the shore. The booty is divided equitably among the tribes, who have now recovered the treasure which was rightfully Joseph's.

Several anomalies appear in the text if it is read in this order. From a scene of violent action the poet passes to what seems to be a reference to the laws of Moses and the book of Deuteronomy, and then into a general moralizing peroration on Judgment Day, which seems to lead to a definite climax in l. 548 (MS). Then he returns to a description in terms of physical action, telling of Moses' speech and the emotions and behavior of the Israelites. In other words, he generalizes on the significance of the scriptures and the meaning of a Christian life and *then* goes on to finish his story.

A simple transposition of the two passages in question improves the sense immeasurably. The story then unfolds logically to its natural end in the gathering of booty from the drowned Egyptians, and the poet concludes with an appropriate reference to the laws of Moses (which, it will be remembered, were referred to in the opening lines of the poem) and a brief homily which (again like the beginning of the poem) lays stress on the specifically Christian world and future life. A strong point in favor of putting the homily at the end is the fact that so many OE Christian poems have very similar endings. Mention of the joys of heaven, the exhortation to hope for and to strive to attain these joys, the reference to the Last Judgment—all these details appear again and again.[3]

---

3. The following poems have conclusions resembling this passage in at least one detail: *Andreas, Fates of the Apostles, Dream of the Rood, Elene,* each of the three parts of *Christ, The Seafarer, Guthlac (A),* and a number of minor poems and fragments. The phrase *tō wīdan feore,* which concludes the homiletic passage in *Exodus,* is found frequently in these conclusions.

Gollancz [4] suggested a rearrangement essentially like this one; but he placed ll. 580–90 after l. 515, followed by ll. 549–79 and then by ll. 515–48. This arrangement places the homily at the end, but the shift of ll. 580–90 does not seem necessary and involves an elaborate hypothesis explaining the confusion. Krapp discusses this suggestion at some length [5] but eventually rejects it in the belief that such a rearrangement would tend to damage the poem and make it anticlimactic. While it may be granted that many readers might feel this to be true, it remains a fact that a large number of OE poems are anticlimactic in exactly the same way. Krapp's defense of the MS order does not outweigh this consideration nor is it very plausible in itself.

Doubt has been raised concerning the genuineness of the homiletic passage, especially ll. 523–48 (MS). Craigie says of them: "We have here a concluding portion of a moralizing poem which has no connexion with the theme of the *Exodus*." [6] Proof can hardly be furnished for either side in this question. It must be admitted that the style of the passage is rigidly conventional and trite in a way that the rest of the poem certainly is not. The striking figure of the two arch-thieves old age and early death, who share the rule over this world, is the only detail reminiscent of the imagination which the *Exodus* poet has shown elsewhere. The passage seems to have little direct connection with *Exodus*, although a case could be made for a rather tenuous connection; it is the kind of general statement which could be attached to almost any Christian poem. On the whole there is no reason to doubt that it is genuine, although it is perhaps displeasing to modern taste.

Several conjectures might be made as to the reason for the disarrangement of the two passages. It would be simplest to imagine a loose leaf in a previous MS, perhaps containing the 42 lines from 549 to 590, with about 21 verse-lines on each side. This leaf, originally meant to follow l. 515, was misplaced so that it followed the actual conclusion of the poem at l. 548. Or perhaps the leaf containing ll. 516–48 was the one misplaced. No more elaborate reconstruction of the error is really needed.

III. Sources

THE great bulk of the narrative material in *Exodus* is drawn from the 13th and 14th chapters of the book of Exodus, which describe the departure of the Israelites from Egypt, the journey to the Red Sea, the crossing of the Israelites, and the drowning of the pursuing Egyptian host. In general the poet has followed this source with some faithfulness but has rearranged his version of the incident extensively in order to

4. *The Cædmon Manuscript*, p. lxxv.
5. *The Junius Manuscript*, pp. xxix–xxxi.
6. "Interpolations and Omissions in Anglo-Saxon Poetic Texts," *Philologica*, 2 (1925), 9.

make an independent poem out of what appears in the Bible as merely one link in a continuous narrative. The poet has made use, in one place or another, of almost every phrase from Exod. 13:17 to the end of chap. 14. The events preceding the exodus are summarized in a remarkably brief fashion; no mention is made of the references to unleavened bread and passover ritual which make up so much of chap. 12, and only the tenth plague is brought in.

Two aspects of the poem, however, have led scholars to search further for a possible single source. The strong impression of form and unity which *Exodus* undeniably gives, on the one hand, and the appearance of a great many details which are not to be found in the basic scriptural source, on the other, have given rise to the belief that the poem was based on a previous literary composition. The only literary work which has been seriously proposed as this source is the Latin poem *De Transitu Maris Rubri,* written in the fifth century by Avitus, Bishop of Vienne.[1] In 1883 E. J. Groth [2] suggested that an acquaintance with this poem on the part of the OE poet was "unzweifelhaft" but saw a direct influence only in the description of the pillar of cloud. In 1899 Gerhard Mürkens, in his detailed study of the poem,[3] went much further than Groth in attributing a considerable number of details in the OE poem to the influence of Avitus. This theory was accepted, with a few reservations by some scholars, until 1911, when Samuel Moore published an article in which he took each of the supposed resemblances mentioned by Mürkens and demolished them in turn.[4] He pointed out that some of them were very dubious indeed and others were facts or ideas which the OE poet could have taken from other parts of the Bible or from well-known commentaries. After stating decisively that the poem by Avitus was in no sense to be called the source of *Exodus,* he admitted that he could find no single source for it in Latin commentary and Christian literature.

Moore's careful study of the isolated factual matters in the case did not include a comparison of the larger aspects, in particular the tone and general treatment, of the two poems. As a rule the Latin poem follows the Bible in much greater detail, beginning with a long account of the ten plagues, bringing in all the details concerning the unleavened bread, emphasizing the disputes in Pharaoh's court among the ministers, and adding in some places specifically Christian interpretations of the meaning of incidents. As a whole it bears little resemblance to the OE poem. Its somewhat florid Vergilian style is far removed from that of *Exodus.*

---

1. Ed. R. Peiper, in *Monumenta Germaniae Historica, Aviti Opera Poematum V;* also to be found in Migne, *Patrologia Latina, 59.*

2. *Composition und Alter der altenglischen (angelsächsischen) Exodus* (Göttingen, 1883), pp. 17–18.

3. *Untersuchungen über das altenglische Exoduslied,* Bonner Beiträge zur Anglistik, 2 (Bonn, 1899), pp. 68–77.

4. "On the Sources of the Old English *Exodus,*" *MP, 9* (1911), 83–108.

Of other Latin poems of the same sort which might have been available to an Anglo-Saxon poet, only a poem by Cyprianus Gallus,[5] of the beginning of the fifth century, bears any resemblance in general tone and treatment to the OE poem. But it resembles it no more than the poem by Avitus, being a very close paraphrase of the biblical text.

In 1912 James A. Bright suggested that the primary source of the poem *Exodus* was to be found in the Catholic service for Holy Saturday, especially in the scriptural passages which were selected to be read on that day.[6] Bright's theory, which he presented with great assurance, has never been discussed in detail by other critics.[7]

The twelve scriptural passages, or "prophecies," as they are called, for Holy Saturday in the modern Roman version include the essential account of the crossing of the Red Sea (No. 4: Exod. 14:24–15:1), the story of Noah (No. 2, chosen from the 5th, 6th, 7th, and 8th chapters of Genesis), and Abraham's offering of Isaac (No. 3: Gen. 22:1–19). All these are to be found in some form in the poem. In addition to these, the story of creation is found in No. 1 (Gen. 1:31–2:1–2), a story which is at least referred to in ll. 25–7 of the poem. Bright also points to some details which the poet might have used from the other prophecies; the unusual expression in ll. 427–31 concerning the powers of God's word he thinks stems from the fifth prophecy (Isa. 55:8–11), and in No. 8 (Isa. 4:5–6) he sees the ultimate source (out of many possible ones) of the idea that the pillar of cloud was a protection from heat.[8] Actually one might add to such examples. In the passage just cited, the phrase *in umbraculum diei ab aestu* might possibly shed some light on the puzzling *dægscealdes hleo (dægscead[w]es?)* of l. 79. The description of the rich princes going down to hell in No. 6 (Baruch 3:9–38) might possibly have influenced the poet's account of the death of the first-born in ll. 41–8. No. 9 (Deut. 31:22–30), describing Moses giving the book of the law to his successors and warning them against evil ways, might be connected with the obscure passage at the end of the poem. The other prophecies have no possible relevance to the poem, although Bright went so far as to regard the passage from Daniel about the fiery furnace (No. 12: Dan. 3:1–24) as significant. He believed that the poem *Daniel* had been deliberately placed after *Exodus* in the MS and in fact had probably been written by the *Exodus* poet himself. But this is going too far, since the differences in style and poetic method between *Exodus* and *Daniel* are very great.

---

5. *Exodus*, ed. R. Peiper, *Corpus Scriptorum Ecclesiasticorum Latinorum, 23.*

6. "The Relation of the Cædmonian *Exodus* to the Liturgy," *MLN, 27* (1912), 97–103.

7. Gollancz (p. lxxiii) rejects it flatly but without discussing it at much length. C. W. Kennedy, *The Earliest English Poetry* (New York, 1943), pp. 177–80, approves of Bright's theory, however.

8. See the Note to l. 72. Hereafter references to the explanatory Notes will be given in the form *See Note, 72.*

It must be conceded at the outset that the poet, especially if, as is very likely, he was connected with a religious order, was familiar with the impressive Holy Saturday service. It was primarily a baptismal service and provided an occasion in the early church when catechumens were instructed in the full significance of the new life they were entering. The various medieval forms of the service [9] did not differ essentially, at least for the purposes of this examination, from the modern form; all of them give prominence to the Red Sea passage and most of them include Abraham's temptation and the creation story, although in some the order is rearranged and sometimes only four or five of the passages are used.

But on the whole one is tempted to draw a sharp distinction between kinds of influence and to define more precisely what is meant by "source." Bright believed that the liturgical service represented an actual source for the poem, and at the end of his article he tries to develop to some extent the mystical significance of the poem in an attempt to show that their basic purposes are essentially the same. He holds that *Exodus* is a *carmen paschale* like the celebrated work of Sedulius. The Holy Saturday service, as has been said, is intended to bring into prominence the theme of baptism. It is implemented throughout with interpretations and prayers which stress the significant points in each of the prophecies. An extraordinary symbolism is created around the Paschal Candle as bringer of new light into the world; it is connected especially and persistently with the pillar of fire.

It may be maintained, however, that the general similarity of material in both the poem and the liturgical service need not imply the same use of that material. While no one could deny that the service is dominated by the theme of baptism, no sane reader would be likely to call *Exodus* a poem about baptism. *Exodus* is very different indeed from the liturgy and from such poems based on it, or at least using some of its symbolism, as Sedulius' *Carmen Paschale* or Avitus' *De Transitu Maris Rubri* in that it is so historical and is devoted to the story as story, drawing no analogies, pointing out no specific doctrine. The action it represents may indeed be suggestive of larger general ideas, but they are ideas which need not, in fact, cannot, on the evidence of the poem itself, be interpreted in any precise doctrinal sense.

As for the use of the Noah, Abraham, and Moses stories together, it is not necessary to assume that the liturgy provides the only source for the connection of the three ideas. The relationship of the three covenants is made clear enough in the Old Testament itself; even so, it is doubtful whether an Anglo-Saxon read his Bible unaccompanied by commen-

9. See J. W. Tyrer, *Historical Survey of Holy Week: Its Services and Ceremonial* (London, 1932), pp. 156–60, who gives the various versions of the prophecies in the Gallican, Ambrosian, and other rites as well as the Roman.

taries. Nor is there any real need to go to the commentaries. The 11th chapter of the Epistle to the Hebrews, which deals with numerous examples of faith, contains references to Noah, Abraham, and Moses and to Joseph as well, among other Old Testament figures. This is certainly as likely and as familiar a "source" as the liturgy. Indeed the similarities between the various stories are made much clearer in Hebrews than in the liturgy, and the general tone of the chapter, with its emphasis on those who endured hardships and subdued kingdoms by faith, resembles not a little the tone of *Exodus*.

Lacking other evidence, we must assume that the poem is in organization essentially the work of the Anglo-Saxon poet. The first of the two kinds of source which might be suspected, a literary source where the material·has already been shaped for a later poet's use, has not been discovered and there are some grounds for doubting that such a source ever existed. A Latin literary source especially is to be regarded as unlikely. Latinisms of any kind are not to be found in the poem other than a few obviously suggested by the Vulgate itself. On the contrary, the poem seems to be particularly "native" in style and spirit. Its general resemblance to the earlier heroic poetry, its rich store of "Germanic antiquities," its abundance of epic terminology and detail, are all much more comparable to what is found in *Beowulf* than in Cynewulf's somewhat Latinized poems.

The second kind of source, on the other hand, one of factual material, a collection of the many fragments of fact and legend which are not to be found in those two chapters of Exodus which provide the main foundation for the poem, is much more likely to have existed. No such source has been discovered, at least not among the better known commentaries which might have been available. Perhaps if such a collection of information existed it was a more humble collection of notes and cullings from the fathers, something local and anonymous which vanished without trace. But, while it might be tempting to believe that the poet knew such a collection, there is still no absolute necessity to assume the single source of information. It might have been gathered by the poet himself if he were a man of reasonable diligence and moderately wide reading.

An examination of the possible sources for these details was begun by Moore.[1] His search for the sources of such details as the incident of the destruction of the Egyptian idols at the time of the exodus and the statement that the pillar of cloud is a protection against heat—he lists fifteen of these details as the most striking—was admirably thorough. For all but four of them he finds some kind of source in patristic legend or in the Bible itself. These are rarely to be considered actual sources but rather analogues, since many of them are to be found only considerably later in time, in the works of such collectors as Peter Comestor.

1. "On the Sources of the Old English *Exodus*," *MP, 9* (1911), 83–108.

The question which now arises is whether it is possible, taking as a basis the work of Moore and similar investigation which supplements it, to narrow down the scope of material, of possible sources, to a small group of the most readily available. If we say that the basic source of the poem lies in the 13th and 14th chapters of the book of Exodus, there is no question that the source next in importance is the rest of the Vulgate itself. The stories of Abraham, Noah, and Joseph (the last cut short by MS loss) come from the book of Genesis, which the poet obviously knew thoroughly. Other books which he seems to have known well and to which he was probably indebted for much of his information especially on military organization were the books of Numbers and Deuteronomy. It is probable that passages from the Psalms, Isaiah, and I Chronicles as well are reflected in the poem. These last examples, and others that might be mentioned, are actually parallels rather than sources, possibly but not certainly known to him. More important perhaps than the use of specific details is the impression the poet gives throughout that he is soaked in the Old Testament atmosphere and is familiar with the somewhat primitive psychology of the earlier books of the Pentateuch. This familiarity he shows particularly in his careful selection of details from his own native stock of heroic tradition to match biblical details. Thus Pharaoh and his leaders become proud thanes on horseback, as the poet picks up the hint of Exod. 15:19 ("Ingressus est enim eques Pharao cum curribus et equitibus ejus in mare . . ."); the trumpets which are described in chap. 10 of Numbers become indistinguishable from Anglo-Saxon horns. The phrase *be sǽm twēonum* (see Note, 443), probably once a reference to the seas of northern Europe, here indicates the seas bounding the Promised Land. It is the accuracy of such a merging of traditions which argues that the poet must have known his Bible well.

It is much more difficult to deal with possible nonbiblical sources. Investigation has turned up a score of authorities for various details in the poem ranging from undoubted ultimate sources to very unlikely ones. In general it may be said that the most obvious sources have scarcely been touched, while odd bits of information, almost always of a factual nature, have been gathered from the most diverse authorities.

As an illustration of this we might begin by taking up a subject not treated in detail by Moore but one which is among the most interesting in the study of sources, the nature of the geographical information found in the description of the march of the Israelites to the sea. We find clear additions to the biblical source in the following statements of the author: (1) Moses led the host through a country of hostile tribes to the land of the *Gūðmyrce,* a land which was apparently covered by a cloud; (2) after leaving the camp at Etham they were forced to travel to the north, since they knew that the country of the Ethiopians lay to the south of them; (3) the heat was so intense that they had to be protected from it by a pillar of cloud which God furnished them. In view of the usual reliance on authority of some kind found elsewhere in the poem—the poet was imaginative, to be sure, but the process was always one of elaboration around a core of hard fact rather than sheer invention—it is more than probable that the poet had in mind some source for his mention of these geographical features. Because of the extreme vagueness of his own descriptions and the unsatisfactory nature of the geographical lore available to him, it is difficult to determine what sources he may have known.

Probably the most readily accessible authorities at the time, if we may judge from the sources known to Bede, were Orosius, Isidore, Solinus, and probably Pliny's *Natural History* (part of which at least Bede was familiar with).[2] But none of these can be established as a definite source for the poet. Almost all of them mention the area in question. The region between Egypt and the Red Sea was sometimes considered as part of Egypt, sometimes as part of Arabia. Ethiopia was an ill-defined district lying generally south of Egypt and extending throughout the southern part of Africa. Accurate knowledge of it was lost even in later Roman times and was replaced by extraordinary fables of outlandish tribes and beasts. The feature mentioned by all writers was the torrid climate, which was believed to be so inclement that the southern regions were absolutely uninhabitable. All this, however, may fairly be termed common knowledge, and it is impossible to tell the source. The one author of those just mentioned who may be reflected in details of the poem is Pliny, and the actual probability even there is small (see Notes, 56, 70).

Yet while the expected sources seem to furnish no help in this case, the one possible source which seems most to resemble some of the details in the poem is a surprising one. It is the work on history by the Greek Diodorus Siculus, the third book of which is devoted to a rambling and inaccurate account of Arabia, Ethiopia, and the Red Sea region.[3] Here we find mention of Arabia, the land between Syria and Egypt and home of the Nabataeans, who "lead a life of brigandage, and overrunning a large part of the neighbouring territory they pillage it, being difficult to overcome in war." These may be the hostile tribes the poet mentions, if we can believe that he had any clear idea of the area in question. More pertinent are the descriptions which Diodorus furnishes of the sun in the regions of Arabia. "When out of the midst of the sea . . . it comes into view, it resembles a fiery red ball of charcoal which discharges huge sparks; . . . but at the beginning of the second hour it takes on the

2. All these are included in the list of books known to Bede compiled by M. L. W. Laistner in his article "The Library of the Venerable Bede," *Bede: His Life, Times and Writings*, ed. A. H. Thompson (Oxford, 1935), pp. 263–6.

3. *Diodorus of Sicily*, tr. C. H. Oldfather, Loeb Classical Library, 2 (Cambridge, Mass., 1935).

form of a round shield and sends forth a light which is exceptionally bright and fiery." In this single passage one might find possible sources of the phrase *hātum heofoncolum* 71 and the much disputed *dægscealdes* ('day-shield'?) 79. Diodorus also describes a country in Arabia which is, to be sure, on the eastern shore of the Red Sea rather than the western, that is "not fiery hot, like the neighbouring territories, but is often overspread by mild and thick clouds, from which come heavy showers and timely storms that make the summer season temperate." [4] One is reminded of the mysterious land of the *Gūðmyrce*, which is covered by a cloud (*lyfthelm*).

While as individual resemblances any one of these might be called coincidental, the combination of them may suggest something more. Certainly there is, at any rate, far more similarity between the details in Diodorus and those in the poem than can be found in any of the other geographical works. If one is tempted to accept the influence of Diodorus here, the problem of how an Anglo-Saxon could have been familiar with the work of Diodorus remains a difficult one. Diodorus was certainly not a standard medieval authority; he was not well known, at least as a source of geographical information, in the late classical period. So far as can be discovered, Latin translations of his work were not available until the renaissance period. It is of course possible that an early Latin translation was in circulation—perhaps only a collection of interesting scraps of information and descriptions—but if it existed it was not well known. It would be hard to believe, on the other hand, that the poet himself knew Greek. If the influence of Diodorus is to be accepted, the most natural supposition is that the information came in some way from the small band of learned men who were trained by Theodore and Hadrian at the end of the seventh century, some of whom were still engaged in the study of Greek in Bede's day. [5]

It is certain that the works of Jerome were known to the poet in some form. A Hebrew etymology of Jerome seems clearly to have furnished the basis for the sustained nautical metaphor (see Note, 81), and one of them may be reflected in the reference to Abraham at 1. 353. Jerome is the most likely source for other details—the idea of the pillar of cloud shielding the host from the heat (see Note, 72) and the reference to the Holy Ghost in 1. 96, both probably coming ultimately from his commentary on the Psalter, and the identification of the mountain where Isaac was sacrificed with the mountain of the temple from his commentary on Genesis (see Note, 389–96). The legend of the destruction of the Egyptian idols at the time of the exodus is also found in Jerome (see Note, 46–7).

Josephus' commentary may have been the original source for the

4. *Diodorus of Sicily*, pp. 203, 41–2, 223.
5. Bede, *Eccl. Hist.* 4.1–2.

number of men which the poet postulates for the Egyptian host and for the incident of the looting of the dead Egyptians cast up on the Red Sea shores (see Notes, 184, 547). Philo Judaeus mentions a "south wind" as causing the drying of the sea (see Note, 289) and describes the two "choirs" of men and women who celebrate the successful crossing (see Note, 542). But the legendary material contained in the works of these two writers became common property so early that it would be a mistake to assume that the poet knew them directly; the information may have come through intermediate sources.

Beyond this point it is impossible to name other likely sources. The most striking conclusion which may be drawn from this study has to do with the sources that were not used, whether unknown to the poet or ignored by him. The classic commentaries on Exodus by Jerome, Ambrose, and the other early fathers were heavily, indeed almost exclusively, allegorical expositions with elaborate interpretations of each incident, "type," and even of the proper names (see, for example, Note, 66). Bede's writings on the Pentateuch seem to be a collection of such observations. The Latin poems on the subject follow their authorities painstakingly in pointing out the specific Christian meaning of each event.

Yet in this poet we find a radical departure from such a tradition. He is interested primarily in facts, in recreating historical events as accurately as possible. It is necessary to emphasize this point because of the impression created by Moore to some extent and Gollancz to a much greater extent that the poet of *Exodus* is following rather ignorantly the allegorical tradition. A few phrases in the poem suggest that he was aware of it (for example, see Note, 104, on *lîfweg* and the concluding homiletic passage); but the whole poem shows decisively that he was not interested in it.

One conclusion which may be advanced with some assurance is that the poet was not under the influence of Bede's exegetical works. This belief may have some slight significance in determining the date of the poem, since it might have been difficult for an English ecclesiastic writing in the heyday of Bede's fame to escape his influence.

IV. Dialect and Date

THE placing of the poem in time and general area must begin with an examination of its language and dialect. Like almost all OE poetry, the poem has been transmitted to us in a dialect which is predominantly Late West Saxon. This dialect is not pure, however, and it shows a good number of non-West Saxon traces in phonology, morphology, and vocabulary. Mürkens made a fairly thorough study of the poem from this point of view,[1] but a good many of his conclusions must be revised in the light of more recent knowledge.

1. *Untersuchungen über das altenglische Exoduslied*, pp. 86–94.

That the majority of forms in the MS are LWS hardly needs proof. There is only one occurrence (*onnīed* 149—a word which the scribe may not have understood) of the telltale Early West Saxon *ie* spelling; *y* is the rule throughout for EWS *ie* of whatever origin (e.g., *gyfan* 263, *gyldan* 150, *scyldas* 125, *yrmþum* 265, *yrre* 506). Breaking occurs in most cases, regularly before *r* plus consonant and *h* plus consonant, usually before *l* plus consonant (*eall* throughout, *gesealde* 16, 20, *geweald* 20, 383, *ealdum* 33, etc.). West Germanic *ā* appears in the great majority of cases as *ǣ* (*rǣd* [5×], *wǣpna* 20, *sǣton* 212, etc.). The forms *syllīc* 109 and *gesyllan* 400 are typical late forms.[2]

Mürkens listed examples of non-WS forms under ten headings and attempted to prove a Northumbrian origin for the poem. There are an appreciable number of non-WS forms in the text. WGmc *ā* appears as *ē* in *bēlegsan* 121 and probably in *wērbēamas* 487 and *onsēgon*(?) (MS *onsigon*) 178.[3] *Forgēfe* 153 and *forgēton* 144 could also be LWS.[4] The form *mēce* 414, 495 is Anglian in origin but common in all the poetry. Unbroken *a* (WGmc *a*) before *l* plus consonant, an Anglian feature,[5] is not uncommon, usually in words used frequently in poetry: *Alwalda* 11, *aldor* (4×), *alwihta* 421, *alde* (in the fossilized phrase *alde mēce* 495 but *eald-* elsewhere), *Waldend* 16, 422, 433, *bald* 253, *nalles* 307, and, in syllables less heavily stressed, *hildecalla* 252 and *sincalda* 473.[6] It is conceivable, on the other hand, but not likely, that such unbroken forms are EWS. The *i*-umlaut of *ēa* (*īe, ȳ* in WS)[7] appears as Anglian *ē* in *ēðfynde* 547, *bestēmed* 449, and perhaps in the emended *bēmum* (MS *benum*) 'trumpets' 216 (beside *bȳme* elsewhere) and in the emended *ingēmen*[*d*] 190. Velar umlaut of *a* (supposedly Mercian and Kentish but common in all the poetry in these particular words) occurs in *heaðorincas* 241, *heaðowylmas* 148, *beadumægnes* 329, *beadosearo* 540, *eaferan* 412. Velar umlaut of *i* to *eo*[8] appears in *freoðowǣre* 306, probably in *beodan* (for WS *bidon*) 166, and, in syllables with secondary stress, in *sǣleoda* 374 and *burhhleoðu* 70 (beside *beorhhliðu* 449). The *i*-umlaut of *ēo* is found as non-WS *ēo* in *dēore* 186. Possibly there is a Northumbrian confusion of *ea* and *eo* in the form *beorna* 401.[9]

Unsyncopated verbal forms in the third singular present indicative are corroborated by the meter in *wyrceð* 282, *dēmeð* 585, and *lǣdeð* 522, 586; such forms are usually considered Anglian. The full ending *-ed* in the past participles of weak verbs of the first class is preserved as shown by the meter in *gelǣded* 535, *oðlǣded* 537, *gemynted* 197, *ge-*

---

2. Karl D. Bülbring, *Altenglisches Elementarbuch* (Heidelberg, 1902), §304.

3. Eduard Sievers and Karl Brunner, *Altenglische Grammatik* (Halle, 1942), §62.

4. Sievers-Brunner, §§391, 123.

5. Bülbring, §134; Sievers-Brunner, §85.

6. There is a doubtful example of *æ* in the form *ælfere* 66 (for **eall-fare?*).

7. Sievers-Brunner, §104.

8. Non-WS before dentals; cf. Bülbring, §§235, 239 and Sievers-Brunner, §111.

9. The poem *Seasons for Fasting*, ed. E. V. K. Dobbie, *Anglo-Saxon Poetic Records*, 6, has *beorn* for *bearn* 68, 178 and *weord* for *weard* 153.

swīðed 30, *swīðed* 517, and *gecȳðed* 420.[1] In *eftwyrd cymð* 582 the longer form *cymeð* is clearly indicated.[2] The third singular of *habban* appears as *hafað* in 523 and 569—Anglian or poetical.[3] The emended *onsēgon* (MS *onsigon*) 178 might be Anglian (WS would ordinarily have *onsāwon*), but *gesāwon* occurs elsewhere regularly.[4] In one case (*forhtigende* 453) the Anglian present participle in -*ende* would be metrically preferable.[5] The metrically short half-line in 568, *rǣd forð gǣð*, requires a dissyllabic *gǣð* but may have originally had the usual Anglian *gangeð*.

The use of *in* instead of *on* has been regarded as an Anglian characteristic; *in* appears 16 times, *on* about 70. Similarly the use of *mid* with the accusative has been called Anglian; it appears with that case three times in the poem (9, 416, 486) and seems to be substantiated by the meter in the first and third instances, while it takes the dative or instrumental 15 times.

These surviving Anglian forms point to an origin in Anglian territory; such an assumption is strongly backed by the evidence of vocabulary. A number of words appear in *Exodus* which do not occur in WS prose, although some of them, the so-called Anglian-poetical words, may appear occasionally in poetry of WS origin. A list of these words, taken from several studies of Anglian and Saxon vocabulary,[6] follows:

> *bēacen* 'signum' (Rauh—poetic)
> *bepeccan* 'cover, protect' (Rauh)
> *ealdor* (as in *tō aldre* 425) 'sempiternum' (Rauh—poetic)
> *hagosteald* 'virgo' (Rauh)
> *hlēoðor* 'voice' (Jordan, Scherer)
> *līxan* 'shine' (Scherer)
> *morðor* 'murder' (Rauh)
> *nymðe* 'nisi' (Jordan, Scherer)
> *sǣlan* 'tie up' (Rauh) (also *onsǣlan*)
> *wæccan* 'waken' (Rauh)

To this list may be added *penden* (Rauh) on the grounds that it is glossed in the margin of the MS (at l. 245 of *Genesis,* where *þa hwile*

---

1. Sievers-Brunner, §402.2.
2. Sievers-Brunner, §358.2.
3. Sievers-Brunner, §417 An. 1.
4. Sievers-Brunner, §391 An. 8.
5. Sievers-Brunner, §412 An. 10.
6. Richard Jordan, *Eigentümlichkeiten des Anglischen Wortschatzes* (Heidelberg, 1906); Günther Scherer, *Zur Geographie und Chronologie des angelsächsischen Wortschatzes, im Anschluss an Bischof Wærferth's Übersetzung der 'Dialoge' Gregors* (Weimar, 1928); Hildegard Rauh, *Der Wortschatz der altenglischen Übersetzungen des Matthaeus-Evangeliums* (Berlin, 1936); cf. also R. J. Menner, "Vocabulary of the Old English Poems on Judgment Day," *PMLA,* 62 (1947), 583–97, and "Anglian Vocabulary of the Blickling Homilies," *Philologica: The Malone Anniversary Studies* (Baltimore, 1949), pp. 56–64.

is written). Two of the words in Rauh's lists which she regards as Anglian and found in *Exodus* are to be rejected: she lists *segne* 'seine, net' for l. 552, but the meaning there is almost certainly *segn* 'banner'; and she lists *tān* 'sors' for 281, where the MS reading *tācne* is passable enough (she follows Grein's emendation to *tāne*). No purely Saxon words are to be found in the poem.

Mürkens wished to show Northumbrian origin of the poem, but it is not possible to establish that by linguistic evidence. The evidence for Anglian origin is convincing, however, and on other grounds one would expect the poem to have been written in Northumbria rather than in Mercia. Even if we choose to write off much of Bede's story of Cædmon as mere legend, we must conclude from it that men were writing religious poetry in the vernacular in the closing years of the seventh century, not only at Whitby but at other religious centers in Northumbria. The tradition of Christianity in Northumbria extends much farther back than that in Mercia, and the former is recognized as the probable place of origin of the earlier poetry.

The date of composition of *Exodus* is not to be determined with much accuracy. We might set as the extreme limits within which the poem must fall the year 650, on the one hand, as the earliest possible date for a Christian poem in Anglian territory (but probably later, since Northumbria was not nominally Christianized until about 625, and Mercia not until 655), and on the other hand, as the latest possible date, about the year 1000, roughly the date of the MS we possess. In general, it might be ventured that the composition of a poem of this kind would have been unlikely after a century of Christianity. A comparison with the Cynewulfian poetry will show the lack of sophistication, from a doctrinal point of view especially, of *Exodus*. There is very little explicit Christian phraseology and thought in *Exodus,* which resembles *Genesis A* and *Daniel* in that respect; they are all to be contrasted in style and psychological atmosphere with the liturgical lyrics and saints' lives of the Cynewulfian "school." There is reason to believe that a poet of the ninth century or later would almost inevitably have made far more of the traditional Christian allegorization which overlaid the story of the exodus as interpreted by the fathers of the church.

From another point of view, the style itself gives some indications of stemming from an earlier period. The vigor of the old heroic language is remarkable; it is characterized by fresh and vivid metaphors and the coining of original kennings. The style of *Exodus* is unlike the epic passages of the Cynewulfian and later Christian poetry. It seems to be closer to the original oral epic tradition, whereas Cynewulfian poetry has become something quite different and perhaps closer to continental Latin traditions.[7] The *Exodus* poet was working as a shaper of traditional

7. This impression may be partly confirmed by some statistics compiled by C. T. Carr (*Nominal Compounds in Germanic,* St. Andrews University Publications, No. 41

materials and one has the strong impression that the tradition must have been still living and still esteemed at his time. One might reply to this argument by citing the undeniable vigor of a late tenth-century poem like *Maldon*. But the strength of *Maldon* lies in its unadorned and stark narrative style rather than in such traditional features of the older epics as nominal compounds and kennings.

Such impressions as these of a fairly early date are confirmed by the various linguistic tests which have been applied over the years to the poem with the intention of determining its date, either in relation to other poems or absolutely. Barnouw, in his study of the use of the definite article and the weak adjective, found that *Exodus* was hardly to be distinguished from *Beowulf* in this respect.[8] He placed *Beowulf* at about 660, *Exodus* and most of the Riddles at from 680 to 700, with *Genesis A* at 740. Morsbach, in dating *Beowulf*, declared that it could not have been written before 700, since final *u* after long stressed syllables did not disappear until that date.[9] Neither *Beowulf* nor *Exodus* contains any cases where the insertion of final *u* would make a metrically acceptable reading. Richter applied this criterion and several others to the rest of the OE poetry. He placed *Genesis A* and *Daniel* at 700, *Beowulf* between 700 and 730, and *Exodus* at about 740.[1] In the linguistic details which he treats, *Beowulf* and *Exodus* again agree very closely; his chief

---

[Oxford, 1939], p. 415). Listing the proportion of repeated compounds in the principal OE poems, he finds that in *Exodus* and *Beowulf* only 12% of the noun-compounds are used more than once, as compared with 20.8% in *Christ* and 22% in *Elene*.

8. A. J. Barnouw, *Textkritische Untersuchungen nach dem Gebrauch des bestimmten Artikels und des schwachen Adjectivs in der altenglischen Poesie* (Leiden, 1902). This study regards as older phenomena the use of the weak adjective without article, the use of the definite article in its original demonstrative sense, and the infrequent use of the definite article plus weak adjective plus noun. All three of these characteristics are to be found rather consistently in *Exodus*. Barnouw's subjective method of interpreting the evidence is, however, a distinct drawback.

9. L. Morsbach, "Zur Datierung des Beowulfepos," *Nachrichten der K. Gesellschaft der Wissenschaften zu Göttingen, Philologischhistorische Klasse* (1906), pp. 251–77. For objections to the evidence on which Morsbach bases this criterion, see H. M. Chadwick, *The Heroic Age* (Cambridge, 1912), 66 ff.

1. Carl Richter, *Chronologische Studien zur angelsächsischen Literatur auf Grund sprachlich-metrischer Kriterien* (Halle, 1910). The other criteria were: (*a*) long diphthongs (early) vs. short diphthongs (late) in words where antevocalic *h* after *r* or *l* had been lost (e.g., in *Exodus*, the meter shows *fēora* to have a long diphthong in *lēofost fēora* 384 and in two other cases, *fēores* 404 and *mēara* 171, while the diphthong is short in *tō wīdan feore* 590); (*b*) monosyllabic forms (early) vs. dissyllabic forms (late) in words with vocalic *r, l, m, n* (e.g., *wundor:wundr;* Richter counts 5 monosyllabic, 19 dissyllabic forms in *Exodus*, but included in the latter are a number of words which never appear as monosyllabic in the poetry; see F. Seiffert, *Die Behandlung der Wörter mit auslautenden ursprünglich silbischen Liquiden oder Nasalen und mit Kontraktionsvokalen in der Genesis A und im Beowulf* [Halle, 1913] for a criticism of Richter's method here); (*c*) uncontracted forms (early) vs. contracted forms (late) in words where intervocalic *h* was lost (e.g. in *Exodus*, *lǣste nēar* 308, where the word *nēar* must have been originally dissyllabic [originally **neahur?*—Bülbring, §216]; Richter counts 5 dissyllabic forms to 2 monosyllabic forms [or 3?] in *Exodus*).

reason for assigning *Exodus* to a later date seems to be his conviction that *Exodus* was influenced by *Beowulf,* a belief which has yet to be proved.

Other attempts to place the poem in relation to other poems have been made with varying and sometimes conflicting results. It can, however, be said that one comes away from an examination of this linguistic evidence with the strong impression that *Exodus* should be assigned to the same general period as *Beowulf,* which it resembles more closely than any other poem both linguistically and, to some extent, stylistically. Fr. Klaeber places *Beowulf* in "the first half of the eighth century" and the so-called Cædmon poems (*Genesis A, Daniel,* and *Exodus*) "in the neighborhood of 700." [2] He is convinced that *Genesis A* and probably *Daniel* preceded *Beowulf,* since there may be traces of their influence on the latter poem.

Controversy has raged for a long period of time over the significance of the striking verbal correspondences between *Exodus* and *Beowulf,* but no general agreement has been reached.[3] Did the *Exodus* poet borrow some of his phrases from *Beowulf,* was the process the reverse, or are the similarities merely coincidental? The first of these hypotheses has been the most popular among scholars in the past. L. L. Schücking's heretical suggestion that the *Beowulf* poet may have borrowed from *Exodus* arose in his discussion of the most frequently mentioned parallel, the line *enge ānpaðas, uncūð gelād* (*Ex.* 58, *Beow.* 1410).[4] Klaeber, in the most elaborate article on the subject, made an extensive examination of all possible parallels in wording and concluded that "the balance of probability inclines at least slightly in favor of the priority of *Exodus.*" [5] The controversy, still centered on the single line mentioned, did not end here. Imelmann claimed to have found a Vergilian source for the line in *Beowulf,* a fact which, if true, would suggest strongly the priority of *Beowulf.*[6] On this evidence Klaeber retracted his stand and stated that *Beowulf* must have preceded *Exodus.*[7] The last word came from Schücking, who still believed in the priority of *Exodus* and considered that even

---

2. *Beowulf and the Fight at Finnsburg* (3d ed. with suppl., New York, Heath, 1941), p. cxiii.

3. Cf. Joseph Strobl, "Angelsächsische Studien," *Germania, 20* (1875), 292 ff.; Groth, *Composition und Alter der altenglischen Exodus,* pp. 29 ff.; Gregor Sarrazin, *Beowulf-Studien* (Berlin, 1888), pp. 158 ff.; Alois Brandl in *Grundriss der germanischen Philologie,* p. 1009.

4. *Untersuchungen zur Bedeutungslehre der angelsächsischen Dichtersprache* (Heidelberg, 1915), pp. 38 ff.

5. "Concerning the Relation between 'Exodus' and 'Beowulf,'" *MLN, 33* (1918), 224.

6. Rudolf Imelmann, *Forschungen zur altenglischen Poesie* (Berlin, 1920), p. 419. The passage is *Æneid* xi 524–5:

> tenuis quo semita ducit,
> angustaeque ferunt fauces aditusque maligni.

7. *Anglia, 50* (1926), 202–3.

if the *Beowulf* poet had known the *Æneid* passage, he took the phrasing of his imitation from *Exodus*.[8]

The problem remains a difficult one, but the most probable solution, although not the most satisfying, is that there was no direct influence either way, that the parallel passages are essentially coincidental. It is always difficult to bear in mind that the portion of OE literature which we possess represents probably only a relatively small proportion of the whole, especially if we imagine all the lays and epic poems which were never written down at all. The much discussed *enge ānpaðas, uncūð gelād,* if we assume it to be a traditional phrase, might well have been one which would stick in a poet's mind. When the opportunity to use it came, as in describing a perilous journey through unknown ways, perhaps a journey into exile, he would employ it for its emotional connotation. It may well be mere chance that we have only two poems surviving in which the phrase is used. It is appropriate enough in both *Exodus* and *Beowulf*. Other parallels are more interesting, but in nearly every case each phrase or passage fits the poem it is in surprisingly well. The descriptions of blood in the water—the blood of the dying Egyptians in *Exodus,* the blood that rises to the surface of Grendel's mere in *Beowulf* —are similar in many phrases, although never startlingly so. Yet each seems appropriate in its context; the *Exodus* poet is evidently playing, in an obscure way, with the idea of the *Red* Sea. Certainly in this case it is possible to imagine a stock of poetic phrases like *holm heolfre spāw* (*Ex.* 450) or *holm heolfre wēoll* (*Beow.* 2138). The Anglo-Saxons were both warriors and seafarers; there must have been at least a few poems in oral circulation celebrating sea fights and gory battles on the beaches which might have provided a plentiful stock of such descriptive phrases. Similarly the description of feats of horsemanship probably stems from the same epic source.[9] In some cases of resemblance, the *Exodus* passage clearly has a source in the phraseology of the Vulgate; the phrases *ne ðǣr ǣnig becwōm herges tō hāme* 456–7 and *forðām þæs heriges hām eft ne cōm . . . ǣnig tō lāfe* 508–9 translate Exod. 14:28: *nec unus quidem superfuit ex eis. Beow.* 2365–6 reads: *lȳt eft becwōm fram þām hildfrecan hāmes nīosan.* Similarly the phrase *þurh mīne hand* represents the literal situation in *Ex.* 262 (cf. Exod. 14:16: *extende manum tuam*), where Moses' hand is mentioned as the immediate cause of the opening of the sea; in *Beow.* 558–9 the same expression seems no more appropriate.

8. "Noch einmal: *enge ānpaðas, uncūð gelād,*" *Studies in English Philology, a Miscellany in Honor of Frederick Klaeber* (Minneapolis, 1929), pp. 213–16.

9. *Ex.* 170–1: *Beow.* 864–5. Hwīlum heaþorōfe hlēapan lēton
            on geflit faran   fealwe mēaras
     and 916–17. Hwīlum flītende   fealwe strǣte
            mēarum mǣton.
Here it should be noted that Pharoah's men were mounted, according to the Bible (Exod. 15:19).

Most of the other parallels found by Klaeber are probably to be considered clichés of little importance. The evidence does not seem to justify any conclusion that either poet was borrowing from the other.[1] The examination of these passages brings out more fully an aspect of the *Exodus* poet's talent already mentioned, his uncanny ability in matching biblical references with the appropriate epic phrase.

Unfortunately nothing very conclusive can be said about the relation of *Exodus* to other OE poems. It is not possible to say on stylistic grounds whether *Exodus* came before or after *Genesis A* or *Daniel* or whether there is any possibility of minor borrowing. *Exodus,* if one may judge from the religious terms found in it (the kennings for God, for example), seems to follow in an already established tradition of religious verse; but there were probably a number of other religious poems besides the ones which have survived. It can be said with certainty that the three poems were written by different poets. *Genesis A* is a paraphrase, owing whatever form it has to the source it follows so closely; *Exodus* is a deliberately conceived and constructed poem based on a single incident and drawing in references and allusions to other biblical stories to reinforce its central theme. Nowhere in *Genesis A* do we find evidence of such an essentially artistic mind or traces of such brilliant if erratic style. *Daniel* is perhaps more like *Exodus* in the method of treating a scriptural subject; but, fundamentally and inescapably, the important difference between *Daniel* and *Exodus* is the difference between the inferior and superior in poetic quality.

Perhaps mention should be made of the possibility that *Exodus* was being imitated or rather recollected in a passage in *Guthlac* (*B*) (see Note, 107b–111a). The description of the apparition of heavenly light which shines at the time of Guthlac's death has some points of resemblance to the description of the pillar of fire in *Exodus*. The resemblance is by no means conclusive, however, and may stem simply from the fact that the objects described are similar.

Altogether it must be concluded that in many ways *Exodus* resembles *Beowulf* more than it resembles any other poem—sometimes in style and often in vocabulary and certain linguistic features. When the suspicion of direct influence or imitation is rejected as quite unproven, the facts remain and seem to suggest that it is possible the two poems may have originated in the same or similar literary climates, perhaps at the same time in history and in the same general area of England.

What can be safely said about the authorship of *Exodus*? We have the name of only one poet, Cædmon, available to us for the period in which it seems to have been written. If we believe what Bede tells us of Cædmon, then it is fairly certain we must believe that he was not the author of

---

1. If borrowing is to be insisted on, *Exodus* has certainly as good a claim to priority as *Beowulf* in many cases, particularly those which reflect phrases in the Bible.

Exodus. According to Bede's account, Cædmon had never composed
poetry before and had had no training in it whatever. He was apparently
illiterate and had to have the stories or lessons which he was commis-
sioned to versify recited to him by learned men. Now if this was actually
the case, there is perhaps some temptation to think that, if not Cædmon
himself, a person like him may have been the author of *Exodus*. Such
a hypothesis would provide an explanation for the erratic appearance of
bits of fact and legend which can be traced to no single source, together
with the strange lack of doctrine, especially of the direct and obvious
allegorizing kind which abounds in the commentaries. There is always,
too, the statement of Bede that among the songs which Cædmon sang
was one on the exodus of Israel out of Egypt.

This theory is not supported, however, by the evidence of the poem
itself. It is simply not to be believed, in the first place, in view of the
extraordinarily precise knowledge of the Bible which the poet seems to
have, that he was illiterate. While he may not have been extensively
learned or well read, and one has the impression that he was not, cer-
tainly he was quite capable of reading and understanding the Vulgate.
The few Latinisms which we find in the poem clearly come from the
Vulgate. There is too great a homogeneity of tone in the poem for us
to believe that such evidences of Latin origin might have been added
later by a tinkering reviser; they clearly stem from the original author.
Furthermore, it is not credible that this poet was unfamiliar with the
older poetry, as Cædmon was said to have been; on the contrary, *Exodus*
shows a wide acquaintance with epic themes and phrases. Although the
poet seems to be limited in some ways in the range of his vocabulary,
certainly he has the very feel of the heroic tradition.

Bede tells us that other Englishmen after Cædmon tried their hands at
composing religious poems. The poet of *Exodus* must have existed some-
where among these shadowy figures. He was probably a Northumbrian
and was almost certainly connected with the church, probably a monk or
priest. The linguistic tests cannot help us to date the poem scientifically;
it would not contradict them and it would be consistent with historical
probability to imagine that *Exodus* was written in the earliest years of
the eighth century, in the first or second generation after Cædmon.

V. *Structure and Style*

IT is in some ways difficult to apply the usual standards of criticism
to a poem which we know to be lacking sizable sections and which
we may suspect of lacking others. Yet it seems possible, since we can
make a fair guess at what is missing, to regard *Exodus* as essentially an
organic unit and to make some observations on its basic theme and
structure.

The central theme of the poem is the march of the Children of Israel under God's guidance to the Promised Land, a progress which the poet has chosen to represent by one chief incident, the escape from Pharaoh in the crossing of the Red Sea. On one level the poem is clearly to be seen as a religious allegory, but it is made all the more effective in that the poet does not generalize in so many words the concept of the relationship between God and man but presents his story consistently in terms of action and the specific event. Avitus, in treating the same subject, dulls the impact of the sheerly dramatic by his constant drawing of morals and his preoccupation with the theological and moral significance of each incident as it arises.

What may be called the dogmatic content of the story seems to involve two complementary ideas: first, the need for (and difficulty of) obeying God; and second, the reward which comes to those who trust and obey him. The first is shown us most clearly in the main action where the Israelites become fainthearted at the moment of crisis until they are rebuked by Moses, but it appears as well in the Abraham and Isaac episode where the temptation to disobey is much stronger, and even by implication in the Noah story. Each of these stories involves a promise on God's part, then a test of faith and obedience, and finally a reward.

Thus from this point of view it may be said that the action of the poem is a single action and that the Abraham and Noah episodes serve to reinforce the central significance of that action. It is the story of a single movement, a mass movement on both physical and spiritual levels. The lack of individualization of characters, which has often been noted in the poem, emphasizes the mass. The people move, are frightened, and rejoice as one. Such stressing of the group, which is in this case a whole race and at its widest extension humanity itself, adds something to the universality of the poet's theme, a universality suggested simply but effectively by the large actions of large masses. Whether or not the poet was aware of the widespread allegorical interpretation of the exodus as man's progress to salvation—there is some definite evidence that he was [1]—the effect of the poem as a whole almost inevitably suggests something of the kind. Yet what is perhaps more important is the fact that he does not choose to employ much of this easily available material. He seems far more interested in the story as story.

As we have seen, there is little characterization of individuals in the poem. Moses is endowed with some of the traits of the epic hero, but he is hardly comparable in interest to Judith or the Satan of *Genesis B* and is even less comparable to Beowulf or Hrothgar. He is most often glorified as the *folctoga,* the leader of the people, and the people emerge as more important than he. Of the very few other characters, only Abraham

1. See Note, 104, on *līfweg,* and Note, 81, on the sail metaphor. The passage placed in this edition at the end of the poem (especially ll. 565–80) seems to emphasize, in a somewhat clumsy fashion, the universal lesson to be obtained from the story. See Note, 576, on *ēðellēase.*

could be said to be individualized at all, and his actions are almost ritualistic in their symbolic significance. Such characters as Pharaoh and the herald exist solely as figureheads or symbols. It may be noted that Avitus shows far more interest in Pharaoh as a character.

It is remarkable that the more one contemplates the poem as a whole the more one tends to feel that the role of epic hero and king has been filled by the person of God himself. The term *cyning,* so often applied to the Deity, seems to carry more literal meaning than usual in this poem. All the emotional associations which clustered around the Germanic concepts of the necessity of loyalty to one's lord, the emphasis on warfare and stern performance of duty, and the munificent reward for faith and obedience have been transferred, and on the whole convincingly transferred, to the religious ties which bind man to God. Such a poetic device is certainly not uncommon in OE religious poetry, but it is not always successful. Perhaps *Genesis B* is the only other poem in which the joining of the heroic and the Christian in this sense is similarly effective. In *Exodus,* furthermore, God is no abstraction. He helps his loyal followers by comfort and miracle when it is necessary and descends to wield his ancient sword in the climactic onslaught on the Egyptians—a gory and essentially physical representation of spiritual conflict and a truly impressive one.

Other heroic aspects of the poem are evident on every hand. The atmosphere of battle and preparation for war is consistently maintained. Though there is never an actual battle, the poet provides a spectacular setting for one. Indeed, when the Egyptians are drowned, their struggle is put into the terms of battle, a bloody and desperate war between them and the sea, or, more properly, between them and God (*hīe wið God wunnon!* 515). While it may be thought that the underlying moral conflict justifies such warlike references, the emphasis on the Hebrews' prowess in war is important also in that several allusions are made to the future when they will have to rely on their own warfare to win a homeland from foreign tribes. On the other hand, the might of the Egyptians is obviously built up so that the grand and awful scale of their destruction may be more clearly pictured. Even the vast and unimaginable armies are broken down by the poet into units which the Anglo-Saxon could comprehend, into war bands under personal leadership. And the battle ends traditionally and satisfyingly with the looting of the fallen enemy.

Heroic features are also to be found in the use of motives springing from kinship. The rivalry between Israelites and Egyptians becomes a blood feud in which the Egyptians are impatient to avenge their brothers' deaths. Similarly the enormity of Abraham's crime in attempting to kill his own son is heightened by the same emotional connotations.

Yet, as the Notes point out in many individual instances, the poet shows unerring taste and judgment in selecting heroic details which reinforce his biblical theme without conflicting with it. One need only recall the inappropriateness of much of the epic and martial imagery which surrounds the figure of the more spiritual warrior Andreas to appreciate the much more highly developed fusion of physical and spiritual, the joining of warlike tone to a basically warlike story in *Exodus*.

Another typical motif in OE poetry may be mentioned here in connection with heroic features which at the same time will lead us into a discussion of some other aspects of the poet's style. This is the nautical imagery, which is used often in the poem and which recalls the many fine sea passages elsewhere in OE poetry. Most interesting is the sustained metaphor, an unusual device in OE poetry, which is developed from the comparison of the pillar of cloud to a sail. The figure is based ultimately on an etymology of Jerome (see Note, 81) and is carried out relatively fully; the Israelites are sailors, Reuben's sons are *sæwīcingas* striding over the salt marsh, the road the host follows is the *flōdweg,* while the Egyptians are referred to (perhaps contemptuously) as "land-men." Not only are we to think of the crossing of the Red Sea as a kind of voyage, which expert sailors (with God's help) can achieve whereas landlubbers come to grief, but in a wider sense the metaphor of life, especially the religious life, as a voyage is suggested. The Noah episode reinforces this idea by implication. Here again we find evidence of the poet's gift for seizing on a detail in a recognized authority which is usable for his purpose and which he can develop in his own idiom for a legitimate poetic effect.

Connected with this voyage theme is the series of references to the Promised Land of the Israelites, the *ēðel* promised to Moses by God at the outset of the poem, toward which they yearn in the midst of despair. The climax of the Abraham episode is the promise by the voice from heaven of a land stretching from sea to sea. Moses reminds them of this promise in his speech after the crossing. In the jubilation following Moses' speech, the phrase *folc wæs on lande* seems to bring together the voyage and homecoming themes in one exultant phrase.

The poet has a gift for narrative technique, not only in the wider sense already mentioned but in the dramatic presentation of action. Perhaps the best example of this may be found in the description of the oncoming Egyptians (ll. 154–204), a passage which is largely original with the poet, based on three or four verses of the Bible. In this passage real dramatic tension is developed. The poet shifts his focus from the terrified Israelites to the menacing hosts advancing on them and then back to the Israelites. We see the Egyptians emerge as individuals as they draw closer—the warriors riding in advance, the grim king in his armor. An ominous description of the numbers of the host, its organization, and the determination of its warriors follows, and the fear of the Hebrews rises to a climax as the distance is narrowed steadily until the angel of God intervenes at the last moment. The whole episode is clearly visualized and powerfully communicated. The famous description of the drowning of the Egyptians shows a different method. Unfortunately it is greatly damaged by textual corruption, but in it too we can see the same sharp perception of detail and imaginative insight into mass emotion. From the standpoint of chronological order the scene is chaotic; beginning, middle, and end seem to be presented simultaneously, but in this case the impression of confusion conveys the dominant aspect of the scene itself.

The verbal style and diction of *Exodus* are, however, perhaps its most striking features and those which have occasioned the most comment.[2] It may be said quite safely that no other OE poem has such violent metaphors or so many new and startling kennings. This individual quality of the poet's language may be seen in many forms: in such word play as *flōd blōd gewōd* 463, in the bewildering series of metaphors in which he speaks of the guiding pillar (it is a canopy, a net, a storm cloud, a sail, and a tent in the space of twelve lines, 73–85), in such bold phrases as *ecg grymetode* 'the sword roared like a wild beast' 408 and *nacud nȳdboda . . . fāh fēðegāst* 475–6, of the destroying sea which falls on the Egyptians, or in such packed compounds as *flōdblāc* 498 and *gyrdwīte* 15.

The effectiveness of some of his phrases cannot be doubted. In the line *wǣron hleahtorsmiðum handa belocene* 43 he has revitalized the figurative compound with *smið,* elsewhere used only conservatively in such words as *wīgsmið,* and made it into something impressive. Typical of the description of the drowning of the Egyptians is:

> *Wicon weallfǣsten,   wǣgas burston,*
> *multon meretorras.* (484–5)

Here we see the style which is perhaps most typical of the poet, the use of many short phrases, usually noun and verb, set in a loose series.

Schücking lists, disapprovingly, almost all these examples and many more; he is puzzled and outraged at what he terms their incomprehensibility and preciosity. In this connection he refers to modern poetry (he mentions Stefan George). Perhaps such an analogy has in fact some significance. To readers of twentieth-century poetry or even of Shakespeare, the metaphors in *Exodus* seem to be if not exactly familiar at least in no way astonishing. The similarity may lie in a fuller exploitation of the meanings of words and in a greater compression or

2. Schücking, *Untersuchungen zur Bedeutungslehre der angelsächsischen Dichtersprache,* pp. 12–18, discusses this subject at great length; see also the remarks of W. F. Schirmer, *Geschichte der englischen Literatur* (Halle, 1937), p. 27, who emphasizes the strained and extreme nature of the poet's rhetoric, and of Fr. Klaeber, "Zum germanischen Sprachstil: Das Nomen," *Archiv für das Studium der neueren Sprachen, 183* (1943), 81, who speaks of the staccato quality of the style.

condensation of meaning in a brief phrase. Yet the fact remains that one finds little of the same use of language in the rest of OE poetry.

The peculiarities of the *Exodus* poet extend even farther. In addition to an extraordinary violence of language at times it is curious to discover, on the other hand, some evidence of a limited vocabulary, or, more precisely, of a disregard for the variations so prominent in other OE poetry. The word *werod,* for example, is used 21 times, not counting such compounds as *lēodwerod; folc* appears 16 times and even more often in compounds, as both first and second element; *mægen* (in the sense of 'army') is used 10 times and in several compound forms. The rhetorical superlative with *mǣst* (e.g., *drihtfolca mǣst*) is used a dozen times; in *Beowulf,* a poem five times as long, it is employed only 8 times. Schücking prints a list of words *not* used in *Exodus* which is of interest even though a number of them must be rejected since it would be nearly impossible to use them in the poem under any circumstances.[3]

The explanation of this apparent contradiction, this combination of unusual boldness of language with a certain carelessness or indifference in the use of it, is not an easy one. If we compare this poet with the *Beowulf* poet, for example, we may gain the impression that for all his familiarity with epic tradition the poet of *Exodus* is in some ways strangely awkward and seems to have made only a limited use of the possibilities of artistic variation in OE verse. The intensity of his search for expression seems to be represented on the one hand by a marked indifference to the minor elegancies of expression and on the other hand by the unexpectedness of many of his phrases and compounds. He may have felt himself compelled to invent his own language much of the time, coining large numbers of phrases and compounds—probably a fair number of the starred *hapax legomena* in the Glossary are coinages—some of which are outstandingly successful and some which the scribes seem to have foundered on and rendered incomprehensible.

The same odd combination of weakness and strength in vocabulary and diction may be paralleled to some extent by a similar phenomenon in the realm of style and syntax. The poet's typical style has already been mentioned; it is what is remembered by the reader as the unique feature of *Exodus.* We see it most clearly in the description of the drowning of the Egyptians, but it is evident as well in some of the other narrative passages (e.g., 54–62, 155–69). It is characterized by rapid, almost breathless, movement and by asyndetic parataxis in syntax—a virtual machine-gun stream of brief and telling phrases. But also noticeable and perhaps equally characteristic of the poet are passages of quite another kind—tortuous and ambiguous in construction, long-winded and involved. Here should be included the opening sentence of the poem, containing a

---

3. Schücking, *Untersuchungen zur Bedeutungslehre der angelsächsischen Dichtersprache,* p. 13; see also Gollancz, *The Cædmon Manuscript,* p. lxviii.

long and remarkably complicated parenthesis; ll. 561–72, a passage even more difficult to unravel satisfactorily; ll. 141–53, containing an allusive and complicated description of the origins of the Egyptians' hostility; and some briefer passages (e.g., ll. 49–53, 114–19). It will be observed that all these passages are more abstract in their subjects than the bulk of the poem. The poet seems to have had little real aptitude for expressing lucidly and gracefully such relatively complex ideas. He tends to load the sentence with more allusions than it can carry.

Undoubtedly some of the peculiar intensity of his language comes directly from the Bible itself. The poetry of the Psalms, for example, seems to have had considerable effect on the general tone of the description of the drowning.

Such suggestions as these seem more plausible than the theory which has been occasionally advanced that the poet was influenced directly by elaborate and precious Latin poetry of the kind made notorious by Aldhelm.[4] Such a contact would argue a greater sophistication, or at least a far different kind of sophistication, than this poet seems to show. Certainly in that event his style would be likely to show traces of Latin rhetoric of the sort we can find extensively in the works of Cynewulf. But the only Latinisms of any kind in the poem are minor verbal echoes of the Vulgate itself and of no great importance.

A few general conclusions may be offered on the poet of *Exodus*. He was, as has been suggested above, certainly a monk, or in some way connected with a religious establishment. He was literate and seems to have known the Bible fairly well, having read it in an independent fashion. While he was doubtless familiar with the conventional allegorization of Old Testament narrative, he seems to have been less interested in ingenious abstract interpretations than in the stories themselves. This is not to say that he was not cognizant of the total symbolic effect of the exodus story; but he was concerned with dramatizing it as a whole rather than in parts. A stock of curious and out-of-the-way information was available to him, material not collected in any known single work. He made good use of such legendary and apocryphal material, employing it on the whole effectively in the artistic sense and not in a mere show of learning. Perhaps like Cædmon he was furnished with information by more learned monks and scholars around him.

We may believe that he lived in an exciting intellectual atmosphere where strange lore of all kinds was everywhere and had as yet been scarcely formulated or digested. It was in all probability the early years of the so-called Northumbrian Renaissance, in which Bede was later to be the great figure.

Despite a certain lack of discipline and an occasional lack of ease and

---

4. See, for example, Gollancz, *The Cædmon Manuscript*, p. lxviii f., and Schirmer, *Geschichte der englischen Literatur*, p. 27.

grace, the author of *Exodus* was a true poet. Against the background of the OE poetry which has survived, his work stands out as one of the very few first-rate poems. He had an architectonic ability rare among poets of his age. Without using, so far as can be discovered, a structural model, he succeeded in writing a poem which is unified both formally and emotionally. Perhaps his greatest achievement is the way he has retold the tremendous story of the exodus without merely paraphrasing and without distorting his original. As a poet he has heightened and enhanced the spiritual significance of his theme, and to the power inherent in that story he has infused creatively the vigor of his own idiom and poetic tradition.

SELECTED BIBLIOGRAPHY

I. Manuscript

Gollancz, Israel. *The Cædmon Manuscript of Anglo-Saxon Biblical Poetry, Junius* XI *in the Bodleian Library*. Facsimile ed. London, Oxford University Press, 1927.

II. Descriptions of Manuscript

Clubb, M. D. *Christ and Satan*. New Haven, 1925. Pp. xi–xiii.

Ellis, Henry. *Account of Cædmon's Metrical Paraphrase of Scriptural History, an Illuminated Manuscript of the Tenth Century, Preserved in the Bodleian Library at Oxford*. London, 1833.

Keller, Wolfgang. *Angelsächsische Palaeographie*. Palaestra, 43, Teil 1. Berlin, 1906. P. 39.

Krapp, George Philip. *The Junius Manuscript. Anglo-Saxon Poetic Records, 1*. New York, Columbia University Press, 1931. MS described in Introduction, *passim*.

——— *The Vercelli Book. Anglo-Saxon Poetic Records, 3*. New York, Columbia University Press, 1932. List of accents in Junius MS, pp. lxv–lxxiv.

Lawrence, John. "On Codex Junius XI," *Anglia, 12* (1889), 598–605.

Sievers, Eduard. "Collationen angelsächsischer Gedichte," *Zeitschrift für deutsches Altertum, 15* (1872), 456–67. *Exodus* described on p. 458.

Stoddard, F. H. "The Cædmon Poems in MS. Junius XI," *Anglia, 10* (1888), 157–62.

Timmer, B. J. *The Later Genesis*. Oxford, 1948.

Wanley, Humphrey. *Antiquæ literaturæ septentrionalis liber alter, seu Humphredi Wanleii librorum vett. septentrionalium, qui in Angliæ bibliothecis extant . . . Catalogus*. Oxford, 1705. P. 77.

III. Editions

(IN CHRONOLOGICAL ORDER)

With the exception of a few, excerpts in readers and grammars of OE are not listed; Krapp's Bibliography in *The Junius Manuscript* contains a full list of such excerpts to 1930.

Junius, Francis. *Cædmonis Monachi Paraphrasis Poetica Genesios ac præcipuarum Sacræ paginæ Historiarum, abhinc annos* M.LXX. *Anglo-Saxonicé conscripta, & nunc primum edita . . .* Amsterdam, 1655.

Thorpe, Benjamin. *Cædmon's Metrical Paraphrase of Parts of the Holy Scriptures, in Anglo-Saxon*. London, 1832.

Bouterwek, Karl W. *Cædmon's des Angelsachsen biblische Dichtungen*. Theil 1, Gütersloh, 1854; Theil 2, Elberfeld, 1851.

Grein, Christian W. M. *Bibliothek der angelsächsischen Poesie*. Bd. 1. Göttingen, 1857.

Körner, Karl. *Einleitung in das Studium des Angelsächsischen*. Teil 2, Heilbronn, 1880. Contains *Exodus* 1–67, 252–306.

Hunt, Theodore W. *Cædmon's Exodus and Daniel*. Edited from Grein. Boston, 1883. 3d ed., Boston, 1888.

Kluge, Friedrich. *Angelsächsisches Lesebuch*. Halle, 1888. Contains *Exodus* 1–361.

Wülker, Richard P. *Bibliothek der angelsächsischen Poesie*. Bd. 2. Leipzig, 1894. Pp. 445–75.

Blackburn, Francis A. *Exodus and Daniel, Two Old English Poems Preserved in MS. Junius 11 in the Bodleian Library of the University of Oxford, England*. Boston and London, Heath, 1907.

Sedgefield, W. J. *An Anglo-Saxon Verse Book*. Manchester, The University Press, 1922. Contains *Exodus* 1–361, 477–590.

Krapp, George Philip. *The Junius Manuscript. Anglo-Saxon Poetic Records, 1*. New York, Columbia University Press, 1931.

IV. Translations

Bouterwek, Karl W. See under III; German translation with his edition.

Gordon, Robert K. *Anglo-Saxon Poetry*. London and Toronto, 1927. Contains *Exodus* 1–306, 447–590.

Grein, Christian W. M. *Dichtungen der Angelsachsen stabreimend übersetzt*. Bd. 1. Göttingen, 1857.

Johnson, William S. "Translation of the Old English *Exodus*," *JEGP, 5* (1903), 44–57.

Kennedy, Charles W. *The Cædmon Poems. Translated into English Prose*. London, G. Routledge & Sons, 1916.

Thorpe, Benjamin. See under III; line-by-line translation with his edition.

V. Textual Studies and Notes

Barnouw, A. J. In *Germanic Review, 6* (1931), 400 f. Review of Krapp's edition.

Baum, Paull F. "The Character of Anglo-Saxon Verse," *MP, 28* (1930–31), 143–56. Uses *Exodus* as an example; defends MS *har hæð* 118a.

Binz, Gustav. In *Anglia Beiblatt, 14* (1903), 356–8. Review of Mürkens.

Bloomfield, Leonard. "Old English Plural Subjunctives in -E," *JEGP, 21* (1930), 100–13.

Bradley, Henry. "The Numbered Sections in Old English Poetical MSS.," *Proceedings of the British Academy, 7* (1915–16), 165–87.

Bright, James W. "Notes on the Cædmonian *Exodus*," *MLN, 17* (1902), 424–6.

—— "On the Anglo-Saxon Poem *Exodus*," *MLN, 27* (1912), 13–19.

Bryan, W. F. "*Ǣrgōd* in *Beowulf*, and Other Old English Compounds of *ǣr*," *MP, 28* (1930–31), 157–61. Note on *ǣrglade* 293.

Craigie, W. A. "Interpolations and Omissions in Anglo-Saxon Poetic Texts," *Philologica, 2* (1925), 5–19.

Cosijn, P. J. *Aanteekeningen op den Béowulf*. Leiden, 1892. P. 1.

Cosijn, P. J. "Anglosaxonica," *Beiträge, 19* (1894), 441–61. Pp. 457–61.

――― "Anglosaxonica II," *Beiträge, 20* (1895), 98–116. Pp. 98–106.

Dietrich, Franz. "Zu Cädmon," *Zeitschrift für deutsches Altertum, 10* (1856), 310–67. Pp. 339–55 on *Exodus*.

Ebert, Adolf. "Zum Exodus," *Anglia, 5* (1882), 409–10.

Graz, Friedrich. "Beiträge zur Textkritik der sogenannten Cædmon'schen Dichtungen," *Englische Studien, 21* (1895), 1–27.

Grein, C. W. M. "Zur Textkritik der angelsächsischen Dichter," *Germania, 10* (1865), 416–29. P. 418.

Holthausen, Ferdinand. In *Anglia Beiblatt, 5* (1895), 231. Review of Wülker's edition.

――― In *Anglia Beiblatt, 30* (1919), 3. Review of Kock JJJ.

――― In *Literaturblatt für germanische und romanische Philologie, 21* (1900), 62–3. Review of Mürkens.

――― "Studien zur altenglischen Dichtung," *Anglia, 46* (1922), 52–62.

――― "Zu altenglischen denkmälern," *Englische Studien, 51* (1917–18), 182–3.

――― "Zu altenglischen Dichtungen," *Anglia, 44* (1920), 353.

――― "Zu alt- und mittelenglischen denkmälern," *Anglia Beiblatt, 29* (1918), 283.

――― "Zur altenglischen Literatur," *Anglia Beiblatt, 18* (1907), 202.

――― "Zur altenglischen Literatur," *Anglia Beiblatt, 21* (1910), 12–14.

Hulbert, J. R. "A Note on Compounds in *Beowulf*," *JEGP, 31* (1932), 506–7.

――― "On the Text of the Junius Manuscript," *JEGP, 37* (1938), 533–6.

Klaeber, Fr. In *Englische Studien, 41* (1909–10), 105–13. Review of Blackburn's edition.

――― In *JEGP, 19* (1920), 409–13. Review of Kock JJJ.

――― "Zu altenglischen Dichtungen," *Archiv, 113* (1904), 146–7.

Kock, E. A. "Interpretations and Emendations of Early English Texts IV," *Anglia, 42* (1918), 99–124. P. 121.

――― "Interpretations and Emendations of Early English Texts V," *Anglia, 43* (1919), 298–312. Pp. 305–7.

――― "Interpretations and Emendations of Early English Texts VII," *Anglia, 44* (1920), 245–60.

――― "Interpretations and Emendations of Early English Texts VIII," *Anglia, 45* (1921), 105–31. Pp. 124–5.

――― "Interpretations and Emendations of Early English Texts X," *Anglia, 46* (1922), 173–92. P. 184.

――― "Jubilee Jaunts and Jottings. 250 Contributions to the Interpretation and Prosody of Old West Teutonic Alliterative Poetry," *Lunds Universitets Årsskrift*, N. F., Avd. 1, Bd. 14, Nr. 26 (1918).

――― "Plain Points and Puzzles. 60 Notes on Old English Poetry," *Lunds Universitets Årsskrift*, N. F., Avd. 1, Bd. 17, Nr. 7 (1922).

Konrath, M. "Zu Exodus 351b–353a," *Englische Studien, 12* (1889), 138–9.

Napier, Arthur S. "The Old English 'Exodus,' ll. 63–134," *MLR, 6* (1911), 165–8.

Rieger, Max. "Die alt- und angelsächsische verskunst," *Zeitschrift für deutsche Philologie, 7* (1876), 1–64.

Routh, James E., Jr. *Two Studies on the Ballad Theory of the Beowulf.* Baltimore, 1905. Pp. 54–5.

Sedgefield, W. J. In *MLR, 26* (1931), 352–5. Review of Krapp's edition.

——— "Suggested Emendations in Old English Poetical Texts," *MLR, 16* (1921), 59–61.

Sievers, Eduard. "Zu Codex Junius XI," *Beiträge, 10* (1885), 195–9.

——— "Zur Rhythmik des germanischen Alliterationsverses. II," *Beiträge, 10* (1885), 451–545.

——— "Zur Rhythmik des germanischen Alliterationsverses. III," *Beiträge, 12* (1887), 454–82.

Sisam, Kenneth. "Notes on Old English Poetry," *RES, 22* (1946), 257–68. P. 264.

——— "The Cædmonian *Exodus* 492," *MLN, 32* (1917), 48.

Strobl, Joseph. "Angelsächsische Studien," *Germania, 20* (1875), 292–305. Chiefly concerns the question of unity and interpolation.

Thomas, P. G. "The OE. *Exodus,*" *MLR, 12* (1917), 342–5.

Von Schaubert, Else. "Zur Erklärung Schwierigkeiten bietender altenglischer Textstellen," in *Philologica: The Malone Anniversary Studies.* Baltimore, Johns Hopkins University Press, 1949. Pp. 41–2.

Williams, O. T. "A Note on 'Exodus,' ll. 56 ff.," *MLR, 4* (1909), 507–8. On *Gūðmyrce* 59.

VI. General

A. DATING AND AUTHORSHIP

Balg, Hugo. *Der Dichter Cædmon und seine Werke.* Bonn, 1882.

Barnouw, A. J. *Textkritische Untersuchungen nach dem Gebrauch des bestimmten Artikels und des schwachen Adjectivs in der altenglischen Poesie.* Leiden, 1902. Pp. 80–9, 233.

Girvan, Ritchie. *Beowulf and the Seventh Century.* London, 1935. Review of dating methods, pp. 1–25.

Götzinger, Ernst. *Ueber die Dichtungen des Angelsachsen Caedmon und deren Verfasser.* Göttingen, 1860.

Groth, Ernst J. *Composition und Alter der altenglischen (angelsächsischen) Exodus.* Göttingen, 1883.

Imelmann, Rudolf. *Forschungen zur altenglischen Poesie.* Berlin, 1920. Chiefly on *enge ānpaðas* 58; pp. 382–420.

Klaeber, Fr. "Beowulfiana," *Anglia, 50* (1926), 202–3. Comment on *enge ānpaðas* 58.

——— "Concerning the Relation between 'Exodus' and 'Beowulf,'" *MLN, 33* (1918), 218–24.

Marquardt, Hertha. "Zur Entstehung des *Beowulf,*" *Anglia, 64* (1940), 152–8. On the relationship of *Beowulf* to the Cædmonian poems.

Mürkens, Gerhard. "Untersuchungen über das altenglische Exoduslied,"

Bonner Beiträge, 2 (1899), 62–117. Includes textual notes on pp. 113–17.

Richter, Carl. *Chronologische Studien zur angelsächsischen Literatur auf Grund sprachlich-metrischer Kriterien.* Halle, 1910. Pp. 16–18.

Sarrazin, Gregor. *Von Kädmon bis Kynewulf.* Berlin, 1913. Esp. pp. 38–9.

—— "Zur chronologie und verfasserfrage angelsächsischer dichtungen," *Englische Studien, 38* (1907), 145–95.

Schücking, L. L. "Noch einmal: *enge ānpaðas, uncūð gelād,*" *Studies in English Philology, a Miscellany in Honor of Frederick Klaeber.* Minneapolis, 1929. Pp. 213–16.

B. TECHNICAL STUDIES (GRAMMAR, METER, STYLE)

Carr, C. T. *Nominal Compounds in Germanic.* St. Andrews University Publications, 41. Oxford, 1939. Esp. p. 415.

Graz, Friedrich. *Die Metrik der sog. Cædmonschen Dichtungen mit Berücksichtigung der Verfasserfrage.* Weimar, 1894.

Hofer, Oscar. "Der syntaktische Gebrauch des Dativs und Instrumentals in den Cædmon beigelegten Dichtungen," *Anglia, 7* (1884), 355–404.

Kempf, Ernst. *Darstellung der Syntax in der sogenannten cædmon'schen Exodus.* Leipzig, 1888.

Klaeber, Fr. "Zum germanischen Sprachstil: Das Nomen," *Archiv, 183* (1943), 73–94. Esp. p. 81.

Pope, John Collins. *The Rhythm of Beowulf.* New Haven, Yale University Press, 1942.

Schmitz, Theodor. "Die Sechstakter in der altenglischen Dichtung," *Anglia, 33* (1910), 1–76, 172–218. Esp. 26–7, 217.

Schücking, L. L. "Heldenstolz und Würde im Angelsachsen," *Abhandlungen der Philologisch-Historischen Klasse der Sächsischen Akademie der Wissenschaften,* Bd. 42, Nr. 5 (1933). Moses as epic hero, pp. 3–13.

—— *Untersuchungen zur Bedeutungslehre der angelsächsischen Dichtersprache.* Heidelberg, 1915. Esp. pp. 12–18.

Strauss, Otto. "Beiträge zur Syntax der im Codex Junius enthaltenen altenglischen Dichtungen," *Die neueren Sprachen, 6* (1925), 172–82.

Wieners, Reinhold. *Zur Metrik des Codex Junius* XI. Bonn, 1913.

Ziegler, Heinrich. *Der poetische Sprachgebrauch in den sogen. Cædmonschen Dichtungen.* Münster, 1883.

C. SOURCES

Baring-Gould, S. *Legends of the Patriarchs and Prophets and Other Old Testament Characters.* New York, 1872.

Bright, James W. "The Relation of the Cædmonian *Exodus* to the Liturgy," *MLN, 27* (1912), 97–103.

Bunbury, E. H. *A History of Ancient Geography.* London, 1879. 2 vols.

Diodorus of Sicily. Tr. and ed. C. H. Oldfather. Loeb Classical Library. Cambridge, Mass., Harvard University Press, 10 vols. Vol. 1, 1933, Vol. 2, 1935.

Ginzberg, Louis. *The Legends of the Jews.* Philadelphia, The Jewish Publication Society of America, 1909–28. 7 vols.

Holthausen, Ferdinand. "Zur Quellenkunde und Textkritik der altengl. Exodus," *Archiv, 115* (1905), 162–3.

Kimble, George H. T. *Geography in the Middle Ages.* London, 1938.

Laistner, M. L. W. "The Library of the Venerable Bede," in *Bede: His Life, Times, and Writings.* Oxford, 1935. Pp. 237–66.

Moore, Samuel. "On the Sources of the Old-English *Exodus,*" *MP, 9* (1911), 83–108.

Rau, Max. *Germanische Altertümer in der Angelsächsischen Exodus.* Leipzig, 1889.

Smalley, Beryl. *The Study of the Bible in the Middle Ages.* Oxford, 1941.

D. LITERARY CRITICISM

Brandl, Alois. *Englische Literatur: A. Angelsächsische Periode,* in *Grundriss der germanischen Philologie,* hrsg. von H. Paul, Bd. 2^1, 2d ed., pp. 980–1024, Strassburg, 1908. Pp. 1028–9.

Legouis, Emile. *A History of English Literature.* Tr. Helen Douglas Irvine. New York, Macmillan, 1929. Pp. 39–40.

Kennedy, Charles W. *The Earliest English Poetry.* Oxford, 1943. Pp. 175–83.

Ker, W. P. *The Dark Ages.* New York, 1904. P. 260.

Malone, Kemp. *A Literary History of England.* Ed. A. C. Baugh. New York, 1948. Pp. 64–5.

Schirmer, Walter F. *Geschichte der englischen Literatur.* Halle, 1937. P. 27.

Ten Brink, Bernhard. *Geschichte der englischen Literatur.* 2d ed., Strassburg, 1899. Bd. 1, pp. 52–3.

Wülker, Richard. *Geschichte der englischen Literatur.* 2d ed., Leipzig, 1906. Bd. 1, p. 35.

ABBREVIATIONS AND CUE TITLES

I. Editions and Commentaries

THE following list includes not only the editions but the more important collections of textual notes; see Bibliography for full citations.

Bl	Blackburn's edition, 1907.
Bou	Bouterwek's edition (text), 1854.
Bou2	Bouterwek's *Erläuterungen.*
Br	Bright, in *Modern Language Notes, 17,* 1902.
Br2	Bright, in *Modern Language Notes, 27,* 1912.
Cos	Cosijn, in *Beiträge, 19,* 1894.
Cos2	Cosijn, in *Beiträge, 20,* 1895.
Diet	Dietrich, in *Zeitschrift für deutsches Altertum, 10,* 1856.
Goll	Gollancz, Introduction, *The Cædmon Manuscript,* 1927.
Graz	Graz, in *Englische Studien, 21,* 1895.
Gr	Grein's edition, 1857.
Gr2	Grein, in *Germania, 10,* 1865.
Groth	Groth, *Composition und Alter,* 1883.
Junius	Junius' edition, 1655.
Kock JJJ	Kock, "Jubilee Jaunts and Jottings," 1918.
Kock PPP	Kock, "Plain Points and Puzzles," 1922.
Klu	Kluge's partial edition, 1888.
Kr	Krapp's edition, 1931.
Krn	Körner's partial edition, 1880.
Mrk	Mürkens, *Untersuchungen* (pp. 113–17), 1899.
Nap	Napier's partial edition, *Modern Language Review, 6,* 1911.
Se	Sedgefield's partial edition, 1922.
Se *MLR*	Sedgefield, *Modern Language Review, 16,* 1921.
Siev	Sievers, *Beiträge, 10* (195–9), 1885.
Siev2	Sievers, *Beiträge, 10* (451–545), 1885.
Siev3	Sievers, *Beiträge, 12,* 1887.
Th	Thorpe's edition, 1832.
Wlk	Wülker's edition, 1894.

II. Periodicals and Standard Works

Angl	*Anglia.*
AnglBeibl	*Anglia Beiblatt.*
Archiv	*Archiv für das Studium der neueren Sprachen und Literaturen.*
Beitr	*Beiträge zur Geschichte der deutschen Sprache und Literatur.*
B-T	Bosworth and Toller, *Anglo-Saxon Dictionary.*

BTS	Supplement to B-T.
CSEL	*Corpus Scriptorum Ecclesiasticorum Latinorum.*
EETS	Early English Text Society.
ESt	*Englische Studien.*
Ettmüller, *Lex*	*Vorda Vealhstôd Engla and Seaxna. Lexicon Anglo-saxonicum.*
Germ	*Germania.*
G-K	Grein's *Sprachschatz der ags. Dichter,* ed. Köhler (& Holthausen).
Gr Spr	Grein's *Sprachschatz der ags. Dichter,* 1861–64.
JEGP	*Journal of English and Germanic Philology.*
MLN	*Modern Language Notes.*
MLR	*Modern Language Review.*
MP	*Modern Philology.*
OED	*Oxford English Dictionary.*
PG	*Patrologia Graeca.*
PL	*Patrologia Latina.*
PMLA	*Publications of the Modern Language Association of America.*
RES	*Review of English Studies.*

III. Old English Poems

An.	*Andreas.*
Beow.	*Beowulf.*
Dan.	*Daniel.*
El.	*Elene.*
Ex.	*Exodus.*
Gen.	*Genesis.*
Guth.	*Guthlac.*
Meters	*Meters of Boethius.*
Rid.	Riddles.
Sol. and Sat.	*Solomon and Saturn.*

EXODUS

Note on Text

IN the text, letters or words which have been added by emendation
are placed in brackets. The alteration of words or letters by emenda-
tion is indicated by italics. Asterisks indicate gaps in the text,
whether physically verified or assumed. No attempt is made to reproduce
the appearance of the text in the MS other than the preservation of the
MS large capitals at the beginning of sections. The small capitals in the
MS, not always easily discernible, are not indicated. (See Krapp's Intro-
duction, p. xlii, for a table of small capitals in *Exodus*). The abbreviation
"Edd" means "all editors since . . ." or "all other editors"; "em."
stands for "emended by . . ." where the emendation has been adopted
in the text.

HWÆT, WĒ FEOR AND NĒAH   gefrigen hab[b]að
ofer middangeard   Moyses dōmas,
(wrǣclīco wordriht   wera cnēorissum—
in uprodor   ēadigra gehwām
5   æfter bealusīðe   bōte līfes,
lifigendra gehwām   langsumne rǣd)
hæleðum secgan!   Gehȳre sē ðe wille!

Þone on wēstenne   weroda Drihten,
sōðfæst Cyning,   mid His sylfes miht
10   gewyrðode,   and him wundra fela,
ēce Alwalda,   in ǣht forgeaf.
Hē wæs lēof Gode,   lēoda aldor,
horsc and hreðerglēaw,   herges wīsa,
freom folctoga.   Faraones cyn,

1 Begins p. 143; large ornamental capital *H*
  hab[b]að: MS habað, so Wlk, Bl, Kr; em. Gr, Klu, Se
3 *wrǣclīco:* wrǣtlīcu Bou2,   wrǣtlīco Se
  wordriht: word dryhtnes Bou2
4 *uprodor:* uproder (erroneously) Gr, Krn, Klu
6 *lifigendra:* lifgendra (erroneously) Gr, Krn
8 *weroda:* MS werode, so Bl; em. Th, Edd
11 *forgeaf:* with a dot over and a dot under the *a;* presumably the *a* was deleted and
   then restored
14 *freom:* from Klu

·XLII·

ÞÆT PE FEOR 7 NEAH

gefrugen habað · oþer middan geard ·
moyses domas · þræclico poþð
þuht · þþa onforþuþþum · inup rodoþ
tuoiзna geþþam · æptiþ bealu riðe · bote liþþþ ·
liþiзðioþa geþþam · lanз þumne · þ ped · hæleduᵐ
reczan · zeþyþe reðe pille · þone onþþchine ·
þþuode oþulrch · roð þaþ cyninз · mid hir þylþþ
miht zeþynðode · 7 him þunoþa þela ðe alpalda ·
in echt þoþ zþit · heþaþ ltop зode · lþða alopθ
hoþþc 7 þedði зlaup · liþiзþ þiþa þrtoᵐ þolc
togæ þaþa oneþ · cyn · зodþ andþaca · зyþð þæ
kaþo · þæþ him зeþalde · þiзoþa palolþo · moð
зuᵐ maзo þaþþuþ hiþ maзa þþonh · onþiþt et
lth· abþahamþ þunum · hðah þæþ þ hand lðan
7 him hola þiþa зeþalde · þæþna зþþbild · þið
þþuðþa зþyne · oþth coᵐ mid þy campe · cnþ maⁿ
зa þela þþonda þþonda þolc þuht · ða þæþ þoþ
ma þið · þ hine þþioða зod · þoþðum nægðe · þæþ
he hiᵐ зeþæзde · þoð þunoþa þela · hu þaþ þoþuld
þoþhte þraз oþulrch· bonðan ymb hþyþþt · 7 up
rodoþ · зþæte þiзe þuce · 7 hiþ þylþþ namaⁿ ·
ðone yloo beaþþ · æþ necyoon · þþoð þæðþa
cyn · þþah hie þela piþoᵐ ·

THE FIRST PAGE OF *EXODUS* (LINES 1–29)
MS Junius XI in the Bodleian Library, Oxford

15   Godes andsaca[n],   gyrdwīte band.
Þǣr him gesealde   sigora Waldend,
mōdgum magorǣswan, his māga feorh,
onwist ēðles Ābrahames sunum.
Hēah wæs þæt handlēan and him hold Frêa,
20   gesealde wǣpna geweald wið wrāðra gryre,
ofercōm mid þȳ campe cnēomāga fela,
fēonda, folcriht. Ðā wæs forma sīð
þæt hine weroda God wordum nǣgde:
þǣr Hē him gesǣgde sōðwundra fela,
25   hū þās woruld worhte wītig Drihten,
eorðan ymbhwyrft and uprodor,
gesette sigerīce, and His sylfes naman,
ðone yldo bearn ǣr ne cūðon,
frōd fædera cyn, þēah hīe fela wiston.
30   Hæfde Hē þā geswīðed sōðum cræftum
and gewurðodne werodes aldor,
Faraones fēond, on forðwegas.

Þā wæs ingere ealdum wītum
dēaðe gedrenced drihtfolca mǣst.
35   Hordwearda hryre hēaf wæs genīwad,
swǣfon seledrēamas, since berofene.
Hæfde mansceaða æt middere niht
frēcne gefylled frumbearna fela,
ābrocene burhweardas. Bana wīde scrāð,
40   lāð lēodhata; land drysmyde

---

15 *andsaca[n]*: MS andsaca, so Bl ("Nthb form"); em. Th, Edd; andraca Gr2
17 *magorǣswan*: MS magoræswum; em. Gr, Edd
   māga feorh: mearchofu Diet
18 *onwist*: on wist Th, Bou; ondwist? Bou2
20 *gesealde wǣpna*: gesealde him wǣpna Krn
22 *fēonda, folcriht*: MS feonda feonda folcriht; fēonda folcriht Edd; fēonda, frēonda Krn; fēonda folcdriht Cos
28 *yldo*: ylda Mrk
30 *Hæfde*: begins p. 144
31 *werodes*: weroda Bou2
33 *ingere*: so Th, Bou, Mrk, Bl, Kr; iūgēra Bou2; iū gēre Gr, Wlk; ungēre (ungēara?) Klaeber (*Archiv 113*:146); ungēra Se
   ealdum wītum: geald unwītum Cos
34 *gedrenced*: renced written in another hand over an erasure; gedēmed Groth, Mrk; gedrecced Cos, Br2, Se; gedrēfed? Bl (n.)
35 *hordwearda*: hordweardra (erroneously) Bl
36 *seledrēamas*: seledrēame Bou2
37 *mansceaða*: MS mansceaðan; mansceaða Bou2, Mrk, Br2
39 *ābrocene*: ābrotene Cos, Se
   burhweardas: burhweallas Bou2
40 *drysmyde*: MS dryrmyde; so Th, Bou; dryrgede Bou2; drysmyde Diet, Gr, Wlk, Kr; drysmode Se; þrysmyde Krn

dēadra hrǣwum; dugoð forð gewāt,
wōp wæs wīde, worulddrēama lȳt.
Wǣron hleahtorsmiðum handa belocene;
ālȳfed lāðsīð lēode grētan,

45 folc fērende (frēond wæs berēafod),
hergas on helle. Heofon þider becōm,
druron dēofolgyld. Dæg wæs mǣre
ofer middangeard þā sēo mengeo fōr.
Swā þæs fæsten drēah fela missēra,

50 eald[or]wērige, Ēgypta folc,
þæs þe hīe wīdeferð wyrnan þōhton
Moyses māgum, gif hīe Metod lēte,
on langne lust lēofes sīðes.
Fyrd wæs gefȳsed, from sē ðe lǣdde,

55 mōdig magorǣ[s]wa, mǣgburh heora.
Oferfōr hē mid þȳ folce fæsten[n]a worn,
land and lēodgeard lāðra manna,
enge ānpaðas, uncūð gelād,
oðþæt hīe on Gūðmyrce gearwe bǣron,

60 (wǣron land heora lyfthelme beþeaht),
mearchofu mōrheald. Moyses ofer þā,
fela meor[r]inga, fyrde gelǣdde.

[H]EHT þā ymb twā niht tīrfæste hæleð,
siððan hīe fēondum oðfaren hæfdon,

44 *lēode:* lāde Bou2
 grētan: grēttan Se
45 *folc:* begins p. 145
 frēond: fēond Th, Bou2, Edd
46 *hergas on helle:* hergas onǣlde Cos; h. on healle Holthausen (*AnglBeibl* 5:231),
 Mrk; hergas (i.e. heargas 'altars') Kock PPP, Br2
 heofon þider becōm: heofon þistro becōm Diet; heofon-þider 'servitium' Gr; hēofon
 'lamentation' Gr2, Krn; hēofung Bl (n.), Kr
49 *þæs fæsten:* þæt f. Th, Bou; þæs (þās?) fǣhðan Mrk
50 *eald[or]wērige:* MS ealdwerige; þæt ealdwērige Gr; þæt ealwērige Cos; eald-
 wērigra Siev2
51 *wīdeferð:* wīde fyrde Bou2
53 *on langne:* ondlangne? Bou2; onlangne Gr, Wlk, Bl, Se
 lust: lāst? Klu
55 *magorǣ[s]wa:* MS magorǣwa; em. Th, Edd
 heora: frēora or fēora Bou2
56 *fæsten[n]a:* MS fæstena; em. Siev2, Graz, Mrk, Se
57 *lēodgeard:* MS leodweard; em. Gr (n.), Se
59 *gearwe:* geatwe Se *MLR*, Se
61 *mōrheald:* mōr hēald (i.e. hēold) Th, Br2; mōrhealde Bou2; mārheald Goll lxxxi
62 *fela meor[r]inga:* MS fela meoringa; fela meorringa Mrk, Br, Se; foldan mearcunge
 Bou2; fēle Mēring (i.e. fǣle Mǣring) Goll lxxxi
63 EHT begins p. 146; space is left for a large capital; Edd read Heht
 twā niht: twāniht Se
 tīrfæste: MS tirfæstne; em. Bou2, Krn, Cos, Mrk, Se, Kr

65   ymbwīcigean werodes bearhtme
      mid ælfere Æthānes byrig,
      mægnes mǣste mearclandum on.
      Nearwe genȳddon on norðwegas,
      wiston him be sūðan Sigelwara land,
70   forbærned burhhleoðu, brūne lēode,
      hātum heofoncolum. Þǣr hālig God
      wið fǣrbryne folc gescylde,
      bælce oferbrǣdde byrnendne heofon,
      hālgan nette hātwendne lyft.
75   Hæfde wederwolcen wīdum fæðmum
      eorðan and uprodor efne gedǣled,
      lǣdde lēodwerod, līgfȳr ādranc,
      hāte heofontorht. Hæleð wāfedon,
      drihta gedrȳmost. Dægsce*a*des hlēo
80   wand ofer wolcnum. Hæfde wītig God
      sunnan sīðfæt *seg*le ofertolden,
      swā þā mæstrāpas men ne cūðon,
      nē ðā seglrōde gesēon meahton,
      eorðbūende ealle cræfte,
85   hū āfæstnod wæs feldhūsa mǣst.
      Siððan Hē mid wuldre geweorðode
      Þēodenholde, þā wæs þridda wīc
      folce tō frōfre. Fyrd eall geseah
      hū þǣr hlīfedon hālige seglas,
90   lyftwundor lēoht; lēode ongēton,
      dugoð Israhela, þæt þǣr Drihten cwōm,
      weroda Drihten, wīcsteal metan.
      Him beforan fōran fȳr and wolcen
      in beorhtrodor, bēamas twēgen,
95   þāra ǣghwæðer efngedǣlde

66 *ælfere:* MS ælf ere, so Th, Bou; wælhere Bou2; æl-fere (i.e. eal-fare 'the whole
    army') Gr Spr *1, 57*; ælfare Se
67 *mægnes:* mægne (mægna?) Nap
68 *genȳddon:* genēðdon Diet, Gr (not Gr2)
69 *Sigelwara:* Sigelwarena Mrk
70 *burhhleoðu:* beorhhleoðu Th (n.), Bou; cf. Nap, Kock (*Angl 45:*124 f.)
73 *bælce:* bælge Holthausen (*Archiv 115:*163)
77 *ādranc:* ācwanc Bou2
78 *hāte:* hāt Gr; hǣte Bou2; but hāte is a noun, cf. Mrk, Se, Kr, *Beow.* 2605
79 *Dægsceades:* MS dægscealdes; dægsceades Kr; dægsce(a)ldes 'day-shield' Cos, Bl
    (n.), Thomas (*MLR 12:*344), Holthausen (*AnglBeibl 29:*283), Se; dægstealdes
    Holthausen (*AnglBeibl 5:*231); dægsweal(o)ðes Holthausen (*Archiv 115:*163);
    dæges-cealdes 'day-cold' Br2; see Note
81 *seg*le: MS swegle; em. Th (n.), Edd except Bou
87 *þridda:* þridde Nap
    Þēodenholde: þēoden holde Th, Bou, Gr, Se
95 *efngedǣlde:* efn gedǣlde Klu; efne gedǣlde Cos2

héahþegnunga   Hāliges Gāstes,
dēormōdra sīð   dagum and nihtum.
þā ic on morgen gefrægn   mōdes rōfan
hebban herebȳman   hlūdan stefnum,
100   wuldres wōman.   Werod eall ārās,
mōdigra mægen,   swā him Moyses bebēad,
mǣre magorǣswa,   Metodes folce,
fūs fyrdgetrum.   Forð gesāwon
līfes lātþēow   līfweg metan;
105   *seg*l sīðe wēold,   sǣmen æfter
fōron flōdwege.   Folc wæs on sālum,
[H]LŪD heriges cyrm.   Heofonbēacen āstāh
ǣfen[n]a gehwām,   ōðer wundor,
syllīc, æfter sunnan   setlrāde behēold,
110   ofer lēodwerum   līge scīnan,
byrnende bēam.   Blāce stōdon
ofer scēotendum   scīre lēoman,
scinon scyldhrēoðan,   scea*do* swiðredon;
nēowle nihtscuwan   nēah ne mihton
115   heolstor āhȳdan.   Heofoncandel barn;
nīwe nihtweard   nȳde sceolde
wīcian ofer weredum,   þȳ lǣs him wēstengryre,
hār hǣð[brōga],   holmegum wederum
o[n] fērclamme   ferhð getwǣf[de].
120   Hæfde foregenga   fȳrene loccas,

96 Begins p. 147
104 *lātþēow:* lāttēow Se
   līfweg: liftweg (i.e. lyftweg) Diet, Gr, Klu, Wlk, Se; liðweg or lidweg Bou2
105 *segl:* MS swegl; em. Bou2, Gr, Wlk, Se; cf. 81
106 *flōdwege:* foldwege? Gr
   sālum is the last word on p. 147
107 LUD, with a small *h* added in the margin, begins p. 148; space is left for a large
   capital
   heriges: a dot appears in the MS under the *i*
108 *ǣfen[n]a:* MS æfena; em. Graz, Mrk
109 *sunnan:* sunne Br, Kr
   behēold: behēoldon Bou2, Goll lxx; ongann? Nap
   setlrāde: seglrād Se *MLR*
110 *līge scīnan:* līges scīman? Cos
113 *sceado:* MS sceaðo, so Bl (n.); em. Th (n.), Edd
   swiðredon: sweðredon Se
115 *heolstor:* heol(u)stras? Cos
   barn: bearn Klu
118 *hār hǣð[brōga]*: so Cos, Kr; MS har hæð; hāres hǣðes Siev2, Klu, Mrk, Se; hārre
   hǣðe Graz; hār hǣðstapa Rieger ("Verskunst," p. 46), Br
119 *o[n] fērclamme:* MS ofer clamme; fērclamme Diet; ō fērclamme Gr, Wlk, Bl; on
   fērclamme Klu, Kr; on fǣrclamme Se
   getwǣf[de]: MS getwǣf; em. Th, Edd

blāce bēamas,   *bē*legsan hwēop
in þām hereþrēate,   hātan līge,
þæt hē on wēstenne   werod forbærnde,
nymðe hīe mōdhwate   Moyses hȳrde.

125   Sceān scīrwerod;   scyldas līxton,
gesāwon randwigan   rihte strǣte,
segn ofer swēoton,   oðþæt sǣfæsten
landes æt ende   lēo[d]mægne forstōd,
fūs on forðweg.   Fyrdwīc ārās;

130   wyrpton hīe wērige,   wiste genǣgdon
mōdige meteþegnas,   hyra mægen bēt[t]on.
Brǣddon æfter beorgum,   siððan bȳme sang,
flotan feldhūsum.   Þā wæs fēorðe wīc,
randwigena ræst,   be þan Rēadan Sǣ.

135   Ðǣr on fyrd hyra   fǣrspell becwōm,
ōht inlende.   Egsan stōdan,
wælgryre weroda.   Wrǣcmon gebād
lāðne lāstweard,   sē ðe him lange ǣr
ēðellēasum   onnīed gescrāf,

140   wēan wītum fæst.   Wǣre ne gȳmdon,
ðēah þe se yldra cyning   ǣr ge

*   *   *   *   *

[Þ]Ā wearð yrfeweard   ingefolca,

121 *bē*l*egsan:* MS bell egsan; so Th ('cry of dread'), Bou; bǣlegsan Bou2, Gr;
bǣlegesan Se; bēllegsan Wlk, Kr
hwēop: spēaw Bou2
122 *in:* omitted by Gr
124 *hȳrde:* hȳrden? Klu; hȳrden Nap, Br2; see Note
125 *sceān scīrwerod:* sceān scīr werod Edd; sceān on scīr werod Bou2
126 *rihte:* rihtre Gr
127 *swēoton:* swēotum Bou, Gr, Graz, Mrk
128 *lēo[d]mægne:* MS leo mægne; em. Edd; lēode mægne? Bl (n.)
129 *fūs on forðweg:* fūsne forðweg Bou2; fūse on forðweg Mrk; fūson (i.e. fūsum)
forðweg Klaeber (*ESt 41:*110), Nap
131 *bēt[t]on:* MS beton; bētton Mrk, Se; bētan Gr
133 *flotan:* flotana Bou2
134 *þan:* þām Gr
135 *hyra:* frēcne Groth
136 *inlende:* inlendes Bou2
139 *onnīed:* ōhtnīed Gr, Klu, Wlk, Se; see Note
141 For gap in MS following ǣr ge, see Introduction, p. 6
yldra: ylda Bou2
ǣr ge: ǣr getiþode Diet, Gr; gelȳfde Klu, Mrk; gesealde Se; all assume no greater
loss
142 A wearð begins p. 149, with space left for a capital; Edd read þā; þā hē Gr
ingefolca: in gefolca Th, Bou (assuming a MS gap after this word); yrre folce or
yrre folca herge (or hēape) Diet

manna æfter māðmum, þæt hē swā miceles geðāh.
Ealles þæs forgēton siððan grame wurdon
145 Ēgypta cyn ymb antþigða;
hēo his mægwinum morðor fremedon,
wrōht berēnedon, wære fræton.
Wæron heaðowylmas heortan getenge,
mihtmōd wera; mānum trēowum
150 woldon hīe þæt feorhlēan fācne gyldan,
þætte h[ī]e þæt dægweorc drēore gebohte,
Moyses lēode, þær him mihtig God
on ðām spildsīðe spēde forgēfe.
Þā him eorla mōd ortrȳwe wearð,
155 siððan hīe gesāwon of sūðwegum
fyrd Faraonis forð ongangan,
oferholt wegan, ēored līxan
(gāras trymedon, gūð hwearfode,
blicon bordhrēoðan, bȳman sungon),
160 þūfas þunian, þēod mearc tredan,
on hwæl * * * * * * * * *
*hr*ēopon herefugolas, hilde grædige,

143 *þæt:* þæs? Klu
145 *ymb antþigða:* MS ymb án twíg·ða; ymb antþigða Kock PPP; others take
ða in next line; ymb ān twig ('the rod of Aaron') Th, Bou(?); ymb ān wīg? Diet;
ymb āne wīg Mrk; ymb andwīg Gr; ymb ānwīg Gr2, Wlk; ymb antwig seredon
Cos; ymb antwīge (i.e. andwīg 'warfare') Bl (n.); ymb ānes wīg Se *MLR;* ymb
āne twīgþe (twīþe?) Klu; ymbe ānwīg Br; ymbe antwīg (i.e. andwīg) Kr; ymb
ānwīge Br2
146 *hēo:* MS heo heo; hēo Edd
hēo his: iosephis(?) Bl (n.)
147 *berēnedon:* berēnodon Gr (silently)
fræton: brǣcon Br
149 *mānum trēowum:* mannum twēonum Br2
151 *h[ī]e:* MS he; hīe Gr, Bl (n.), Kr
156 *Faraonis:* Faraones Gr
forð ongangan: forðor gangan Bou2
157 *oferholt wegan:* ofer holt wegan Th, Bou; ofer holtwegon (i.e. -wegum) Klu;
eoferholt 'boar-spear'? Se (n.)
157–60 Gr places 160 after 157, followed by Klu, Bl (n.), Se
158 *gūð:* gūðweard Bou2; gūðfana Gr2, Cos
160 *þēod mearc:* þēodmearc Th, Bou, Gr2, Graz, Mrk
161–2 There is no indication of loss in the MS, which reads: on hwæl·hwreopån·here
fugolas·hilde grædige·Siev reads hreopan wrongly for hwreopan; on hwæl
hwreopon / here-fugolas / hilde grǣdige Th, with no indication of loss; on hwæl
hrēopon herefugolas / hilde grædige gūðes gifre Bou (gūðe gifre Bou2); hwēol
'circle' for hwæl Diet; Klu omits on hwæl; on hwæl hrēopon herefugolas / hilde-
grǣdige, hræfen gōl Gr; on hrǣ hrēopon on here fugolas / hildegrǣdige hræfn
sweart āgōl Mrk; on hwælmere hrēo wæron ȳða (159), hrēopan herefugolas hilde
grædige (162) Bl (n.); on hwæl hrēopon herefugolas / hilde grædige hræfn uppe
gōl Br; Wlk leaves blank half-line after hildegrædige (162 in his text); Bl, Se, Kr
leave blank half-line after on hwæl (161); Holthausen (*Archiv 115:*163), who
omits on hwæl, adds herge on lāste, hræfn uppe gōl

dēawigfeðere, ofer drihtnēum,
wonn wælcēasega. Wulfas sungon
165 atol æfenlēoð ætes on wēnan,
carlēasan dēor, cwyldrōf beodan
on lāðra lāst lēodmægnes fyl;
hrēopon mearcweardas middum nihtum,
flēah fæge gāst, folc wæs geh[n]æged.
170 Hwīlum of þām werode wlance þegnas
mæton mīlpaðas mēara bōgum.
Him þær segncyning wið þone segn foran,
manna þengel, mearcþrēate rād;
gūðweard gumena grimhelm gespēon,
175 cyning cinberge, (cumbol līxton),
wīges on wēnum, wælhlencan sceōc,
hēt his hereciste healdan georne
fæst fyrdgetrum. Frēond onsēgon
lāðum ēagan landmanna cyme.
180 Ymb hine wǣgon wīgend unforhte,
hāre heorowulfas, hilde grētton,
þurstige þræcwīges, þēodenholde.
Hæfde him ālesen[e] lēoda dugeðe

163 *drihtnēum:* drihtwerum Groth
164 P. 150 blank; wonn begins p. 151
wonn wælcēasega: wonne wælcēasge Holthausen (*AnglBeibl* 5:231); Bl takes wonn as pret. of winnan 'hasten'
166 *beodan:* beodan or bidon Gr
167 *fyl:* MS ful; fyll Bou2, Diet; fyl Klu, Edd except Wlk; fal Gr2
168 *middum:* MS midum, with a second *d* added above the line and a caret-mark after *d*
169 *geh[n]æged:* MS gehæged; gehnæged Bou2, Diet, Se; genæged Gr (Gr2 like MS); geǣged Cos2
172 *segncyning:* sigecyning Gr, Klu; secga cyning Diet
173 *mearcþrēate:* mearc þrēate Th, Bou; mearhþrēate Bou2
175 *cyning:* So MS; cining Th, Bou, Gr
176 *wælhlencan:* MS hwæl hlencan, so Th; wælhlencan Bou, Edd; wælhlence onsceōc Bou2
177 *hēt:* heht Th, Bou, Gr; hel (misprint?) Siev, Klu
178 *fyrdgetrum:* MS syrdgetrum; misread as fyrdgetrum by early Edd; correctly by Siev, Wlk, Bl (n.), Se, Kr
frēond onsēgon: MS freond onsigon, so Th (but Th [n.]: fēond onsāwon?); so also Bou, Bl (n.) (onsigon 'approached'); frēond onsēgon Diet, Kr; frēond on sēgon Klu; frēond on sǣgon Se; fēond onsēgon Gr, Wlk
179 *ēagan:* ēagum Gr (silently)
lāðum ēagan: lāðan ēagum? Klu
180 *wǣgon:* wǣron Se *MLR*, Se
wīgend: wigan Siev2, Graz, Mrk
181 *heorowulfas:* MS heora wulfas; herewulfas Th (n.), Bou; heorawulfas Wlk; heorowulfas Gr, Mrk, Se, Kr; heoruwulfas Gr Spr, Klu
hilde grētton: hildegeatwe Cos2 (obj. of wǣgon)
182 *þēodenholde:* þēoden holde Th, Bou
183 *ālesen[e]:* MS alesen; ālesene Siev2, Klu, Mrk

tīrēadigra   twā þūsendo,

185 þæt wǣron cyningas   and cnēowmāgas,
on þæt ēade riht   æðelum dēore.
Forðon ānra gehwilc   ūt ālǣdde
wǣpnedcynnes   wigan ǣghwilcne
þāra þe hē on ðām fyrste   findan mihte.

190 Wǣron ingēmen[d]   ealle ætgædere,
cyningas on corðre.   Cūð oft geb[ē]ad
horn on hēape   tō hwæs hægstealdmen,
gūðþrēat gumena,   gearwe bǣron.
Swā þǣr eorp werod,   ēcan lǣddon,

195 lāð æfter lāðum,   lēodmægnes worn,
þūsendmǣlum,   þider wǣron fūse.
Hæfdon hīe gemynted   tō þām mægenhēapum
tō þām ǣrdæge   Israhela cynn
billum ābrēotan   on hyra brōðorgyld.

200 Forþon wæs in wīcum   wōp up āhafen,
atol æfenlēoð;   egesan stōdon,
weredon wælnet,   þā se wōma cwōm,
flugon frēcne spel;   fēond wæs ānmōd,
werud wæs wīgblāc,   oðþæt wlance forscēaf

205 mihtig engel,   sē ðā menigeo behēold,
þæt þǣr gelāðe mid him   leng ne mihton
gesēon tōsomne.   Sīð wæs gedǣled!
Hæfde nȳdfara   nihtlangne fyrst,
þēah ðe him on healfa gehwām   hettend seomedon,

184 *twā þūsendo:* twā hund þūsendo Br2
186 *þæt ēade riht:* þæs ēades riht Br
 ēade riht: eorðrīce? or eardrīce? Th (n.); ealde riht Klu, Se
 dēore: drēore Bou2
190 *ingēmen[d]:* MS ingemen, so Th, Bou, Klu, Mrk, Kr; incgemen 'vasalli' Bou2;
 inge men 'young men' Diet, Gr, Wlk, Bl (n.), Se; see Note
191 *cyningas:* cyninges Bou2
 cūð oft: cūð eft Bou; cūðost Gr
 geb[ē]ad: MS gebad; gebēad Gr, Bl (n.), Se
192 *horn on:* horum or hārum Bou2
193 *gearwe:* geatwe Se *MLR*, Se
194 *ēcan lǣddon:* ēc anlǣddon Th, Bou, Gr2, Wlk; ēcan (i.e. ēacan) Gr, Klu, Se, Kr;
 ēcan from ēce Bl (Glossary); ēacan 'increased, great' Br2
197 P. 152 blank; hæfdon begins p. 153
 tō: omitted by Cos2, Br
199 *brōðorgyld:* brōðra gyld? Th (n.)
200 *in:* on Gr (silently)
202 *weredon wælnet:* weredum wælnēd Cos; weredum wælnet Mrk; weredon 'wore'
 Br2; see Kock JJJ, and Note
204 *wlance:* wlence Gr (n.)
206 *þæt þǣr gelāðe:* þæt þæt gelād Bou2; Th, Bou, Diet read gelāðe erroneously for
 gelāðe
207 *gesēon:* gescēon Diet
208 Begins p. 154

210   mægen oððe merestrēam; nāhton māran hwyrft.
       Wǣron orwēnan   ēðelrihtes,
       sǣton æfter beorgum in blacum rēafum,
       wēan on wēnum. Wæccende bād
       eall sēo sibgedriht somod ætgædere
215   māran mægenes, oð Moyses bebēad
       eorlas on ūhttīd ǣrnum bēmum
       folc somnigean, frecan ārīsan,
       habban heora hlencan, hycgan on ellen,
       beran beorht searo, bēacnum cīgean
220   swēot sande nēar; snelle gemundon
       weardas wīglēoð. Werod wæs gefȳsed,
       brūdon ofer burgum, (bȳman gehȳrdon),
       flotan feldhūsum, fyrd wæs on ofste.
       Siððan hīe getealdon wið þām tēonhete
225   on þām forðherge fēðan twelfe
       mōde rōf[r]a; mægen wæs onhrēred.
       Wæs on ānra gehwām æðelan cynnes
       ālesen under lindum lēoda duguðe
       on folcgetæl fīftig cista;
230   hæfde cista gehwilc cūðes werodes
       gārberendra, gūðfremmendra,
       tȳn hund geteled, tīrēadigra;
       þæt wæs wīglīc werod! Wāc[e] ne grētton
       in þæt rincgetæl rǣswan herges
235   þā þe for geoguðe gȳt ne mihton
       under bordhrēoðan brēostnet wera
       wið flāne fēond folmum werigean,
       nē him bealubenne gebiden hæfdon
       ofer linde lǣrig, līcwunde swo*l*,
240   gylpplegan gāres. Gamele ne mōston,

---

212 *blacum:* blācum Edd; see Note
215b oð ðæt Moyses bebēad Se
216 *bēmum:* MS benum; em. Th, Edd
218 *habban heora hlencan:* habban heorahlencan Sisam (*RES 22:*264n.)
220 *sande:* sunde? Gr (n.)
222 *burgum:* beorgum Gr
224 *tēonhete:* tēonhetend Bou2
226 *mōde rōf[r]a:* MS mode rofa, so Bl (n.) (rōfa Nthb for rōfan); mōde rōfra
     Bou2, Gr (n.), Klu, Graz, Mrk, Se; mōderōfra Kr
227 *æðelan:* æðeles Gr (silently); æðelestan Holthausen (G-K, 873)
232 tȳn *hund:* MS . x . hund; tȳnhund Gr, Klu; tȳn hund Se
233 *wāc[e]:* MS wac; em. Gr, Edd
237 *flāne:* fāne Klu
    fēond: fēonda? Th, Bou
239 *lǣrig:* lærg Graz
    *swo*l: MS swor; swol Se *MLR,* Se; spor? Gr (n.), Bl (n.)

hāre heaðorincas,   hilde onþēon,
gif him mōdhēapum   mægen swiðrade,
ac hīe be wæstmum   wīg[þrēat] curon,
hū in lēodscipe   læstan wolde
245   mōd mid āran;   ēac þan mægnes cræft
* * * * * * *   gārbēames feng.
þā wæs handrōfra   here ætgædere,
fūs forðwegas.   Fana up [ge]rād,
bēama beorhtost;   bidon ealle þā gēn
250   hwonne sīðboda   sæstrēamum nēah
lēoht ofer lindum   lyftedoras bræc.
ĀHlēop þā for hæleðum   hildecalla,
bald bēohata,   bord up āhōf,
heht þā folctogan   fyrde gestillan,
255   þenden mōdiges meðel   monige gehȳrdon.
Wolde reordigean   rīces hyrde
ofer hereciste   hālgan stefne,
werodes wīsa   wurðmyndum spræc:

"Ne bēoð gē þȳ forhtran,   þēah þe Faraon brōhte
260   sweordwīgendra   sīde hergas,
eorla unrīm.   Him eallum wile
mihtig Drihten   þurh mīne hand

241 onþēon begins p. 155
   onþēon: on tēon Bou2
242 *gif:* git Th (n.)
   mōdhēapum: mōdhæpum Gr (n.) ; see Note
   swiðrade: sweðrade Se
243 *wīg[þrēat] curon:* MS wig curon; wīghēap curon? or wīgþrēat curon? Bl (n.) ;
   wīghēap curon Se; him þā wīg curon Holthausen (*AnglBeibl 5:231*) ; him wīg curon
   Graz; wīgende curon Mrk; on wīg curon Br2, Kr
244 *hū:* hwā Bou2
245 *āran:* æran Wlk (misreading of MS)
246 No indication of loss in MS. Wlk, Se indicate missing first half-line, Kr missing
   second half-line; gegān mihte gārbēames feng Gr; gārbēames feng grētan mihte
   Klu, Graz, Mrk
248 fūs forðweges, fana wæs ufrad Bou2
   fūs forðwegas: fūs on forðwegas Klu
   fana up [ge]rād: MS fana up rad; em. Siev2, Graz, Mrk, Se, Kr
249 *bēama:* bēacna Cos2
   beorhtost: so MS; beorhtest Th, Bou, Gr
   bidon: MS buton; bufon? Th (n.), Bou; bugon Bou2; bidon Gr, Edd
251 *lyftedoras:* lyfte doras (-u?) or lyftdoras (-u?) Mrk
   bræc: bræce Gr, Cos2
252 Begins p. 156; plain large capital *A* in ĀHlēop
   ĀHlēop: āhlēow Bou2
253 *bēohata:* bodhāta Bou2, Kr (?) ; bēahhata Diet; bēothāta Ettmüller (*Lex.* 203), Gr;
   beohāta (i.e. bihāta) Gr2, Se; bēohāta Nthb for bēah-hāta 'promiser of treasure'
   Bl (n.)
   up āhōf: MS up hof, with *a* added above the line and hof written over an erasure
   (barely visible in facsimile)

tō dæge þissum   dædlēan gyfan,
þæt hīe lifigende   leng ne mōton
265 ægnian mid yrmðum   Israhela cyn.
Ne willað ēow andrǣdan   dēade fēðan,
fǣge ferhðlocan;   fyrst is æt ende
lǣnes līfes.   Ēow is lār Godes
ābroden of brēostum.   Ic on beteran rǣd,
270 þæt gē gewurðien   wuldres Aldor,
and ēow Līffrēan   lissa bidde,
sigora gesynto,   þǣr gē sīðien.
Þis is se ēcea   Ābrahames God,
frumsceafta Frēa,   sē ðās fyrd wereð,
275 mōdig and mægenrōf,   mid þǣre miclan hand!"

Hōf ðā for hergum   hlūde stefne
lifigendra *lēoð,*   þā hē tō lēodum sprǣc:

"Hwæt, gē nū ēagum   on lōciað,
folca lēofost,   fǣrwundra sum,
280 hū ic sylfa slōh   and þēos swīðre hand
grēne tācne   gārsecges dēop!
Ȳð up fǣreð,   ofstum wyrceð
wæter *on* wealfæsten.   Wegas syndon drȳge,
haswe herestrǣta,   holm gerȳmed,
285 ealde staðolas,   þā ic ǣr ne gefrægn
ofer middangeard   men gefēran,
fāge feldas,   þā forð heonon
in ēce [tīd]   ȳðe þeahton.

265 *ægnian:* ængian (i.e. engan 'oppress') Kock JJJ; egian Bou2; æglian (i.e. eglian) Diet; eglan Holthausen (*Angl 46:*54), Cos2; ǣgnian (i.e. āgnian 'own') Br2, Holthausen (G-K, 873); ōgnian Se *MLR,* Se

269 *on:* con Cos2, Mrk?; Mrk also rearranges 269b to read rǣd ic on beteran *rǣd:* rǣde Diet, Klu

271 *bidde:* bidden? Klu

272 *sigora:* sigoran Bou2

275 *hand:* handa Bou2, Klu

276 Begins p. 157

277 *leoð:* MS þeod; lēoð Br2; lēod Bou2, Edd; þēode? Th (n.); þēoden? Bl (n.); þēodne Goll lxxi

278 MS hwæt ge nu eagum to on lociað: tō omitted Br2, Se (n.)

280 *slōh and þēos:* slēa mid þās Bou2

281 *tācne:* tāne Bou2, Diet, Edd except Bl (n.), Kr

283 *on:* MS abbreviation for "and"; on Gr; in Br; omitted by Th (n.), Gr2, Graz, Mrk, Br2, Se, Kr; Diet reads wæteren wealfæsten for 283a

285 *þā:* þǣr? Th (n.)

287 *fāge:* fāmge Gr
feldas: felda? Bou2
feldas ends p. 157; þā begins p. 158

288 *in ēce* [*tīd*]: MS in ece; in ēce tīd Holthausen (*AnglBeibl 5:*231), Kr; in ēce Gr, Wlk; iū ǣr ēce Cos2; in ēcnysse Klu, Graz, Mrk; in ēcnesse Se *MLR,* Se

Sælde sægrundas   sūðwind fornam,
290   bæðweges blæst;   bri*m* is ārēafod,
sand sǣcir spā*w*.   Ic wāt sōð gere
þæt ēow mihtig God   miltse gecȳðde,
eorlas ǣrglade!   Ofest is sēlost
þæt gē of fēonda   fæðme weorðen
295   nū se Āgend   up ārǣrde
rēade strēamas   in randgebeorh.
Syndon þā foreweallas   fægre gestēpte,
wrǣtlīcu wǣgfaru,   oð wolcna hrōf."

Æfter þām wordum   werod eall ārās,
300   mōdigra mægen.   Mere stille bād.
Hōfon herecyste   hwīte linde,
segnas on sande.   Sǣweall āstāh,
uplang gestōd   wið Israhelum
āndægne fyrst.   Wæs sēo eorla gedriht
305   ānes modes * * * * * * *
fæstum fæðmum   freoðowǣre hēold.
Nalles hī*e* gehyr[w]don   hāliges lāre
siððan lēofes lēoþ   lǣste near
swēg swiðrode   and sances bland.
310   Þā þæt fēorðe cyn   fyrmest ēode,
wōd on wǣgstrēam,   wigan on hēape,
ofer grēnne grund,   Iūdisc fēða,
on ōnette   uncūð gelād

289 *sǣlde:* sealte Th, Bou2; sīde Cos2
   sūðwind: sund wind Cos2, Se
   fornam: fornimð Bou2
290 *brim:* MS bring; em. Th, Edd
291 *spāw:* MS span; āspāu? Bou2; spāu Gr, Wlk, spāw Kr; spen Diet; Se recon-
   structs 291a as: sandsǣ āspranc
293 *ǣrglade:* ǣr glade Th, Bou, Gr
295 *Āgend:* āgendfrēa Bou2, Mrk, Se
296 *rēade:* rēde (rēðe?) Diet
297 *syndon:* synt Graz, Mrk
298 *wǣgfaru:* wǣgfaroð Bou2
305 No indication of loss in MS. Wlk, Se indicate missing half-line; 2d half-lines sup-
   plied as follows: ȳða weall Gr; hīe ēce drihten Gr2; swylce him ȳða weall Klu,
   Graz, Mrk; him ȳða weall Br; hīe ȳða weall Bl (n.)
307 *hīe:* MS hige; hī or hīe Th (n.), Bou, Klu, Graz, Mrk, Se
   gehyr[w]don: MS gehyrdon; gehyrwdon Gr, Klu; gehȳndon Gr2
308 siððan lēodes lēoð lǣte nearwode Bou2
309 *sances:* sanges Diet, Gr, Klu, Graz, Mrk, Se
   sances bland: sanc āblann Bou2
313 *on ōnette:* MS an on orette; on ōrette Kr; anon ōnette Th; anon ōrette Bou; ān
   on ōrette Klu; ān on ōnette Bou2, Gr2; ān onōrette Diet, Gr, Wlk, Bl; an
   ōre ōnette Cos2; ān ōnette Se
   gelād: gelāð (pret. of gelīðan?) Klu
   uncūð gelād: on uncūð gelād Kr

for his mǣgwinum;   swā him mihtig God
315   þæs dægweorces   dēop lēan forgeald,
siððan him gesǣlde   sigorworca hrēð,
þæt hē ealdordōm   āgan sceolde
ofer cynerīcu,   cnēowmāga blǣd.
HÆFdon him tō segne,   þā hīe on sund stigon,
320   ofer bordhrēoðan   bēacen ārǣred
in þām gārhēape,   gyldenne lēon,
drihtfolca mǣst,   dēora cēnost.
Be þām herewīsan   hȳnðo ne woldon
be him lifigendum   lange þolian,
325   þonne hīe tō gūðe   gārwudu rǣrdon,
ðēoda ǣnigre.   Þracu wæs on ōre,
heard handplega,   hægsteald mōdige,
wǣpna wælslihtes,   wīgend unforhte,
bilswaðu blōdige,   beadumægnes rǣs,
330   grimhelma gegrind,   þǣr Iūdas fōr.

Æfter þǣre fyrde   flota mōdgade,
Rūbēnes sunu;   randas bǣron
sǣwīcingas   ofer sealtne mersc,
man[na] menio,   micel āngetrum
335   ēode unforht;   hē his ealdordōm
synnum āswefede,   þæt hē sīðor fōr
on lēofes lāst.   Him on lēodsceare
frumbearnes riht   frēobrōðor oðþah,
ēad and æðelo;   hē wæs gearu swā þēah.

340   Þǣr [forð] æfter him   folca þrȳðum

318 *cynerīcu:* cynrunu Cos2
319 P. 159 blank; Hæfdon, with plain large capital *H,* begins p. 160
321 *gyldenne:* gyldene Bou, Gr, Klu
    lēon: MS leor; em. Th, Edd
326 *þracu:* MS þraca; em. Gr, Edd except Wlk; þracra Bou2
327 *handplega:* MS hand apparently written over a partially erased heard by scribe
    hægsteald mōdige: hægstealdas mōdge Cos2, Bl (n.) ; hægstealda mōd Br2
328 *wælslihtes:* wælslihtas Cos2
    wīgend: wigan Siev2, Graz, Mrk
329 *blōdige:* blōdig Siev2
331 *flota mōdgade:* fēða mōdgode Br
333 *sǣwīcingas:* sǣwīcinge Gr (but Gr2 like MS)
334 *man[na] menio:* MS man menio; manna menio Siev2, Graz, Mrk, Bl (n.), Se, Kr;
    man-menio? Mrk
    micel āngetrum: micelan getrume Klu (n.)
338 *oðþah:* oðtēah Bou2
339 *gearu:* earu Diet, Gr (but not Gr2)
340a No indication of loss in MS. þǣr forð æfter him Gr, Cos2, Kr; þǣr æfter him
    fōron Se; fōr þǣr æfter him Mrk; þǣr æfter him fūse Holthausen (*AnglBeibl*
    5:231)

sunu Simeōnes   swēotum cōmon,
þridde þēodmægen   (þūfas wundon
ofer gārfare)   gūðcyste onþrang
dēawig sceaftum.   Dægwōma becwōm
345   ofer gārsec*ge*,   Godes bēacna sum,
morgen meretorht.   Mægen forð gewāt;
þā þǣr folcmægen   fōr æfter ōðrum,
īsernhergum,   (ān wīsode
mægenþrymmum mǣst,   þȳ hē mǣre wearð),
350   on forðwegas,   folc æfter wolcnum,
cynn æfter cynne.   Cūðe ǣghwilc
mǣgburga riht,   swā him Moises bēad
eorla æðelo.   Him wæs ān fæder;
lēof lēodfruma   landriht geþah,
355   frōd on ferhðe,   frēomāgum lēof.
Cende cnēowsibbe   cēnra manna
hēahfædera sum,   hālige þēode,
Israela cyn,   onriht Godes,
swā þæt orþancum   ealde reccað,
360   þā þe mǣgburge   mǣst gefrūnon,
frumcyn fēora,   fæderæðelo gehwæs.
Nīwe flōdas   Nōe ofer lāð,
þrymfæst þēoden,   mid his þrīm sunum,
þone dēopestan   dren[ce]flōda
365   þāra ðe gewurde   on woruldrīce.
Hæfde him on hreðre   hālige trēowa;
forþon hē gelǣdde   ofer lagustrēamas
māðmhorda mǣst,   mīne *ge*frǣge,
On feorhgebeorh   foldan hæfde

341 *sunu:* suna Se
343 *gūðcyste onþrang:* gūðcyst onþrang Gr, Klu, Graz; gūðcyston (-um) þrang Cos2
344 *dēawig sceaftum:* dēaðwīgsceaftum Se *MLR,* Se
345 *ofer gārsec*ge: MS ofer gar secges; ofer gārsecge Graz, Mrk, Br2, Se, Kr; ofer
    gārsecges gin Bou; ofer g. begong Gr, Kock PPP; ofer g. grund Klu; ofer g. dēop
    (strēam?) Cos2; ofer geofones begong Graz
346 *meretorht:* MS mǣretorht; meretorht Klu(?), Graz, Se; mǣre morgentorht? Klu
349 *mægenþrymmum:* mægenþrymma Br
350a fōr on forðwegas Gr
    æfter is last word on p. 160; wolcnum begins p. 161
    wolcnum: folcum Th, Bou, Se; folce Br
352 *Moises:* so MS; Moyses Th, Bou, Gr
353 *æðelo:* ēðel Ebert (*Angl* 5:409)
354 *lēodfruma:* landfruma Klu
358 *onriht:* on riht Th, Bou; ānriht Se *MLR,* Se
362 *ofer lāð:* so Bl; other Edd oferlāð
364 *dren[ce]flōda:* MS dren floda; drencflōda Th (n.), Bou, Gr, Wlk; drenceflōda
    Cos2, Graz, Mrk, Kr; þāra (ealra?) drencflōda Siev2
368 *gefrǣge:* MS fr fræge; em. Th, Edd
369 *foldan:* folden Gr

370   eallum eorðcynne   ēce lāfe,
        frumcnēow geh[w]æs,   fæder and mōder
        tuddortēondra,   geteled rīme
        mis*senlīc*ra   þonne men cunnon,
        snottor sǣleoda.   Ēac þon sǣda gehwilc
375   on bearm scipes   beornas feredon,
        þāra þe under heofonum   hæleð bryttigað.
        Swā þæt wīse men   wordum secgað
        þæt from Nōe   nigoða wǣre
        fæder Ābrahames   on folctale.

380   Þæt is se Ābraham   sē him engla God
        naman nīwan āsceōp;   ēac þon nēah and feor
        hālige hēapas   in gehyld bebēad,
        werþēoda geweald.   Hē on wrǣce lifde.
        Siððan hē gelǣdde   lēofost fēora
385   Hāliges hǣsum;   hēahlond stigon
        sibgemāgas,   on Sēone beorh.
        Wǣre hīe þǣr fundon   (wuldor gesāwon),
        hālige hēahtrēowe,   swā hæleð gefrūnon.
        Þǣr eft se snottra   sunu Dāuides,
390   wuldorfæst cyning,   witgan lārum
        getimbrede   tempel Gode,
        al*h* hāligne,   eorðcyninga
        se wīsesta   on woruldrīce,
        hēahst and hāligost,   hæleðum gefrǣgost,
395   mǣst and mǣrost,   þāra þe manna bearn,
        fīra æfter foldan,   folmum geworhte.
        Tō þām meðelstede   magan gelǣdde
        Ābraham Īsaac.   Ādfȳr onbran
        fyrst ferhðbana   (nō þȳ fǣgra wæs);
400   wolde þone lāstweard   līge gesyllan,

370 *ēce lāfe:* ēcende lāfe Th; ēgelāfe Gr; ēagorlāfe Holthausen (*AnglBeibl 5:231*)
371 *geh[w]æs:* MS gehæs; em. Junius, Edd
373 *missenlīcra:* MS mismicelra; missenlīcra B-T (*s.v.* mismicel); mislīcerra Cosijn
    (*Aanteekeningen op den Beowulf, p.* 1)
373b *mā þonne men cunnon* Gr (n.)
374 *sǣleoda:* sǣlida? Th (n.)
381 *feor:* MS for, with *e* added above the line
384 *gelǣdde:* altered in MS from gelifde; *if* changed to *æ, d* added above line
385 *stigon:* stīgan Th (n.), Bou
386 Begins p. 162
    on Sēone: onsēone Mrk
391 *Gode:* drihtne Graz, Mrk; gōde Bl (n.)
392 *alh:* MS alhn; em. Bou, Edd
399 *fyrst:* fūs Klaeber (*Archiv 113:147*)
    fǣgra: fægenra Cos2, Klaeber (*Archiv 113:147*), Br2, Kr

in bǣlblyse beorna sēlost,
his swǣsne sunu tō sigetībre,
āngan ofer eorðan yrfelāfe,
fēores frōfre, ðā hē swā forð gebād,
405 lēodum tō lāfe, langsumne hiht.
Hē þæt gecȳðde, þā hē þone cniht genam
fæste mid folmum, folccūð getēag
ealde lāfe, (ecg grymetode),
þæt hē him līfdagas lēofran ne wisse
410 þonne hē hȳrde Heofoncyninge.
[Þā Ābraham] up ārǣmde,
se eorl wolde slēan eaferan sīnne
unweaxenne, ecgum rēodan
magan mid mēce, gif hine *Metod* lēte.
415 Ne wolde him beorht Fæder bearn ætniman,
hālig tīber, ac mid handa befēng.
Þā him stȳran cwōm stefn of heofonum,
wuldres hlēoðor, word æfter spræc:

"Ne sleh þū, Ābraham, þīn āgen bearn,
420 sunu mid sweorde! Sōð is gecȳðed,
nū þīn cunnode Cyning alwihta,
þæt þū wið Waldend wǣre hēolde,
fæste trēowe, sēo þe [tō] frē*ode* sceal
in līfdagum lengest weorðan,
425 āwa tō aldre unswīciendo.
Hū þearf mannes sunu māran trēowe?
Ne behwylfan mæg heofon and eorðe
His wuldres word, wīddra and sīddra
þonne befæðman mæge foldan scēattas,
430 eorðan ymbhwyrft and uprodor,
gārsecges gin and þēos gēomre lyft.

---

401 *beorna:* bearna Barnouw (*Textkritische Untersuchungen*, p. 87)
404 *ðā:* ðēah Gr
  forð gebād: forðgebād Wlk
405 *lāfe:* lāre Bou, Gr
411–12 Printed as one line Gr, Wlk. No indication of loss in the MS. For 411b Kr supplies Abraham þā, Bl (n.) Abraham sweorde
413 *ecgum:* MS eagum; em. Th, Edd
414 Metod: MS god; metod Gr, Cos2, Graz, Mrk, Bl (n.), Kr
415 *ætniman:* æt niman Siev2, Graz, Bl
419 Begins p. 163
423 [tō] *frē*ode: MS freoðo; frēode Graz; furðor Holthausen (*ESt 51*:183).; frēolīc Holthausen (G-K, 882)
428 *wīddra:* written over an incomplete erasure; *id* written over *or,* according to Bl
429 *scēattas:* scēatas Diet, Gr
431 *gēomre lyft:* eormenlyft Cos2

Þē āð swereð engla Þēoden,
wyrda Waldend and wereda God,
sōðfæst sigora, þurh His sylfes līf,
435 þæt þīnes cynnes and cnēowmāga,
randwiggendra, rīm ne cunnon
yldo ofer eorðan ealle cræfte
tō gesecgenne sōðum wordum,
nymðe hwylc þæs snottor in sefan weorðe
440 þæt hē āna mæge ealle gerīman
stānas on eorðan, steorran on heofonum,
sæbeorga sand, sealte ȳða;
ac hīe gesittað be sǣm twēonum
oð Ēgipte ingeðēode
445 land Cananea, lēode þīne,
frēobearn fæder, folca sēlost."

* * * * * * * * * * *

FOLC wæs āfǣred, flōdegsa becwōm
gāstas gēomre, geofon dēaðe hwēop.
Wǣron beorhhliðu blōde bestēmed,
450 holm heolfre spāw, hrēam wæs on ȳðum,
wæter wæpna ful, wælmist āstāh.
Wǣron Ēgypte eft oncyrde,
flugon forhtigende, fǣr ongēton,
woldon hereblēaðe hāmas findan,
455 gylp wearð gnornra. Him ongēn genāp
atol ȳða gewealc, nē ðǣr ænig becwōm
herges tō hāme, ac behindan belēac
wyrd mid wǣge; þǣr ǣr wegas lāgon,
mere mōdgode, mægen wæs ādrenced.
460 Strēamas stōdon, storm up gewāt
hēah tō heofonum, herewōpa mǣst;
lāðe cyrmdon, (lyft up geswearc),
fǣgum stæfnum; flōd blōd gewōd.

432 þē: MS ne; þē Kock JJJ, Holthausen (AnglBeibl 30:3); nū Br2; hē Th, Edd
434 sigora: sigora weard Diet, Gr
437 yldo: ylde Gr
442 sand: MS sund; em. Th, Edd
444 ingeðēode: MS incaðeode; ingeðēode Gr, Wlk; incre þēode Bou2
446 P. 164 is blank except for "tribus annis transactis" written on it in a later hand; a
leaf has been cut out following it (see Introduction, p. 10); p. 165 is blank
447 Begins p. 166. Folc has a large plain capital F
453 forhtigende: forhtende Siev2, Mrk
454 hereblēaðe: here bleaðe (i.e. blīðe?) Th (n.)
455 genāp: gehnap Gr (but Gr2 like MS)
457 behindan: hīe hindan Gr (but Gr2 like MS)
463 stæfnum: flǣscum Gr (n.); stefnum Se

Randbyrig wæron rofene,   rodor swipode
465   meredēaða mæst;   mōdige swulton,
cyningas on corðre,   cyre swiðroðe
wæges æt ende,   wīgbord scinon.

Hēah ofer hæleðum   holmweall āstāh,
merestrēam mōdig;   mægen wæs on cwealme
470   fæste gefeterod,   forðganges nep,
searwum *āsæled*.   Sand bā*sn*odon
witodre *wy*rde,   hwonne waðema strēam,
sincalda sæ,   sealtum ȳðum,
æflāstum gewuna,   ēce staðulas,
475   nacud nȳdboda,   nēosan cōme,
fāh fēðegāst,   sē ðe fēondum genēop.

Wæs sēo hæwene lyft   heolfre geblanden;
brim berstende   blōdegsan hwēop
sæmanna sīð,   oðþæt sōð Metod
480   þurh Moyses hand   mōdge rȳmde,
wīde wæðde,   wælfæðmum swēop.

Flōd fāmgode,   fæge crungon,
lagu land gefēol,   lyft wæs onhrēred;
wicon weallfæsten,   wægas burston,
485   multon meretorras,   þā se Mihtiga slōh
mid hālige hand,   heofonrīces [God],
Weard wērbēamas,   wlance ðēode.

---

466 *cyre:* cyrr Diet, Gr (but Gr2 like MS); cyrm Cos2, Se *MLR,* Se; cyre 'choice' Imelmann (*Forschungen,* p. 403)
467 *wæges:* MS sæs; wæges Gr, Klu, Graz, Mrk
470 *forðganges nep:* forðganges hnepde Bou2; forðganges ner Gr2; forðgange nēh Mrk; forðgang esnes Se *MLR,* Se; forðganges weg Br2, Kr
471 *āsæled:* MS æsæled; āsæled Junius, Edd except Bl, Kr
    bāsnodon: MS barenodon; bāsnodon Diet, Gr2, Wlk, Klaeber (*ESt 41:*110), Kr; bāsnode Br, Br2; berēnod on Bou2; hīe rēnodon Se *MLR,* Se
472 *wyrde:* MS fyrde; wyrde Diet, Wlk, Klaeber (*ESt 41:*110)
474 *æflāstum gewuna:* æglāstum or ægflotum Bou (n.); ēalāstum or wæglāstum gewunad Bou2; æflāst-ungewuna Cos2
476 *fāh fēðegāst:* fāh fæge gāst or flēah fæge gāst Th (n.); fāh wæs se gāst Bou
    genēop: gehnēop Diet; gehwēop Se *MLR,* Se
480 Moyses last word on p. 166; hand begins p. 167
    mōdge rȳmde: mōd gerȳmde Th, Bou, Graz, Bl
481 *wælfæðmum:* wæl fæðmum Th, Bou
482 *fāmgode:* fāmgende? Cos2
483 *lagu land:* laguland Diet, Gr (but not Gr2), Klu, Graz, Mrk
486–7 This arrangement suggested by Bl (n.); Bl (text) has heofonrīces weard in 486, werbēamas in 487; other Edd have weard in 486
487a werbēama swēot Holthausen (*AnglBeibl 5:*231); wrāðe werbēamas Mrk; on wægstrēamas Br2; wērge beornas Holthausen (G-K, 782); werbēamas on Se *MLR;* on werbēamas Se, Kr; on wērbēamas ('the protecting columns') Thomas (*MLR 12:*345)

Ne mihton forhabban   helpendra pað,
merestrēames mōd,   ac hē manegum gesceōd
490   gyllende gryre. Gārsecg wēdde,
up ātēah, on slēap; egesan stōdon,
wēollon wælbenna. Wītrod gefēol
hēah of heofonum   handweorc Godes,
fāmigbosma; flōdweard [g]eslōh
495   unhlēowan wæg alde mēce,
þæt ðȳ dēaðdrepe drihte swæfon,
synfullra swēot. Sāwlum lunnon
fæste befarene, flōdblāc here,
siððan him on bōgum brūn' yppinge

*   *   *   *   *   *   *   *

500   mōdwæga mæst. Mægen eall gedrēas,
d[ē]aþe gedre[n]cte, dugoð Ēgypta,
Faraon mid his folcum. Hē onfond hraðe,
siððan [grund] gestāh, Godes andsaca,
þæt wæs mihtigra mereflōdes Weard;
505   wolde heorufæðmum hilde gesceādan,

---

488. *helpendra pað:* helpendran pað Th (n.); hālwendne pað Bou2; helpenda ('elephants') pað Gr; hleopandra ('sea-leopards') pað Kock (*Angl 43:*306); hwelpendra pað Holthausen (*Angl 44:*353), Br (but retracted by Br2); helwarena pað Holthausen (G-K, 885); helpendra paða Mrk; helpendra fæðm Se *MLR,* Se; hālwendra or hælwendra pað? Kr (n.)

491 *up ātēah:* up āstāh Bou2

492 *wælbenna:* wælburnan Bou2; wælbenda? Sisam (*MLN 32:*48)

    wītrod: witod Th (n.); wīterōd Bou; wit-rod Diet, Gr; wīg-trod Gr2, Kock JJJ; wīgrād Br; wīgrōd Se *MLR,* Se; wiþertrod Sisam (*MLN 32:*48)

494 *flōdweard [g]eslōh:* MS flodwearde sloh; flōd wearð geslōh Cos2

498 *befarene:* befangene Bou2

499 siððan hīe on hōgum hrān yrringa Se *MLR,* Se; Edd assume no gap after this line (no indication of one in MS)

    him: MS hie

    on bōgum: onbugon Gr, Wlk; on buge Bl (n.); onbrugdon or onbrūdon Br; on bugon Thomas (*MLR 12:*345), Kr

    brūn': MS brun; brūne Diet; brūn' Thomas (*MLR 12:*345); brēcun Holthausen (*ESt 51:*182)

    brūn' yppinge: brim-yppinge or brim yppende Br2

500 *mōdwæga:* MS modewæga; mōdwæga Gr, Graz, Mrk, Se

501 d[ē]aþe gedre[n]cte: MS ða þegedrecte; dēaðe gedrencte Se *MLR,* Se; ðā hē gedrencte Bou, Gr, Mrk; ðā þe gedrencte Wlk; ðā gedrencte wæron Kr; see Note

502 *onfond:* MS onfeond; em. Th (n.), Edd except Bl

    onfond hraðe: on fēond hrēðde Diet

503 *siððan [grund] gestāh:* MS siððan gestah; grund supplied by Gr, Edd, hē grund by Se

    gestāh: geseah Diet

504 *wæs:* þær Gr

505 *heorufæðmum:* MS huru fæðmum; heorofæðmum Gr; heorufæðmum Klu, Wlk, Se, Kr

yrre and egesfull. Ēgyptum wearð
þæs dægweorces dēop lēan gescēod,
forðām þæs heriges hām eft ne cōm
ealles ungrundes ænig tō lāfe,
510 þætte sīð heora secgan mōste,
bodigean æfter burgum bealospella mæst,
hordwearda hryre, hæleða cwēnum,
ac þā mægenþrēatas meredēað geswealh,
[swā ēac] spelbodan; sē ðe spēd āhte
515 āgēat gylp wera. Hīe wið God wunnon!

Swā reordode ræda gemyndig   (549)
manna mildost, mihtum swīðed,   (550)
hlūdan stefne; here stille bād
witodes willan, wundor ongēton,
520 mōdiges mūðhæl; hē tō mænegum spræc:

"Micel is þēos menigeo, mægenwīsa trum,
fullēsta mæst, sē ðās fare lædeð;   (555)
hafað ūs on Cananea cyn gelȳfed
burh and bēagas, brāde rīce;
525 wile nū gelæstan þæt hē lange gehēt
mid āðsware, engla Drihten,
in fyrndagum fæderyncynne,   (560)
gif gē gehealdað hālige lāre,
þæt gē fēonda gehwone forð ofergangað,
530 gesittað sigerīce be sǣm twēonum,
bēorselas beorna. Bið eower blæd micel!"

Æfter þām wordum werod wæs on sālum,   (565)
sungon sigebȳman, (segnas stōdon),
on fægerne swēg. Folc wæs on lande!
535 Hæfde wuldres bēam werud gelæded,
hālige hēapas, on hild Godes.

509 *ungrundes:* ungerīmedes Bou2
510 *heora:* MS heoro; em. Th (n.), Edd except Bl
511 P. 168 is blank; begins p. 169
514a MS spelbodan; swā ēac spelbodan Se; spelbodan ēac Bl (n.), Kr; spilde spelbodan
   Gr, Graz, Mrk; hȳrde spelbodan Rieger ("Verskunst," p. 46)
516–90 The text is rearranged and renumbered; original numbering in parentheses at
   right; see Introduction, pp. 11–12
520 *mūðhæl:* meðel Th (n.); mūðe hæl Bou2
523 *ūs on:* MS ufon; em. Bou2, Edd except Bl
527 *fæderyncynne:* fædera cynne Gr (n.)
534 *fægerne:* fægenne? Mrk
536 *hild:* hyld Se

* * * līfe gefēon   þā hīe oðlǣded hæfdon   (570)
feorh of fēonda dōme,   þēah ðe hīe hit frēcne genēðdon,
weras under wǣtera hrōfas.   Gesāwon hīe þǣr weallas standan,
540   ealle him brimu blōdige þūhton,   þurh þā heora beadosearo
                                 wǣgon.
Hrēðdon hildespelle,   siððan hīe þām [herge] wiðfōron;
hōfon hereþrēatas   hlūde stefne,   (575)
for þām dǣdweorce   Drihten heredon,
weras wuldres sang;   wīf on ōðrum,
545   folcswēota mǣst,   fyrdlēoð gōlan
āclum stefnum,   eallwundra fela.
Þā wæs ēðfynde   Ēbrisc mēowle   (580)
on geofones staðe   golde geweorðod.
Handa hōfon   halswurðunge,
550   blīðe wǣron,   bōte gesāwon,
hēddon hererēafes,   (hæft wæs onsǣled).
Ongunnon sǣlāfe   segnum dǣlan   (585)
on ȳðlāfe   ealde mādmas,
rēaf and randas.   Hēo on riht sceō[don]
555   gold and godweb,   Iōsepes gestrēon,
wera wuldorgesteald.   Werigend lāgon
on dēaðstede,   drihtfolca mǣ[st].   (590)

Þanon Israhelum   ēce rǣdas   (516)
on merehwearfe   Moyse[s] sægde,
560   hēahþungen wer,   hālige sprǣce,
dēop ǣrende.   Dægword nemnað

537 Edd assume no loss
    gefēon: gefēonde Th; gefēgon Diet, Gr, Edd except Klu
540a brimu him ealle blōdige þūhton Siev3 476; Bl prints 540a and 540b as two normal
    lines
541 þām: hām Se; Gr, Klu, Bl (n.), Kr add herge after þām
    wiðfōron: hildfrumum Bou
544 sang is last word on p. 170; wīf begins p. 171
545 gōlan: MS galan; gōlon Gr; gōlan Wlk, Bl (n.), Se, Kr
547 Ēbrisc: MS afrisc; ebrisc Holthausen (AnglBeibl 21:14), Br2, Goll lxxv
    mēowle: iūweola Bou2; nēowle Bl (n.), Goll lxxv, Kr
549 handa hōfon: hand āhōfon Th, Bou, Gr, Wlk, Se, Kr; handa hōfon Gr (n.), Bou2, Bl
    handa: handum Holthausen (G-K, 884)
550 bōte gesāwon: botlgestrēonum Bou2
552 segnum: secgum Bou2
    dǣlan: lǣdan Klaeber (Archiv 113:147)
554 hēo: heom Gr, Klu, Wlk, Se
    sceō[don]: MS sceo; sceōdon Th (n.), Bl (n.), Kr; scēode Gr, Klu, Wlk, Se
557 mǣ[st]: MS mæ, with erasure following it; mǣst Junius, Edd.
    P. 172 is blank; Daniel begins on p. 173
559 Moyse[s]: MS moyse; em. Th, Edd
561 dægword: MS dægweorc; dægword Goll lxxvii, Kr
    nemnað: nemned Th (n.)

swā gȳt werðēode, on gewritum findað   (520)
dōma gehwilcne, þāra ðe him Drihten bebēad
on þām sīðfate sōðum wordum,
565   gif onlūcan wile līfes wealhstōd,
beorht in brēostum, bānhūses weard,
ginfæstan gōd gāstes cǣgon,   (525)
rūn bið gerecenod, rǣd forð gê̄ð;
hafað wīslīcu word on fæðme,
570   wile meagollīce mōdum tǣcan
þæt wē gēsne ne sȳn Godes þēodscipes,
Metodes miltsa. Hē ūs mā onlȳhð,   (530)
nū ūs bōceras beteran secgað
lengran līfwynna. Þis is lǣne drēam,
575   wommum āwyrged, wreccum ālȳfed,
earmra anbid. Ēðellēase
þysne gystsele gihðum healdað,   (535)
murnað on mōde, mānhūs witon
fæst under foldan, þǣr bið fȳr and wyrm,
580   open ēce scræf yfela geh[w]ylces.
Swā nū regnþēofas rīce dǣlað,
yldo oððe ǣrdēað. Eftwyrd cym[e]ð,   (540)
mægenþrymma mǣst ofer middangeard,
dæg dǣdum fāh. Drihten sylfa
585   on þām meðelstede manegum dēmeð,
þonne Hē sōðfæstra sāwla lǣdeð,
ēadige gāstas, on uprodor,   (545)
þǣr [bið] lēoht and līf, ēac þon lissa blǣd.
Dugoð on drēame Drihten herigað,
590   weroda Wuldorcyning, tō wīdan feore!   (548)

566 *weard:* hord Holthausen (*Angl 44:*353)
567 *ginfæstan:* MS ginfæsten; ginfæstan Gr2, Cos2; ginfæst Bou, Gr; ginfæsta Siev2; ginfæste Mrk
    cǣgon: cǣgum Klu
568 *gê̄ð:* gangeð Mrk
571 *gēsne:* so MS; Edd except Bl, Kr misread as gesine
574 *līfwynna:* MS lyft wynna, so Th, Gr, Wlk; līfwynna Th (n.), Cos2, Kr; lȳfwynna Bl (n.); lystwynna Bou
575 *āwyrged:* āwyrded Diet
    wreccum: wræccum Gr (n.); the word is somewhat obscured by a wrinkle in the MS and was read by Th as wineccum, by Siev as wirecum
577 *healdað:* MS healdeð; healdað Gr, Klu, Wlk, Kr
580 *geh[w]ylces:* MS gehylces; em. Junius, Edd
581 *regnþēofas:* rægl (i.e. hrægl) þēofas Bou2
582 *ǣrdēað:* ǣr dēað Th, Bou
    eftwyrd: eft wyrd Th, Bou
    cym[e]ð: MS cymð; cymeð Th (n.), Siev2, Graz, Mrk
583 *mægenþrymma mǣst:* mægentrumma mǣste Bou2
586 sōðfæs ends p. 169; tra begins p. 170
588 *þǣr [bið] lēoht:* MS þǣr leoht; þǣr is lēoht Gr, Klu, Graz, Mrk, Kr

NOTES

1–7. The general meaning of this introductory passage is fairly clear, but the syntax presents a puzzling problem. A parenthesis of unusual length must be assumed, since *Moyses* is probably to be taken as accusative and subject of the infinitive *secgan*. The whole passage from 3 to 6 represents loosely the message given by Moses; within that passage the phrases may be taken in several ways. *Dōmas, wordriht, bōte līfes,* and *langsumne rǣd* seem to be loosely parallel, with the last two representing distinctions or qualifications. The specifically Christian reference here to the future life is worth noticing; obviously there is no such reference to be found in the O.T. version of the laws of Moses. This beginning bears a resemblance to the "Proem" of the *Meters of Boethius,* the closing phrases being almost identical: *folccūðne rǣd / hæleðum secgan. Hliste sē þe wille!* (9–10). But the *Meters* show no such grammatical complexity as the passage here. The formula itself was probably a familiar one, descended originally from the minstrel's call for attention.

5. *bealusīðe.* A reference to death, the terrible journey. Sedgefield (n.) suggests that the word refers both to the journey of the Israelites through the wilderness and to man's journey through life. But the contrast of *bealusīðe* with *līfes* in the same line seems deliberate, and *lāðsīð* 44, showing the same metaphor, is to be compared with it.

6. *langsumne rǣd.* 'Enduring benefit,' the translation offered by Klaeber (*ESt. 41:109*). Blackburn (n.), taking this phrase with *hæleðum secgan* in the next line, translates 'a benefit which it would take a long time to tell to men.' But *langsumne rǣd* is the reward of the living (*lifigendra gehwām*) as opposed to that of the dead; it is part of Moses' legacy, not all of it. Cf. *langsumne hiht* 405.

8–32. This passage describes primarily God's appearance to Moses in the burning bush on Mt. Horeb (Exod. 3), but references to the first meeting (ll. 8–11, 16–18, 22–9) are interspersed with a running survey of Moses' career.

10. *wundra fela.* Specifically, the ability to perform miracles. Cf. Exod. 4:21: "Vide ut omnia ostenta quae posui in manu tua, facias coram Pharaone." (Is *handlēan* 19 a reflection of the phrase *in manu tua*?)

15. *Godes andsaca[n].* A phrase used elsewhere (e.g., *Christ and Satan* 190) of Satan. The allegorical expositions of the exodus among early commentators almost invariably equate Pharaoh with the devil and Egypt with hell. (See, for example, Bede, *In Pentateuchum Commentarii, Exodus, PL 91:287* ff. and Cyprian, *Opuscula Ad Fortunatum de Martyro, PL 4:686.*) For this reason it might be preferable here to consider the ambiguous *Godes andsacan* as genitive singular in apposition to *Faraones.*

16–18. 'There [or then—presumably on Horeb] the Ruler of Victories gave him (or entrusted to him), the brave prince, the lives of his kinsmen (and) a dwelling place in a native land for the sons of Abraham.' Cf. Exod. 3:17 ff.

19–22. A reference forward in time to the warfare in Canaan with the tribes mentioned in Exod. 3:8–17, 23:23 ff., and elsewhere. The word *him* 19 is dative plural, referring to the sons of Abraham.

22. *folcriht.* In this context the word seems to mean little more than 'property' or 'possessions' (cf. *Beow.* 2608; Schücking, *Bedeutungslehre* 46), even though it is used in more precise senses as a technical term in the various Anglo-Saxon laws with the basic meaning of customary or common law (cf. F. Liebermann, *Die Gesetze der Angelsachsen,* Bd. 2, 2. Hälfte, *s.v. folcriht*).

22–9. The poet seems to state quite clearly that Moses was informed of the story of creation by God at their first meeting, but there is of course no indication of this in the 3d chapter of Exodus. The regular tradition seems to be followed by Ælfric in his treatise "On the Old and New Testament," where he says that the story of the Pentateuch was dictated to Moses by God on Mt. Sinai (*Old English Heptateuch,* EETS O.S. 160, ed. S. J. Crawford [1922], 21). The explanation probably lies in the identification (or confusion) of Horeb with Sinai; Deut. 5:2, in speaking of the giving of the Ten Commandments, reads: "The Lord our God made a covenant with us on Horeb" (cf. Deut. 4:15 and the opening lines of *Paradise Lost* [I, 6–10]:

> Sing, Heav'nly Muse, that on the secret top
> Of *Oreb,* or of *Sinai,* didst inspire
> That Shepherd, who first taught the chosen Seed,
> In the Beginning how the Heav'ns and Earth
> Rose out of *Chaos.*)

27 ff. *His sylfes naman.* The reference is not so much to Exod. 3:13–14 as to Exod. 6:2–3 (a later meeting between God and Moses): "Locutusque est Dominus ad Moysen dicens, Ego Dominus [3] qui apparui Abraham, Isaac, et Iacob in Deo omnipotente et nomen meum ADONAI non indicavi eis." The poet is typically condensing the important features of several interviews into one.

30–2. These lines seem to sum up the preceding lines and look toward the future; *on forðwegas* 32 probably means something very much like 'in his [Moses'] future actions.'

33–53. This passage is in some ways a miracle of compression, but it raises great problems in interpretation. The change of a word in l. 34 to *gedrenced* may be evidence that the passage was not clear to earlier readers, for the corrector must have taken the passage to refer primarily to the drowning of the Egyptian army. The phrase *ealdum wītum* 33 is thought by Bright (*MLN 27*:13) to refer to the threefold punishment of the Egyptians through loss of treasure, death of the first-born, and destruction of idols. This may be true but it cannot be proved. A more plausible meaning for the phrase is obtained if it is taken as referring to the plagues of Egypt, perhaps only the first nine since the rest of the passage seems to be primarily focused on the tenth plague, the death of the first-born. It is the first-born who are the *hordwearda* of l. 35 and who are referred to in the following terms in the rest of the passage: *dugoð* 41, *lēode* 44, *folc fērende* 45, *hergas* 46, and *mengeo* 48. Ll. 44–6 are in fact a logical extension of the well-worn figure of dying suggested in *dugoð forð gewāt.* Such an interpretation not only relieves the reader of the strain of introducing Israelites into the context at l. 44 (and the difficulty of explaining *lāðsīð* and *hergas on helle*) but artistically it provides a very effective contrast between the terrible journey (*lāðsīð*) of the Egyptian first-born to hell and the joyful journey (*lēofes sīðes* 53) of the Israelites to freedom. It also renders more understandable the rather obscure sentence beginning in l. 49.

33. *ingere.* No satisfactory explanation or emendation of this word has been proposed. Both the proposed changes—to *iū gēre* (i.e. *gēara*) 'long ago' or to *ungēra* (i.e. *ungēara*) 'recently'—are somewhat doubtful on grounds of meaning. While a temporal adverb of some sort would certainly be possible here, there has been no standard of time established which would give any real significance to either 'long ago' or 'recently.' Mürkens (p. 92) argues for the retention of the MS reading *ingere,* the *in-* being an intensive prefix, as in *infrōd, Beow.* 2449, the *gere* a form of *geare* (cf. *sōð gere* 291); he would give the compound the meaning 'perfectissime.' This interpretation was supported by Krapp but was called a desperate way out by Klaeber (*Archiv 113*:146). Perhaps such a word did exist with this or a similar meaning. There remains the possibility that *ingere* is merely the remnant of a word not understood by the scribe, perhaps one of the peculiar *in-* nouns found elsewhere in the poem (see Note, 142). *Ingebēod* would be a possible guess.

33. *ealdum wītum.* The word *eald* here probably has connotations of 'long-decided, inexorable.' Klaeber (*Archiv 113*:146) translates it as 'seit langer Zeit bestimmt.' The phrase *ealdum wītum,* even if read this way, is still quite clumsy. A possible emendation would be *ealdorwītum* 'life-punishments,' i.e., fatal punishments. Cf. the emended *eald[or]wērige* 50.

34. *gedrenced.* The original reading has been completely obliterated and the hand which changed it to *gedrenced* is certainly not the scribe's. The original word can only be guessed at. A reference to drowning is out of place here. The poet is speaking either in a general way about the downfall of the entire Egyptian nation (a process of some time) or specifically, in view of what follows, of the death of the first-born. The word *gedēmed* might serve here, although the original reading was probably a longer word. The scribe is usually very neat in keeping his right-hand margin aligned and *gedēmed* might have allowed space for at least the first element of the next word, *drihtfolca.*

Gedrecced is probably to be rejected as a possibility; the usual form would have been *gedreaht*.

36. *since berofene*. Unless this phrase is attached to the following sentence (as suggested by Cosijn, *Beitr 19*:458), a fairly awkward construction, it appears to be syntactically homeless. It must be taken as referring vaguely to the survivors left in Egypt; there would be little point in making it refer to the already dead first-born. So far as we are told in this poem, the Egyptians' treasure was lost in the Red Sea, where the Israelites found it on the shore (see Note, 555). The Israelites also "spoiled the Egyptians" before departing (Exod. 11:2, 12:35–6); but to see a reference to that in this one phrase is perhaps basing too much on slender evidence. The phrase seems rather to be an elegiac cliché, not to be pinned down too exactly.

37. *mansceaða*. The emendation from MS *mansceaðan* makes the word subject of the sentence and roughly parallel with *bana* and *lēodhata* 39–40—the destroying angel. The chief difficulty with the MS reading, which would make the word refer to the first-born as accusative plural, is the furnishing of a suitable subject; the only possible subject would be God in l. 30, a long and awkward carry-over. The first element is here taken to be *man(n)* 'man' rather than *mān* 'criminal, evil,' although the latter would be possible. Ps. 78:49–51 may have suggested the idea of evil angels: "Misit in eos iram indignationis suae: indignationem, et iram, et tribulationem: immissiones per angelos malos. [50] Viam fecit semitae irae suae, non pepercit a morte animabus eorum: et jumenta eorum in morte conclusit. [51] Et percussit omne primogenitum in terra Aegypti: primitias omnis laboris eorum in tabernaculis Cham." While this passage does not actually attribute the killing of the first-born to the evil angels, such a reading of it would be easily understandable.

40. *drysmyde*. The verb *drysmian* appears only in *Beow.* 1375, where the exact meaning of it is uncertain; Klaeber glosses it 'become gloomy.' That meaning would fit the context here. Sedgefield (n.) translates 'was soaked.'

41. *dēadra hrǣwum*. Cf. the book of Wisdom 18:12: "Similiter ergo omnes uno nomine mortis mortuos habebant innumerabiles. Nec enim ad sepeliendum vivi sufficiebant, quoniam uno momento, quae erat praeclarior natio illorum, exterminata est."

dugoð forð gewāt. Blackburn (n.) would take this as referring to the departure of the Israelites, but it is no more than a standard phrase for death. See, among many examples, *Gen.* 1178, 1192, where *þā hē forð gewāt* means simply 'when he died,' and the AS Chronicle, *passim*.

43. *hleahtorsmiðum*. A very general reference seems to be intended here, in keeping with the tone of lament in the preceding lines. Blackburn (n.) is too literal in taking this word to refer to the magicians of Egypt. The 'makers of laughter' are probably minstrels who have fallen silent in the grief-stricken kingdom.

44. A verb must be supplied here. The simplest reading is that proposed by Kock (JJJ 24), where *wæs* is to be understood after *ālȳfed*. Translate 'A hateful journey was permitted to greet the people, the journeying folk . . . armies in hell (or hellish armies?).' *Lāðsīð* is certainly the journey to death, or hell. Cf. *Gen. B* 732–3: *ac hīe tō helle sculon   on þone sweartan sīð; Sol. and Sat.* 353–4: *Ne mæg mon forildan ǣnige hwīle   ðone dēoran sīð, ac hē hine ādrēogan sceall.*

45. *frēond wæs berēafod*. 'The lover was bereaved.' A parenthetical exclamation, in keeping with the tone of the *wōp wæs wīde* sentiment. It seems much more effective read this way, despite the almost universal emendation by the editors to *fēond*.

46. *hergas on helle*. Klaeber (*Archiv 113*:147) translates *on helle* as 'höllisch, verflucht,' as in *Beow.* 101; but in this passage the literal meaning 'in hell' would serve well enough. Kock (PPP 6) begins a new sentence with *hergas* in the sense 'altars' (i.e., *heargas*) and in apposition to *dēofolgyld*. He cites good examples of the pairing of *heargas* and *dēofolgyld* elsewhere, but the change seems unnecessary.

46–7. *Heofon þider becōm, druron dēofolgyld*. It is indeed difficult to see why the reading *heofon* should not be preserved here. The reference is primarily to Exod. 12:12: "Et transibo per terram Ægypti nocte illa, percutiamque omne primogenitum in terra Ægypti . . . et in cunctis diis Ægypti faciam judicia, Ego Dominus." 'Heaven,' in other words, stands for God himself. The legend of the fall of the Egyptian idols on the night of the passover is widespread. While Holthausen (*Archiv 115*:162) and Moore (*MP 9*:104) have pointed out mention of the legend in Bede and

Peter Comestor, an earlier source is to be found in Jerome's *Epistola* LXXVIII.4 (*CSEL* 55:54) : "Illud Hebraei autumant, quod nocte, qua egressus est populus, omnia in Ægypto templa destructa sint, sive motu terrae, sive tactu fulminum." Countless other medieval commentators copy this remark. Ginzberg (*Legends of the Jews, 2,* 367) gives the Jewish tradition referred to by Jerome: "All the idols of the Egyptians were swept out of existence in that night. The stone idols were ground into dust, the wooden idols rotted, and those made of metal rotted away." Blackburn refers to the ME *Genesis and Exodus,* where an earthquake fells the temples and idols (ll. 3195-8, EETS, O.S.7, ed. R. Morris, 1865). A further scriptural source is in Num. 33 : 4: "et sepelientibus primogenitos, quos percusserat Dominus (nam et in diis eorum exercuerat ultionem)."

47. *Dæg wæs mære.* Bright (*MLN 27:*14) calls attention to Exod. 12:42, 13:3, where the Lord tells the Israelites to remember the night (or day) when they were delivered. See also Exod. 12:14, where the Lord, after announcing his intention of slaying the first-born, says: "Habebitis autem hunc diem in monumentum: et celebrabitis eam sollemnem Domino in generationibus vestris cultu sempiterno."

49-53. 'So the people of Egypt endured captivity(?) for many years, weary of soul, for this reason, that they intended to keep Moses' kinsmen a long time, as long as they wished(?), from the longed-for journey—if God had let them.' In spite of several obscurities, this seems to be the sense of this difficult passage. The verb *wyrnan* requires the genitive in the thing refused, which would here be *lēofes sīðes,* and the dative for the person to whom it is refused, here *māgum.* The difficulty lies in the phrase *on langne lust,* which, if the above rule is observed, cannot then be taken as governing *lēofes sīðes.* The only recourse is to take the phrase as a kind of parallel to *wīdeferð;* Krapp translates it 'at their [i.e. the Egyptians'] pleasure, as long as they wished.' The passage as a whole follows what has gone before a good deal more naturally if we assume that the poet has been talking about the first-born, *sēo mengeo* 48. Scholars who have tried to interpret it in other contexts have been forced to desperate measures; see Bright (*MLN 27:*14) and Thomas (*MLR 12:*343).

49. *fæsten.* An ambiguous word here, perhaps conveying the idea of captivity (in hell), or possibly even that of famine, either on earth for the survivors or in hell.

50. *eald[or]wērige.* This emendation for the unmetrical and somewhat strange *ealdwērige* seems justified; even though the word does not appear elsewhere, the synonymous *ferhðwērig* is found several times in the poetry (*Guth.* 1157, *Christ* 830, *El.* 560), as is *wērigferhð.* The *Christ* passage describes sufferings in hell, as a matter of fact : *Þæs hī longe sculon ferðwērige onfōn in fȳrbaðe* (829-30).

56. *fæsten[n]a.* There is a bare possibility that this reflects an observation of Pliny (*Natural History* V.I.1) : "[The natives of Africa] mostly reside in fortresses" (tr. H. Rackham, Loeb Classical Library edition, [1942] *2,* 219).

57. *lāðra manna.* Exod. 13:17-18 says distinctly that God led the Israelites by another route so that they would not pass through the land of the Philistines, lest they should repent leaving Egypt if they came in contact with fighting. Yet here the poet seems to suggest that the Israelites passed through hostile tribes on their way to the Red Sea. Moore (p. 86) includes this passage among the additions or organic changes which the poet has made to his original material and explains it finally as being an invention of the poet, who in typical OE fashion is emphasizing the warlike details of his narrative. But the poet rarely invents such incidents and ordinarily has great respect for authority. This entire geographical passage especially seems to be derived from some strange conception of lands and people and it is very unlikely the poet had invented it. Schücking attempted to show that there was really no disparity between this account and that in the Bible. He interpreted *oferfōr* as meaning not 'passed through' but 'avoided, bypassed' (*Klaeber Miscellany* 214n.). But this would mean that the Israelites avoided the *enge ānpaðas* as well, a reading which would make little sense. Evidently the poet has the Israelites pass through hostile country because he believes on some authority that warlike tribes inhabited the area between Egypt and the Red Sea. What that authority was is difficult to determine, but the reference to the Nabataeans who are "difficult to overcome in war" furnished by Diodorus Siculus would furnish a possible basis for this description. See Introduction, p. 18.

58. This line is identical with *Beow.* 1410 and is discussed in the Introduction, pp. 25-7, in connection with relative dating of the poem. The Vulgate phrase which may

have suggested this is in Exod. 13:18: "Sed circumduxit per viam deserti." This line is hardly a translation of the Latin but rather one which seems to have had associations with loneliness, exile, and making a way through unknown territory.

59. *Gūðmyrce.* 'Warlike border-dwellers' seems the most likely meaning of this word. The words *mearchofu* 61 and *mearclandum* 67, as Blackburn suggests, favor this interpretation. It is impossible to tell whether the poet had a specific tribe in mind. The alternative explanation, favored by Grein (*Sprachschatz 2:*786) and Gollancz (p. lxxx), is to take the word as meaning "war-negroes," comparing it to *ælmyrcna, An.* 432. But there is no indication that the *Gūðmyrce* are Negroes; they are certainly not the Ethiopians mentioned later and probably not the Nubians favored by Gollancz (see following Note).

60. *lyfthelme.* Blackburn is quite mistaken in taking this to refer to the pillar of cloud, which has not yet appeared. Gollancz (p. lxxx) regards this line as evidence that the poet was here thinking of the Nubians and "was playing on the fictitious etymology connecting Nubae, the Nubians, with 'nubes,' a cloud." In ancient geography, according to Gollancz, the Nubians were placed south of Egypt and north of the Ethiopians. But the usual location of the Nubians was far to the south in the region of Meroe (modern Khartoum) or, more often, southwest of Egypt. Strabo (Book 17.1.2) places them on the left (west) bank of the Nile, upland from Egypt; Ptolemy places them well to the southwest of Meroe (see map facing p. 632 in E. H. Bunbury, *A History of Ancient Geography,* Vol. 2, London, 1879). If the poet is referring to Nubians here, we must assume that his knowledge of geography is very inaccurate. The country referred to by Diodorus is perhaps a more likely source, the country which "is overspread by mild and thick clouds" that reduce the burning heat of the region (Diod. III.45.6; quoted in the Introduction, p. 19.

61. *mearchofu mōrheald.* This phrase may be corrupt, but no easy emendation suggests itself. It seems best to retain *mōrheald* as being a possible compound, perhaps an adjective like *frēondheald;* cf. the entries in B-T *s.v. heald,* adj. (e.g., *of dūne healde* 'downwards'). *Heald* has the basic meaning 'inclined'; *mōrheald* might mean little more than 'on the moor, moorland.' Gollancz (p. lxxxi) would read *mārheald* 'securely moored,' citing such words as *mǣrels, mǣrels-rāp,* and Old Frisian *mere* 'rope.' According to his discussion of the itinerary of the Israelites, this is a reference to the encampment at Succoth, a word which is always interpreted (cf. Gen. 33:17) as 'tents' (Lat. tabernacula). Gollancz' emendation is somewhat insecure, but there is no reason to doubt that *mearchofu,* whether fastened by ropes or not, may represent a reference to tents or at least to Succoth, the second stopping place. Mention should be made of a line in *Beowulf* which is oddly reminiscent of this phrase: *mearcað mōrhopu* 450a. This is not mentioned by Klaeber in his list of parallels (*MLN 33*). Perhaps one should read *mearchopu* here, if it were not for the strong suspicion that *mearchofu* represents a reference to Succoth's tents. Both these lines may be transmuted recollections of epic formulas or phrase units.

63. *meor[r]inga.* 'Impediments'(?). The usual interpretation of this word holds that it is cognate with Goth. *marzjan,* possibly related to OE *gemearr* 'hindrance' and with that meaning here. This form would then be a Northumbrian form (properly *meorringa,* not *meoringa*) of a word **mearringa.* The WS *i*-umlauted equivalent would be *mierringa* or *myrringa* (Mürkens, p. 113, Bright *MLN 17:*424), ME *merring, maring, marring* (Mätzner and Bieling, *Altenglische Sprachproben,* p. 469, and see *OED, s.v. marring,* vbl. sb.). This meaning is suitable here. Another reading might be suggested: *mēringa* (i.e. *mǣringa*) 'boundaries, borderlands.' The basis for this is found in the evidence of place names. R. E. Zachrisson ("The Meaning of English Place-Names in the Light of the Terminal Theory," *Studia Neophilologica, 6* [1933–34], 25–89) states on p. 30: "I take *mǣring, (mearcing)* to have the same meaning as OE. *mǣre, mearc,* 'boundary, border, border-land,' perpetuated in Mod. dial. English *mere,* 'boundary, boundary-mark, a road serving as a boundary,' and in *mearing,* 'boundary,' as in *mearing ditch,* Hants." Still another possibility might be **mōringa* 'moor-dwellers,' but it would be much less likely. (See R. E. Zachrisson, "Studies on the *-ing* Suffix," *Studia Neophilologica, 9* [1936–37], 78 for similar constructions). Gollancz' (p. lxxxi) elaborate emendation of *fela meoringa* to *fēle Mēring* (i.e. *fǣle Mǣring*) 'the trusty Amramite,' a reference to Moses (see Num. 3:27), is far too involved to be probable.

63. *tīrfæste.* Both the plural reference in the next line and the fact that Moses is the

only possible subject of the sentence as it stands require this emendation. If *tīrfæstne* were retained, it could refer only to Moses, and then God would have to be furnished as the subject of the sentence.

66. *Æthānes byrig.* This is the only place mentioned by name in this section, but in the course of their journey the Israelites stop at at least three places. Rameses was variously regarded by commentators as the starting place or the first camp; if the reference to two nights has any significance, presumably the poet believed the latter, as is later demonstrated more clearly in his calling the camp on the Red Sea the fourth camp (133-4). Num. 33:3-8 lists the *mansiones* of the Israelites in order: "Profecti igitur de Ramesse mense primo . . . [5] Castrametati sunt in Soccoth. [6] Et de Soccoth venerunt in Etham, quae est in extremis finibus solitudinis. [7] Inde egressi venerunt contra Phihahiroth, quae respicit Beelsephon, et castrametati sunt ante Magdalum. [8] Profectique de Phihahiroth, transierunt per medium mare in solitudinem . . ." The camps are also mentioned, in essentially the same words, in Exod. 12:37, 13:20, 14:2, 14:9. The second camp then would be Succoth, which is not mentioned by name but which may be referred to in the mention of *mearchofu.* Etham is definitely called the *þridda wīc* in 87. The fourth camp is not named but is on the shores of the Red Sea. The allegorical treatment of these separate *mansiones* was an elaborate one at the hands of the early commentators. The allegory is based on Paul's suggestion (I Cor. 10:1-4) of a comparison between the exodus and the process of baptism. Specific treatment of it may be found in Ambrose's *De* XLII *Mansionibus Filiorum Israel Tractatus* (*PL 17*) and Jerome's *Epistola* LXXVIII (*CSEL 55*), although there are several others differing to some extent in their detailed interpretation. Egypt is represented as the state of sin, from which the human soul proceeds by gradual and well-defined steps (the various *mansiones*) through baptism (in the Red Sea) to ultimate salvation. Some of these stages may be selected from Origen's discussion of them (*Homilia in Exodum,* Homily v, *PG 12:*325 ff., in Latin translation only). The man who wishes to leave Egypt, the land of darkness, error, and sin, must leave from Ramases, which name Origen interprets to mean *commotio tineae* 'the movement of the moth or worm.' These are the perishable treasures which moths can corrupt (Luke 12:33). Then he arrives at Succoth, "tabernacles" or "tents." Here he lives as a nomad, stripped of impediments. (Could this be hinted at in the *fela meorringa* 62?) Etham means *signa eis,* the place where on the significant *third* day he receives a sign (the pillar of cloud and fire) and the mystery is made known. Other commentators use different Hebrew etymologies for the placenames and obtain different results (see Note, 81). But it is clear that this level of interpretation is not used explicitly by the poet, and it is impossible to determine how much he intended to suggest to his audience. The word *līfweg* 104, as Gollancz (p. lxxxiii) points out, does suggest that he had in mind this idea of understanding the journey as a kind of pilgrim's progress.

67. *mearclandum on.* This seems to translate the Vulg. phrase (Exod. 13:20): "[Etham] in extremis finibus solitudinis."

68. *Nearwe genȳddon on norðwegas.* 'Difficulties forced (them) to take the roads to the north.' This is the reading suggested by Napier (*MLR 6:*168). The 'difficulties' were, presumably, the presence of the Ethiopians to the south and more especially the intense heat in the southern regions. Other editors (Grein, Blackburn, Sedgefield) take *nearwe* as an adverb meaning 'with difficulty' and translate *genȳddon* as 'pressed on, hastened,' a meaning which it seems to have in *Soul and Body* I (Vercelli Book), 117. Exod. 14:2 gives a hint of a change of direction, although it gives no such explanation as we find here: "Loquere filiis Israel: *Reversi* castrametentur e regione Phihahiroth."

69. *Sigelwara land.* The land of the Ethiopians. The reference to the Ethiopians is of course not found in the biblical account and no commentary has come to light which connects Ethiopia in any way with this journey to the Red Sea. Moore (p. 105) attempts to explain this allusion by bringing in an old legend found in Josephus and several of the earlier writers which tells how Moses as a youth commanded an Egyptian army which defeated the Ethiopians. But it is not actually said here that the Ethiopians are hostile to Moses or the Israelites, merely that their land is too hot to travel through. Perhaps in a vaguer sense the association of Moses with Ethiopia in legend may have been an underlying cause for the introduction of this reference by the poet.

The word *Sigelwara* was taken, by a kind of popular etymology, to mean 'sun-dwellers.' The older form, however, *Sigelhearwa,* is of obscure etymology. J. R. R. Tolkien, who discusses the occurrences of the word and its probable origin exhaustively (*Medium Aevum* [1932], *1,* 183–96, *3,* 95–111), suggests that the older reading was probably the original one here. It would certainly have been somewhat better metrically.

70. *forbærned burhhleoðu.* 'Scorched hillsides.' Cf. *beorhhliðu* 449. The word also appears in the form *burghleoþum* in Rid. 27, 2, where the meaning is 'hillsides.' The forms *burh* and *beorh* are confused in this poem; *burgum* 222 seems to mean 'hills.' BTS includes this word under *beorhhlið.* See Napier, *MLR* 6:168, Kock, *Anglia* 45:124–5. There may be an echo of a description by Pliny of the inland parts of Cyrenaica on the trade route to Ethiopia: "After these a long range stretches from east to west which our people from its nature call the Black Mountain, as it has the appearance of having suffered from fire, or else of being scorched by the reflection of the sun." (*Nat. Hist.* v.5.35; tr. Rackham, Loeb ed., *2,* 245).

brūne lēode. That the Ethiopians' brown or black color was caused by the burning of the sun was, of course, an ancient and medieval commonplace. The Greek Phaeton myth is mentioned contemptuously by Orosius: "On þære tīde wæs sīo ofermycelo hǣto on ealre worulde: nales þæt ān þæt men wǣron miclum geswencte, ac ēac ealle nytenu swȳðe nēah forwurdon. And ðā sūðmestan Æthiopian hæfdon bryne for ðǣre hǣte, and Sciþþie þā norþmestan hæfdon ungewunelīce hǣton. Þā hæfdon monige unwīse menn him tō worde and tō lēasungspelle þæt sīo hǣte nǣre for hiora synnum, ac sǣdon þæt hīo wǣre for Fetontis forscapunge, ānes mannes" (*King Alfred's Orosius,* EETS O.S. 79, ed. H. Sweet [1883], 40–1). The Christian allegorical interpretation tended to regard the Ethiopians as blackened by sins. See, for example, Paulinus of Nola:

Aethiopum populus non sole perustos,
sed uitiis nigros et crimine nocticolores.
(Carmen XXVIII, 249–50, *CSEL 30:302*)

71. *hātum heofoncolum.* This phrase shows a certain resemblance to the description of the sun in the Red Sea district given by Diodorus (III.48.3): "Because of this [sudden dawn] there is no daylight in those regions before the sun has become visible, and when out of the midst of the sea, as they say, it comes into view, it resembles a fiery red ball of charcoal which discharges huge sparks" (tr. Oldfather, Loeb ed., *2,* 235).

71b–124. This passage, presenting some notable difficulties, is devoted largely to the pillars of cloud and fire. The problem of the sequence of events and the proposed rearrangements are discussed in the Introduction (pp. 4–6). The pillars of cloud and fire (the poet considers them as two separate entities) are here presented in an unusual manner, if we are to regard a departure from the bare account of the book of Exodus as unusual. The pillar of cloud has the primary function of protecting the Israelites from the heat of the sun; secondarily, it indicates camping places (92) and acts as a guide on the march (105). The pillar of fire, in addition to acting as a guide on night marches, serves as a protection from panic which might arise from fear of the wilderness darkness (116 ff.); it also keeps order by threatening with punishment any of the Israelites who might disobey Moses' orders (121 ff.). In most cases, evidence for these functions of the pillars can be brought forward from other parts of the Bible and from the commentaries, as will be shown in the individual Notes which follow.

72. *wið færbryne folc gescylde.* The belief that the pillar of cloud served to protect the children of Israel from the heat of the sun, while not suggested by the source in Exodus, was a fairly common one among the early commentators. Several biblical passages clearly suggest this idea. Bright (*MLN* 17:424) cites Ps. 105:39: "Expandit nubem in protectionem eorum, et ignem ut luceret eis per noctem." He also quotes Isa. 4:5–6: "Et creabit Dominus super omnem locum montis Sion, et ubi invocatus est, nubem per diem, et fumum et splendorem ignis flammantis in nocte; super omnem enim gloriam protectio. Et tabernaculum erit in umbraculum diei ab aestu, et in securitatem, et absconsionem a turbine et a pluvia." Moore (p. 89) adds Wisdom 19:7: "Nam nubes castra eorum obumbrabat." Cf. also Wisdom 18:3 and 10:17, Isa. 49:10, and Ps. 121:6. Moore also quotes what is perhaps more important, Jerome's comment on Ps. 105:39: "Nubem et ignem, Spiritum sanctum dicit: qui nos et ab aestu diei defendit, et in nocturnis tenebris illuminat." Ginzberg (*Legends of the Jews, 2,* 374) gives the Jewish tradition: "In Succoth God enveloped them in seven clouds of glory, four hovering in front, behind and at the two sides of them, one suspended above them, to keep off rain, hail, and the

rays of the sun, and one under them to protect them against thorns and snakes." The tradition is found very widely in later commentators.

78. *hāte.* 'With heat.' For *hāt* as a noun see *Beow.* 2605.

79. *dægsceades hlēo.* This emendation, following Krapp, of the MS reading *dægscealdes,* is offered very tentatively. Perhaps *dægscead[w]es* would be better metrically. 'The protection (preserver?) of day-shadow [i.e. the cloud-canopy itself] wound (passed) over the clouds,' or, as Krapp suggests, more generally, 'across the skies' (as opposed to *under wolcnum,* the common phrase for 'on earth'). In defense of this reading, the suggestion of Krapp that the *l* in *scealdes* might have been written in anticipation of the *l* in *hlēo* is worth consideration. The passage in Isaiah quoted above in Note, 72, (Isa. 4:6) contains the phrase *in umbraculum diei;* occurring as it does in a passage directly concerned with the idea of the cloud as a protection from heat, it may have been known to the poet. On the other hand, one would expect the reference to be to the sun, if the phrase *ofer wolcnum* is to be taken literally. The most common interpretation of *dægscealdes* as being some form of **dægsceld* 'day-shield,' apart from phonetic difficulties, does not make the sentence much clearer. The reference of Diodorus (III.48.3) to the Red Sea sun which "takes on the form of a round shield and sends forth a light which is exceptionally bright and fiery" (tr. Oldfather, Loeb ed., *2,* 235) might support this reading if we really had proof that the poet knew Diodorus. But if *dægsceld* is the sun, then *dægsceldes hlēo* is presumably the cloud, and the difficulty with *ofer wolcnum* remains.

81. *segle.* An obvious emendation of MS *swegle.* Here the poet begins an extraordinary extended metaphor in which he identifies the guiding pillar of cloud with a sail, the Israelites with sailors, their journey with the voyage (cf. 89, 105, 223, 331 ff.). The crossing of the Red Sea might indeed suggest the figure to some extent, but such an explanation would not deal with the appearance of the motif at this point in such direct connection with the pillar of cloud. There seem to be hints in the commentaries of a traditional allegorization resembling that of this poem, however. Among Jerome's lists of Hebrew names and their translations occurs the definition of Etham as "consummatus sive suscipiens navigationem" (Jerome's *Liber de Nominibus Hebraicis, PL 23:787*). Such definitions were often the starting points of ingenious symbolic or allegorical interpretations (cf. Note, 66, on Etham). Bruno Astensis in the twelfth century carried the idea farther in his *Expositio in Exodum (PL 164:264)* : "Merito igitur de Sochot, id est de tabernaculis, venitur in Ethan, quia postquam ad Ecclesiam homo veniens baptizatus est, non otiosus sedere, sed per hujus maris pericula cum apostolis navigare debet. . . . Venit igitur populus de Ethan in Aharoth, quia jam coepta navigatione, quibusdam virtutum gradibus proficiens, venit ad coronam." Here Bruno is obviously making use of Jerome's *navigatio* for Etham. This idea does not seem to be found elsewhere; as can be seen in Origen's interpretation of Etham, other meanings of the word were used. Since it was at Etham that the cloud first appeared, according to both this poem and the usual interpretation, the poet might have expanded his image of the sail either from the bare gloss of Jerome or, perhaps more likely, from a further development of the idea by another commentator.

85. *feldhūsa mæst.* Perhaps the association of the previous camp, Succoth, with tents was in the poet's mind and occasioned this unusual image.

91-2. The unusual repetition in the phrase *þæt þær Drihten cwōm, weroda Drihten* leads one to suspect strongly that the original may have had *weroda Waldend,* in view of the usual OE principles of variation; but an emendation to that effect would scarcely be justified.

92. *wīcsteal metan.* This may be a Latinism, as Klaeber (*MLN 33:222*) suggests, based on the Vulg. *castrametari* (Exod. 13:20, 14:2). It is at any rate an unusual use of OE *metan.* Blackburn mentions the possibility that the poet was influenced here by Deut. 1:32-3: ". . . Domino Deo vestro, [33] qui praecessit vos in via, et metatus est locum, in quo tentoria figere deberetis, nocte ostendens vobis iter per ignem, et die per columnam nubis."

93. *fȳr and wolcen . . . bēamas twēgen.* Exod. 13:21-2: "Dominus autem praecedebat eos ad ostendendam viam per diem in columna nubis, et per noctem in columna ignis, ut dux esset itineris utroque tempore. Numquam defuit columna nubis per diem, nec columna ignis per noctem, coram populo." Moore (pp. 87, 102) lists as one of the "additions"

which the OE poet has made to the Vulgate account the description of the pillar of cloud and fire as two separate pillars. There is the possibility that the poet understood the Vulgate text, which is rather ambiguous, to refer to two columns. As Moore indicates by citing Bede, Bruno Astensis, and a Jewish tradition, there is authority for such an interpretation. Later writers emphasize the unity of the column strongly, thereby implying the existence of different views on the subject; see, for example, Hugo of Saint-Victor (*Exegetica, PL 175:65*) : "Una et eadem columna erat contra calorem obumbrans, et contra tenebros illuminans," and Adamus Scotus (*De Tripartito Tabernaculo,* pars 2, cap. 15, *PL 198:730-1*) for an even firmer insistence on the fact that the column was one.

96. The reference to the Holy Ghost suggests a familiarity on the part of the poet with the usual allegorical glosses on the pillar of fire and cloud. Jerome's comment on Ps. 105:39 (*Breviarium in Psalmos, PL 26:*1139) contains the phrase "Nubem et ignem, Spiritum sanctum dicit."

98–100a. 'Then (so I heard) in the morning bravehearted (men) raised war-trumpets with loud voices, (raised) a sound of glory.' This seems to be the most natural reading of the highly ambiguous forms, even though it involves a mild case of syllepsis. Among other interpretations are Cosijn's (*Beitr 20:*98), who takes *mōdes rōfan* as genitive singular (referring to Moses) and *herebȳman* as accusative, subject of the infinitive *hebban,* and Blackburn's, who takes *herebȳman* to be genitive singular with *stefnum;* both with regard *wōman* as direct object.

99. *herebȳman.* Horns and trumpets seem to be, on the evidence of *Beowulf* and other poems, traditional epic accouterments in OE heroic verse. Here the poet is using them for those associations and, in addition, with characteristic attention to accuracy, using them as they are described in the Bible itself. The most important scriptural basis for the mention of trumpets is Num. 10:1–10. Here the Lord gives explicit directions to Moses on the proper uses of trumpets for assembling the tribes, breaking camp, giving the alarm, and in forms of celebration. In the poem they are used (as here) as a signal for moving on, in 132 as a signal to disband or set up camp, in 215–17 as a signal for a general assembly to hear a speech, and finally to celebrate the successful crossing (*sigebȳman* in 533). Pharaoh's army is also furnished with trumpets (159).

103. *fūs fyrdgetrum.* In apposition with *werod* in 100.

104. *līfes lātþēow.* Probably a reference to the pillar of cloud, especially as considered equivalent to or associated with the Holy Ghost. Cf. Note, 96.

līfweg. It is probable that this word contains a reference to some sort of allegory of spiritual progress (cf. Note, 66). The MS reading, which has been frequently emended to *liftweg* by previous editors and commentators, is certainly defensible on other grounds. As Blackburn and Krapp suggest, it is easy enough to understand *līfweg* simply as the road which the Israelites must take to save their lives in the most literal sense, the road to safety. The repetition of *līf* is paralleled elsewhere in the poem. Cf. *segncyning . . . segn* 172.

105. *segl.* This alteration from *MS swegl* seems necessary, especially since two other nautical terms follow in the same sentence. See Note, 81.

106. *flōdwege.* 'On the road to the sea.' Metaphorically, however, it is the sea itself on which the Israelite sailors are navigating, impelled by their 'holy sails.' Since the MS reading can be defended in this way, there is no need to emend to the more logical *foldwege.*

107b–111a. 'The heaven-sign rose every evening, a second wonder, a strange one, after it had beheld the setting of the sun, to shine in flame over the people, a burning pillar.' This reading of a difficult passage is reasonably satisfactory if it is borne in mind that the pillar is certainly personified (cf. *fȳrene loccas* 120) and can thus properly "behold" the setting of the sun. This seems to be essentially the interpretation offered by Thomas (*MLR 12:*344), who takes *wundor* as subject of *behēold* and makes *sunnan* object of *æfter,* so that it is the pillar which is observing the setting of the sun. Bright, who cites a phrase from Ps. 104:19, "sol cognovit occasum suum" (Vulg.), *sunne hire setlgang healdeþ* (*Paris Psalter* 103:18), emends *sunnan* to *sunne* to make it the subject of the *æfter* clause, and he is followed by Krapp. Sedgefield takes *syllīc æfter sunnan* as a phrase unit, putting *setlrāde behēold* in parentheses. Other scholars have tried to find a suitable subject for *behēold.* BTS (*s.v. behealdan*) takes *folc* 106 as subject; Blackburn sees *wundor* as subject and *beheold . . . scinan* as meaning 'took heed to shine.' Holthausen (*ESt. 51*:182) mentions the possibility of an impersonal and unexpressed subject, "one," for *beheold*—in this case, the onlookers who behold the pillar. He refers to considerable evidence for this type of construction. In Napier's rearrangement of the text, 108 follows immediately after 85; he suggests changing *beheold* to *ongann*.

This description resembles in some details the account in *Guth.* (B) 1277–331 of the bright apparition in the heavens at Guthlac's death. Cf. *Guth.* 1288: *scān scīrwered. Scadu sweðredon* (*Ex.* 125a, 113b); *Guth.* 1309: *bēama beorhtast,* of the light; *Guth.* 1290: *heofonlīc condel,* of the light, not, as is usual, of the sun (*Ex.* 116b). But the differences between the two passages are also quite noticeable, and it would be rash to suggest borrowing by the *Guthlac* poet.

113. *sceado.* Blackburn defends the MS reading *sceaðo* as probably "the same variation as in *mādmas* and *māðmas, hrade* and *hraðe,* etc." But *ð* for *d* is a common enough scribal error, especially in this case where there is an *ð* in the next word.

114–15. 'The deep night-shadows could not conceal any hiding-place near at hand.' To take *nēah* as meaning 'nearby' rather than 'nearly' is perhaps preferable. Blackburn translates 'their hiding-places could not conceal the deep shadows of night'; Sedgefield takes *heolstor* as nominative singular in apposition with *nihtscuwan,* translating 'the intense night-shadows, the darkness, could not nearly hide (any one)'—not a very likely construction.

117b–119b. 'Lest the terror of the wilderness, grey heath-panic, by violent storms snatch their lives from them in its sudden grip.' Three serious errors in the space of two lines suggest that the scribe's comprehension of the passage was limited.

118. *hār hæð[brōga].* Suggested by Cosijn and followed by Krapp. It makes a good parallel to *wēstengryre.* Sievers' emendation *hāres hæðes* is very feeble stylistically and, as Blackburn points out, assumes two faults instead of one. For compounds with -*brōga* see *wæterbrōgan, An.* 197, 456; *sperebrōgan,* Rid. 17, 4; *herebrōgan, Beow.* 462.

118b. *holmegum wederum.* 'By storms of a violence usually only encountered at sea' would be the cautious interpretation here. But metaphorically the poet seems once more to be carrying out his nautical figure which has been so far extended already—these are 'sea-storms' which threaten the Israelite 'sailors' and their ship (of faith, presumably).

121. *bēlegsan.* WS *bǣlegsan.* The probable explanation for the MS form *bellegsan* is that a WS scribe did not recognize the form *bēl* and "corrected" it to *bell.* Similarly *on fērclamme* 119 may have become *ofer clamme* in somewhat the same way. Blackburn suggests that the element *bell-* was related to the word *bellan* 'to roar' and in this case refers to thunder.

123–4. God's fire as an instrument of punishment in the hands of Moses appears in Num. 11:1: "Interea ortum est murmur populi, quasi dolentium pro labore, contra Dominum. Quod cum audisset Dominus, iratus est. Et accensus in eos ignis Domini devoravit extremam castrorum partem." Cf. Num. 16:35, where fire consumes 250 men, and Lev. 10:2, where fire destroys the sons of Aaron. The identification of this fire with the fiery pillar is not made clear in the Bible, however. Several commentators bring the two ideas into conjunction. Paterius (*Liber de Testimoniis, PL 79*:732) remarks on the pillars of cloud and fire: "Quid in igne nisi terror est? In nube autem visionis lene blandimentum. . . . In die ergo per nubem columna monstrata est, et in nocte per ignem, quia omnipotens Deus et blandus justis, et terribilis apparebit injustis." Procopius of Gaza (*Commentarii in Exodum, PG 87,* pars 1, 581) observes that the pillar "praecedebat Israelitas in specie ignis, scilicet in lege, quae condemnat et punit." See also Isidore, *Quaestiones in Vet. Test.: in Exodum* (*PL 83*:296). These quotations suggest that allegorically the pillar of fire was associated with punishment. It remains doubtful whether the poet was following one of the commentaries or independently identified the fiery pillar with the fire mentioned in Numbers and Leviticus.

124. *hȳrde.* '(They) obeyed.' The expected form would, of course, be *hȳrden.* But see L. Bloomfield, "OE. Plural Subjunctives in -E" (*JEGP, 29* [1930], 100–13), for numerous other examples of the -*e* forms, which Bloomfield regards as doubtless archaic. *Gebohte* 151 is probably a similar form. See also Sievers-Brunner §365 An. 2, and Bright, *MLN 27*:15.

125. *scīrwerod.* The usual reading has been *scīr werod,* but cf. *Guth.* 1288a: *scān scīrwered,* in a context where the impossibility of reading *scīr werod* is clearly demon-

strated. It is unlikely that two separate phrases, *scān scīr werod* and *scān scīrwered*, existed concurrently. In the present instance the meaning may be improved by translating the passage 'it [the pillar] shone brightly clad.' The poet in 107–15 has introduced the pillar and emphasized its brightness; he digresses briefly to point out its punitive function; and he now returns to dwell on the gleaming of the pillar, which causes the shields to glitter and enables the Israelites to see clearly the *rihte strǣte*.

126–9a. 'The warriors saw clearly the straight road, (saw) the sign over the hosts, until the sea-fastness at the land's end stood in the way of the army, eager to move forward.' While in translation it is possible to avoid the problem of the precise syntactical location of the phrase *fūs on forðweg,* it seems clear that it belongs in sense with *lēodmægne.* Cosijn (*Beitr 20:*98) and Kock (*JJJ* 25) offer examples of uninflected adjectives and participles which support this interpretation. Indeed, if *werod* is done away with (see previous Note), there is no other possibility. Bright (*MLN 27:*15) believes that *fūs on forðweg* refers to *werod.* Klaeber (*ESt. 41:*110) and Napier (*MLR 6:*168), who read *fūson* (i.e. *fūsum*) for *fūs on,* take *forðweg* to be object of *forstōd.* Blackburn and Sedgefield take *segn* as the subject of *forstōd;* Sedgefield translates 'the banner, eager to advance, high above the hosts, helped the army right up to the sea-fortress [i.e., the shore] at the land's end.'

132–3. The word *brǣddon* here may be taken in the intransitive sense, 'the sailors spread out over the hills,' or, as a more technical term, it may refer to the "stretching" or pitching of the tents. The dictionaries give the latter reading, but the former seems preferable.

133. *fēorðe wīc.* This camp is not named in the poem, but it is clearly the camp "contra Phihahiroth, quae respicit Beelsephon" on the shore of the Red Sea. Cf. Exod. 14:1–2 and Note, 66.

135–47. This passage is chiefly concerned with the causes of the hostility between Egyptians and Israelites. Since there is probably a considerable loss after l. 141 (conceivably as many as 120 verses could have been contained on the 4 missing sides), the reconstruction of the passage and the explanation of some of the references are conjectural. It seems clear, however, that reference is made to the relationship of a former Pharaoh (*se yldra cyning* 141) with Joseph and his father and brothers, a story which is to be found in the 47th chapter of Genesis. The *wǣre* of 140 is probably the old Pharaoh's promise of the Land of Goshen to Jacob and his children (Gen. 47:5–6). The *onnīed* 139, though of doubtful meaning, is probably some form of forced labor or oppression imposed on the children of Israel by the new Pharaoh "who knew not Joseph" (Exod. 1:8). Ll. 142–3 seem to be part of an incomplete sentence and are not very clear; what probably lies behind them is the story of the buying up of all the land of Egypt during the time of famine by Joseph acting for Pharaoh (Gen. 47:19–20). The *yrfeweard* 142 may be either Pharaoh or Joseph himself (taking the word in its literal sense). It is this action on Joseph's part which seems to be called a *feorhlēan* in 150—a granting of life to the starving population of Egypt, since Joseph's prophecy of famine and the measures taken to store grain may be said to have saved the lives of the Egyptians. The word *morðor* 146, if it has a specific reference, may suggest the murder of the Hebrew male children (Exod. 1); similarly, *wrōht* 147, taken in the limited sense of 'injustice,' might refer vaguely to the requirement that the Israelites make their bricks without straw.

137–40. 'The exile waited for the hostile pursuer, who had long before decreed oppression(?) for him when he was homeless [i.e., without a country of his own], and grief (as well), fast-bound in torments.' *Wrǣcmon* is used for the Israelites as a group and *lāstweard* for the Egyptians. *Wēan* is probably in apposition to *onnīed,* accusative singular or plural. The phrase *wītum fæst* would ordinarily convey the idea of torture; if it goes in sense with *wrǣcmon,* the Israelite, it refers to their suffering in slavery in Egypt. Blackburn translates *wītum fæst* 'unyielding in harm, resolute in injury' and regards it as limiting *sē ðe* (i.e., the Egyptians). Sedgefield translates the phrase 'bound up in penalties, i.e., criminal' and apparently connects it directly with *wēan.* The syntax is certainly vague and confusing through much of this section.

139. *onnīed.* Not found elsewhere in OE. Blackburn glosses it 'oppression'; Kock (*PPP* 7) refers to the common ON equivalent *ánauð.* This meaning certainly fits the context better than that of *ōhtnīed,* the usual emendation, which is not found elsewhere

either. At this point the poet is not talking about pursuit but is moving back to the period of slavery *lange ǣr,* as the following fragmentary sentence shows.

141–3. See Introduction (pp. 6–7) for an account of the MS break here. Solely on grounds of meaning, there seems to be some sort of break indicated. To pass from mention of the promise which the former Pharaoh had made to Joseph to a sentence which seems to be concluding or summing up the result of Joseph's industry in saving the land of Egypt seems distinctly abrupt and unlikely. Most editors, however, have assumed the loss of only a few syllables in the word beginning with *ge-* and have variously guessed at it. Ll. 142–3 may be translated 'then became heir of the native race(?), of the men after (having received their) treasure, so that he prospered greatly.' The subject of the sentence is missing; probably the reference is to Pharaoh. If the word *yrfeweard* were taken in the literal sense of 'guardian of property,' the reference might be to Joseph, suggesting Joseph's position as agent or manager in the business of buying up the land in payment for food from the royal granaries. It is certainly true that Joseph prospered by the transaction.

142. *ingefolca.* The first of three *in-* compounds in the poem; cf. *ingēmen[d]* 190 and *ingeðēode* (MS *incaðeode*) 444. The phrase *ōht inlende* 136 is also used in reference to the Egyptians. The dominant idea in all these words (and probably also in *landmanna* 179) is the "inland" or native quality of the Egyptians. The poet is consistently contrasting them in this respect with the Israelites, who are neither natives nor 'land-men' (they are *eðellēase*—cf. 139 and 576), who are sailors, and who are throughout the poem escaping and going out. The concept of Egypt as house of bondage, prison, and even hell (see Note, 66) lends significance to this device.

144. *grame wurdon.* 'Became hostile, oppressive.' Cf. *OE Heptateuch, Exod.* 23:9 (EETS, O.S. 160, ed. Crawford, 270), where the phrase *ne bēo þū elðēodigum gram* translates the Vulg. *peregrino molestus non eris* (cited by Blackburn).

145. *antþigða.* This emendation was suggested by Kock (PPP 8). The MS reading *ymb an twig* makes little sense. What is to be expected here is a word suggesting what the Egyptians really became angry about, namely, the Israelites' prosperity in Egypt. Kock creates the word **andþigð,* from Germanic **andþigiþo* (cf. the OE verb *onþēon*), with the meaning 'getting on, managing, success.' Then the assumption is that MS *an twig ða* represents a corruption of *antþigða,* certainly plausible enough paleographically. Other attempts to explain the phrase are much less satisfactory. If *antwīg* (i.e. *andwīg* 'warfare') is to be read, one is faced with the problem of making a metrical line out of it. *Ymbe antwīg* (Krapp) is not metrical; and *ymb antwīge* is scarcely possible, since *ymb* takes the accusative universally in the poetry. Some of the earlier editors, reading *ān twig,* saw here a highly improbable reference to Aaron's rod. Bright (*MLN 27*:15) reads *ānwīg* 'duel,' seeing a reference to the slaying of the Egyptian by Moses (Exod. 2:11–12). But the slaying, as Blackburn points out, was certainly not the cause of the oppression of the Israelites.

146–53. 'Then they [the Egyptians] committed murder against his [Joseph's?] kinsmen, stirred up strife, broke the treaty. Warlike emotions were in their hearts, the passions of men. By wicked promises they [the Egyptians] fully intended to repay criminally that gift of life, so that Moses' people might have paid for that day's work in blood, if mighty God had only given them [the Egyptians] success in their murderous venture.' Apparently *dægweorc* and *feorhlēan* are roughly parallel in sense, both referring to the action of Joseph (and the Israelites as a whole) in saving the Egyptians from famine. Bright's belief in the 'duel' leads him to take these two words as referring to Moses' action; he apparently retains the MS reading *hē* in 151.

146. For *hēo his* Blackburn suggests *iosephis*—which would make for very strange meter. Bright suggests *Moyses* but remarks that "it would demand of the meter an unusual, if not a forbidden, anacrusis." But if we assume that a good deal of explanatory matter is missing after 141, the apparent vagueness of the reference here is not surprising.

147. *frǣton.* Literally, 'devoured.' Bright (*MLN 17*:425 and *MLN 27*:15) calls the use of it here "inadmissible." He would read *brǣcon.* But the poet is given to expressions as bold as this elsewhere and, while an unimaginative scribe might have substituted the common *brǣcon* for *frǣton,* the process would hardly have been reversed.

148. At this point the poet seems to resume the narrative with a description of the

emotions of the advancing Egyptian army, having concluded his explanation of the causes of the hostility.

149. *mānum trēowum.* Apparently not to be taken quite literally in this context, as it is almost synonymous with *fācne* in the following line. Blackburn translates 'treacherously, faithlessly.' Bright (*MLN 27*:15) reads *mannum twēonum,* referring to the two men engaged in the supposed 'duel' (*ānwīg*); see Note, 145. But even if the idea of the duel is accepted, this emendation seems too violent. Grein, Wülker, and Blackburn take *mānum trēowum* as belonging to the preceding sentence (*Wǣron heaðowylmas,* etc.), placing a colon or period at the end of 149. But the phrase is better taken as parallel with *fācne.*

151. *hīe.* See Note, 124, for another plural subjunctive like *gebohte.* The scribe's "correction" of *hīe* to *hē* makes the passage almost incomprehensible.

dægweorc. Perhaps best taken as parallel with *feorhlēan,* the act of saving the Egyptians from famine. But it may after all be merely a vague way of talking about a possible battle and its result; 'they might have paid for that day's work in blood,' i.e., been massacred by the more powerful Egyptians. Cf. Mürkens, p. 114. Bright takes *dægweorc* as referring to the duel, Blackburn as referring to the death of the first-born.

154 ff. Exod. 14:10: "Cumque appropinquasset Pharao, levantes filii Israel oculos, viderunt Ægyptios post se: et timuerunt valde: clamaveruntque ad Dominum."

155. *sūðwegum.* Cf. *on norðwegas* 68. The Israelites, after marching to the north, turn to find the Egyptians approaching from the south.

157. *oferholt wegan.* The exact meaning of *oferholt* is not clear. On the analogy of *Gen.* 2049, *randas wǣgon,* perhaps the word means 'shield' or 'the covering or protecting wood' (so Krapp and G-K). Blackburn (Glossary) suggests 'forest (of spears),' a suggestion repeated by Sedgefield, who also proposes as the original word *eoferholt* 'boar-spear.' Kluge's reading *ofer holtwegan* (i.e. *holtwegum*) would destroy the alliteration.

158–9. These two lines have been placed after 160 by Grein and Sedgefield. Unless this rearrangement is made, the lines form an awkward but not unheard-of parenthesis. But since 161 shows obvious signs of corruption, perhaps it would be best to leave the text as it is.

158. *gūð hwearfode.* Literally, 'battle turned, moved in a circle.' Sedgefield translates as either 'battle returned' or 'the army wheeled.' B-T translates 'war rolled on,' or possibly, personifying *gūð* as a kind of Valkyrie, 'hovered about.'

161–2. *on hwæl . . .* The MS reading here is *on hwæl · hwreopạn · here fugolas · hilde grædige ·* The word *hwæl* is not clear here, and the form *hwreopan* seems to have been influenced by the preceding *hw;* all editors read *hrēopon* (see 168). It seems obvious that a word or two in 161a and the whole half-line 161b have dropped out. Under these circumstances, it is possible to reconstruct the passage only by guesswork. As Sedgefield points out, the word *hwæl* suggests an original *wæl.* Kluge and Holthausen (*Archiv 115*:163) omit *on hwæl* altogether. Dietrich and Grein take *hwæl* as a form of *hwēl, hwēogol* 'wheel,' translating 'im kreise.' Blackburn, in an elaborate reconstruction of the entire passage 154–63, reads *on hwæl(mere hrēo wǣron ȳða).* Other versions appear at the foot of the text. The line division here indicated (that of Sedgefield and Krapp) is based on the construction in 168, where *hrēopon* also begins a sentence.

163. *drihtnēum.* Both the mention of corpses here and the expression *flēah fǣge gāst* 169 are surprising, since no battle has yet taken place. The phrase *middum nihtum* 168 is not literally accurate, since the time of day seems to be about sunset. This passage (162–9) is a good illustration of one of the most familiar forms of OE epic convention, the description of animals of prey at a battlefield. It may well be supposed that the poet has here, if anywhere, a plentiful traditional stock of ready-made formulas and phrases. The poet's description of wolves and carrion birds is dramatically appropriate in that it heightens, by creating a mood or stock response, the terror of the Egyptians' menacing approach. Yet the effect is naive and the impression remains that a better poet would not have allowed himself to be carried so near absurdity by his enthusiasm at this point.

164. *wonn wælcēasega.* If this phrase is to be taken in the sentence with *hrēopon,* the change from the plural *herefugolas* to the singular here is unusual. The insertion of *hræfn* in some of the reconstructions offered by the editors is intended to avoid this

difficulty. It should be noted that this phrase begins a new page, and a line may have been lost before it. Krapp is inclined to accept the MS reading as "a simple rhetorical device that may have been intended," i.e., the change from plural to singular.

166. *beodan.* Probably a velar-umlauted form of *bidon,* via the form **biodon*(?).

167. *fyl.* Wülker, in preserving the MS reading *ful,* cites as analogous such a pair as *wurt:wyrt.* But in the latter it is a case of the influence of the initial *w* (Sievers-Brunner §118). Sedgefield translates *fyl* as 'the dead,' but it is more likely that it means 'falling in battle, slaughter.'

168. *mearcweardas.* Wolves.

169a. *flēah fǣge gāst.* 'The doomed spirit fled.' This is usually taken to mean that men were dying in battle. Blackburn suggests reading *gǣst* for *gāst,* translating 'the strangers (i.e., the Hebrews) fled affrighted.' But *gāst* 'spirit' seems to fit with *fǣge,* and in any case the Hebrews were unable to flee. Sedgefield takes the phrase as meaning 'ghostly apparitions were seen at night'; but surely this sudden introduction of the supernatural is unwarranted. It may be felt that the phrase is no more appropriate here than the rest of the battle trappings, wolves and ravens; or possibly the poet is trying, somewhat awkwardly, to convey the emotional state of the Israelites—they felt as good as dead, or their hearts sank. Cf. the peculiar use of *dēade fēðan, fǣge ferhðlocan* 266–7.

169b. *geh[n]ǣged.* This emendation seems necessary, since the case for the MS *gehǣged* is not a strong one. B-T suggested that *gehǣged* might be related to *haga* 'enclosure,' and Blackburn accordingly translates it 'hemmed in.' But the meter favors a long vowel here rather than a short one. Another point in favor of the emendation is the fact that *gehnǣgan* is an Anglian word (so listed by Hildegard Rauh, *Der Wortschatz der altenglischen Uebersetzungen des Matthaeus-Evangeliums*) and thus may not have been understood by a WS scribe.

170–1. The mention of horses here was probably suggested by the passage in the "Song of Moses" (Exod. 15) which celebrates the overthrow of the "horse and his rider." Similar passages in *Beowulf* (e.g., 864 ff.) suggest that the display of equestrian prowess was a Germanic epic convention as well.

172. *segncyning.* In order to avoid repetition of the word *segn,* editors have proposed changes in this word. But for similar repetitions in the poem, see 93, 104.

176. *wælhlencan.* As Krapp suggests, the miswriting *hwæl* here may also have occurred in 161.

178–9. *Frēond onsēgon lāðum ēagan landmanna cyme.* 'The friends [i.e., the Israelites] watched the coming of the men of the land with hostile eyes.' An effective shift of focus from the impressive appearance of the Egyptian forces to the trapped and sullen Israelites. (For *landmanna* as applied to the Egyptians cf. Note, 142). The emendation *onsēgon* (Anglian preterite plural of *onsēon*—WS *onsāwon;* cf. Sievers-Brunner §391 An. 8) was adopted by Dietrich and followed by most editors. Blackburn, seeking to preserve the MS reading, renders 'the advance of the men of the land moved toward the friends with hostile looks,' taking *on sigon* as meaning 'approach, come upon.' Thorpe and Grein suggest *fēond* for *frēond*—an unnecessary change.

180. *wǣgon.* The verb *wegan* 'carry, wear' is not recorded elsewhere in an intransitive sense. (Is the word *beran* used in a similar sense in the disputed *ac hēr forþ berað, Finnsburg* 5?) Perhaps a line between 180 and 181 has dropped out. Various solutions have been proposed. Sedgefield simply reads *wǣron* for *wǣgon,* but, as Krapp remarks, this makes a feeble line. BTS would insert the word *wǣpn* before *wǣgon.* Cosijn (*Beitr 20:*100) would change *hilde grētton* 181 to *hildegeatwe* to furnish an object to the verb; but that seems a drastic change.

180b. The meter of this half-line has been called into question. Sievers (*Beitr 10:*511) suggests *wigan,* a lighter word, for *wigend.* The MS accent on *un-* supports this change. But the stress could also be on the second syllable of *unforhte;* cf. 328b.

183. *ālesen[e].* The added *e* makes the line metrical.

184. *twā þūsendo.* The total number of men in the Egyptian army is not stated in the Bible. The relevant verses in Exod. 14 follow: [6] "[Pharao] junxit ergo currum, et omnem populum suum assumpsit secum. [7] Tulitque sexcentos currus electos, et quidquid in Ægypto curruum fuit: et duces totius exercitus . . . [9] Cumque persequerentur Ægyptii vestigia praecedentium, repererunt eos in castris super mare: omnis equitatus et currus Pharaonis, et universus exercitus erant in Phihahiroth contra

Beelsephon." The *duces* mentioned in Exod. 14:7 are presumably the *cyningas* and *cnēowmāgas* of 185. The OE poet's choice of the number 2000 has been a matter of some discussion. Such objections as are raised by Mürkens (p. 72) or Cosijn (*Beitr 20*:100) to the effect that the number is far too small are clearly based on a misunderstanding of the passage. The poet says that Pharaoh had chosen 2000 leaders, each one of whom was to take into battle as many males as he could find in the time available. But there are certainly more than 2000 Egyptians in the whole army. Moore (p. 106) discusses the possible sources for the figure 2000. Josephus (*Jewish Antiquities* II.324), followed by Peter Comestor (*Historia Scholastica*, Exod. 31; *PL 198*:1157), gives the number of Egyptian infantry as 200,000. S. Baring-Gould (*Legends of the Patriarchs and Prophets and Other Old Testament Characters* [New York, 1872], p. 271) gives the number of foot soldiers as 2,000,000. It seems probable that both these figures come from some original containing the figure 2 which may have been known in some form to the poet. Moore suggests that the poet may have thought that the Egyptian leaders each commanded a unit of 1000 men (which is the number in each of the *cista* of the Hebrew force; see 230–2), thus giving a total figure of 2,000,000. One has the impression, on the whole, that the poet is unwilling to commit himself to a precise figure because he has no authority for it in the Bible. Other examples of such a conservative interpretation may be found. Orosius observes: "Se kyningc Pharon hæfde syx hund wīgwægna, and swā fela þæs ōðres heres wæs þæt man mæg þanon oncnāwan, þā him swā fela manna ondrēdon swā mid Moyse wǣron: þæt wæs syx hund þūsenda manna" (Alfred's translation, EETS O.S. 79, ed. Sweet, 38). Ælfric, in his essay "On the Old and New Testament," is even briefer and merely states that Pharaoh followed the Israelites *mid māran fyrde* (*OE Heptateuch*, EETS O.S. 160, ed. Crawford, 29). Cf. *māran mægenes* 215, and the dialogue fragment entitled *Pharaoh* in the Exeter Book.

190. *ingēmen[d]*. This emendation, suggested to me by John C. Pope, offers a highly satisfactory solution of the baffling MS form *ingemen*. In its Anglian form, *ingēmend* ('native rulers'; cf. the following *cyningas on corðre*) might easily have passed unrecognized by a WS scribe. Sievers (*Beitr 10*:195–6) reads *inge men*, a supposedly Kentish form of *ginge men* 'young men.' But there is almost no evidence to suggest Kentish origin of the poem. For the other interesting *in-* compounds in the poem, see Note, 142.

191b–193. 'Frequently sounding, the well-known voice of the horn signalled the host where the war-troop of heroes should bear their arms' (Kennedy's translation, *Cædmon Poems*). *Gebēad* 'ordered, announced' must be read for MS *gebad*. Blackburn mentions the confusion frequent among the scribes of *bād, bēad, bæd*.

194. *eorp werod*. The Egyptians are not called dark in the Bible, at least not in the book of Exodus. This was one of the details which Mürkens (p. 72) believed to have been taken from Avitus (*De Transitu Maris Rubri* 641: "Effertur nigri dux agminis . . ."). Moore (p. 94) calls the resemblance a commonplace. Prudentius, in a hymn in the *Liber Cathemerinon*, "Hymnus ad Incensum Lucernae," uses a similar expression in describing the Egyptian host at the Red Sea: *corpora nigrorum . . . satellitum* 78–9 (Prudentius, ed. H. J. Thompson, Loeb Classical Library edition [1949], *I*, 42).

197. A passable reading of this line may be obtained by omitting the word *tō*, which may have been added by a scribe with his eye on the following phrase *tō þām ǣrdæge*. The phrase *þām mægenhēapum* would then be roughly parallel with *billum*.

199. *brōðorgyld*. I.e., in revenge for their brothers, the first-born. As Blackburn points out, "in sense *hyra* limits *brōðor* rather than *gyld*." Here the motivation of the Egyptians is clearly revenge of a kind instantly understandable by the Germanic mind. The poet does not allude directly to the actual motive for pursuing the fleeing Israelites assigned to Pharaoh by the Bible (Exod. 14:5), namely, to bring them back into servitude rather than kill them.

200. Exod. 14:10: "Cumque appropinquasset Pharao, levantes filii Israel oculos, viderunt Ægyptios post se: et timuerunt valde: clamaveruntque ad Dominum." The complaint of the Israelites to Moses (Exod. 14:11–12) does not appear in the poem, however, although Moses' encouraging reply ("nolite timere") appears in 259 ff.

201b–203a. 'Terrors prevailed, corselets protected, when roar (of battle) came, the terrible news flew.' The syntax of this passage is ambiguous. Kock (JJJ 25), followed by Sedgefield (Glossary) and Krapp, takes *wælnet* to mean 'corselet, coat of mail' (cf.

brēostnet . . . werigean 236–7, *wælhlencan* 176, *wællseax* 'battle-knife' *Beow.* 2703). *Wælnet* has been understood, however, as a highly figurative expression meaning 'the net of death' (cf. G-K, B-T, and Kennedy's translation, 'the nets of death encompassed them about'). The phrase *flugon frēcne spel* is ambiguous, as can be seen by the various translations: 'bold speeches fled' (Blackburn, Gordon); 'they fled the fearful tidings' (Johnson); 'the fatal tidings flew abroad' (Kennedy, Sedgefield). Kock (JJJ 25) thinks that *frēcne spel* is a reference to shafts and arrows.

203b–207. 'The enemy [Egyptian] was resolute, the host was in gleaming armor, until the mighty angel who guarded the multitude drove back the proud ones [Egyptians], so that the hostile forces could no longer see each other. The march (or battle) was interrupted.' This is based on Exod. 14:19–20: "Tollensque se angelus Dei, qui praecedebat castra Israel, abiit post eos: et cum eo pariter columna nubis, priora dimittens, post tergum stetit, inter castra Ægyptiorum et castra Israel: et erat nubes tenebrosa, et illuminans noctem, ita ut ad se invicem toto noctis tempore accedere non valerent." The OE *mid him . . . gesēon tōsomne* is a complicated way of saying 'see each other,' perhaps influenced by the Latin *ad se invicem;* cf. Cosijn (*Beitr 20:*100).

210. *mægen oððe merestrēam.* There is an interesting parallel to this phrase in a sermon attributed to Augustine (*Sermones Supposititii* 1, *PL* 39:1790): "Includuntur persequentibus Ægyptiis Hebraei inter mare et hostes, inter undas et gladios. Hinc mare spumat, inde arma coruscant: hinc aquarum, inde armorum strepitus." The dilemma of the Israelites may well have been formulated in similar terms by two imaginative writers. Cf. Exod. 14:3: "Dicturusque est Pharao super filiis Israel: coarctati sunt in terra, conclusit eos desertum."

212. *blacum rēafum.* 'In black garments.' Bright (*MLN 27:*16) cites the verse *on blacum hrægle,* Rid. 10, 7.

213b–217. 'All that host of kinsmen watched and waited for the greater army, until Moses ordered the warriors to assemble the people at dawn with brazen trumpets, (ordered) the soldiers to arise.'

218. Cf. *Finnsburg* 11: *habbað ēowre linda, hicgeaþ on ellen,* and *Maldon* 4, 123, 128. This parallel renders less likely Sisam's conjecture (*RES 22:*264n.) of *heorahlencan* (i.e. *heoruhlencan*).

219. *bēacnum.* Here 'signals,' i.e., trumpet calls.

222–3. *brudon ofer burgum . . . flotan feldhūsum.* 'The sailors moved with their tents over the hills (or struck their tents?).' See Note, 132–3. *Burgum* is surely for *beorgum* here: see Note, 70.

224–32. The number of able-bodied men in the Israelite fighting force is given in the Bible as 600,000. Exod. 12:37: "Profectique sunt filii Israel de Ramesse in Socoth, sexcenta fere millia peditum virorum, absque parvulis." This is the total figure here in the poem; 12 *fēðan* (tribes) each consist of 50 *cista* and each *cist* is made up of 1000 men. It is not quite clear where the poet found the idea for the internal organization of the 600,000. Kock (JJJ 26) and Blackburn refer to the 1st chapter of Numbers, where an extended account is given of the number (varying widely) of the fighting men in each tribe. The *average* number of warriors in each tribe is, of course, about 50,000— e.g., Reuben 46,500, Simeon 59,300, etc. Moore (p. 102) suggests as a basis for the division into units of 1000 Exod. 18:21–2: "Provide autem de omni plebe viros potentes, et timentes Deum, in quibus sit veritas, et qui oderint avaritiam, et constitue ex eis tribunos, et centuriones, et quinquagenarios, et decanos, qui judicent populum omni tempore." The Vulg. "tribunos" is translated by Ælfric as "ðūsendmen" (*OE Heptateuch*, EETS O.S. 160, 258).

233–46. *wāce ne grētton . . .* Cf. Ps. 105:37: "et non erat in tribubus eorum infirmus." The basis for this idea of careful selection of fighting men on the part of the Israelites can be found in Num. 1–2, where such phrases as this occur: "omne quod sexus est masculini a vigesimo anno et supra, procedentium ad bellum." The OE poet characteristically goes on to explain the exclusion from the army of underage and inexperienced warriors.

239. *lærig.* This word, occurring only here and in *Maldon* (*bærst bordes lærig* 284), is obscure in etymology and meaning. Max Förster discusses the word in his article "Keltisches Wortgut im Englischen" (*Festgabe für Liebermann* [Halle, 1921], p. 171–2). He approves the older etymology, from Lat. *lorica* by way of Welsh *llurig* or

another Celtic form, and takes it as meaning the metal-studded leather covering of the Germanic wooden shield. J. H. Kern (*Anglia 37*:55) connected it with Middle Irish *lerg* 'slope.' The usual interpretation is 'border, rim,' based on a gloss *syn emblærg* [*ede*] for *ambiuntur* 'provide with a border' (see A. Napier, *Old English Glosses* [Oxford, 1900], 170:377, and E. V. Gordon's note on p. 59 of his edition of *Maldon* [London, 1937]).

239b. *līcwunde swol.* 'The burning of a wound,' the phrase roughly parallel to *bealu-benna.* The MS reading *swor* is found nowhere else, and the defense of it by Kock (*Anglia 43*:305) is not based on sufficient evidence. The suggested *spor* is hardly acceptable; *wǣpna spor,* lit. 'mark of weapons,' is a common phrase for 'wound'; but *līcwunde spor* 'the mark of a wound' would make little sense.

240. See Note, 233–46.

242. *modhēapum.* The MS form may be retained with the meaning 'in the (brave) war-bands.' Grein suggested *modhǣpum* 'rich in courage,' which, on the analogy of expressions like *be him lifigendum* 324, would be possible here but probably is not necessary.

243–6. 'But they chose the war-band(?) by stature, (taking into account) how courage would acquit itself with honor among the people, together with the power of strength . . . grip(?) of spear.' Two omissions are evident in this passage: 243b is metrically incomplete, and a half-line is missing in 246. In the first instance, the addition of a second element to *wīg* (Blackburn suggested both *wīgþrēat* and *wīghēap*) would seem to give the best reading. The context indicates that the passage is concerned with the choice by the leaders of the best warriors for their bands. Bright (*MLN 27*:16), who reads *on wīg curon,* cites Num. 1:3: "A vigesimo anno et supra, omnium virorum fortium ex Israel, et numerabitis eos per turmas suas, tu et Aaron." But this passage does not lend much weight to this particular emendation; did he have in mind the reading in A.V. of the same verse: "all that are able to go forth to war in Israel"? The missing half-line in 246 has been variously supplied by editors. Wülker and Sedgefield assume that the first half-line is missing, others that the second is missing; but, as Krapp remarks, it is impossible to tell which has been lost. Krapp, who does not supply anything, suggests taking *cræft* and *feng* as subjects of *wolde* parallel with *mōd;* the exact syntax is not clear without the missing words, however.

248. *forðwegas.* Genitive singular. Sedgefield calls this an archaic Northumbrian form, which is of course possible. It has been suggested that it is rather a LWS dialectal form, a form of back-spelling. Kemp Malone, in his article, "When Did Middle English Begin?" (*Curme Volume of Linguistic Studies* [Philadelphia, 1930], pp. 114–15), lists about 25 cases of levelling in unstressed syllables in the first three poems of the Junius MS, including this form. But the small number of examples in the MS, and the fact that this particular form of levelling (*-es* :-*as*) is hardly to be found even in later MSS, renders somewhat unsafe Malone's assumption that the scribe's own dialect is here emerging.

248b–249. *Fana up* [*ge*]*rād.* The MS reading *fana up rad* is metrically impossible. From the following phrase it is evident that the *fana* is the pillar of cloud, here seen as a battle standard. Cosijn's change of *bēama* 249 to *bēacna* is unnecessary.

249b–51. 'They all remained waiting, until the guide [i.e., the guiding pillar] bright over the shields near the sea shattered the air-barriers.' Cosijn (*Beitr 20*:100) insists on the subjunctive form *brǣce* after *bidon;* but, as Bright (*MLN 27*:16–17) argues, the meaning as well as the meter would be distorted by such a change. The Israelites were not waiting *for* the pillar to move; they were waiting (in despair) when suddenly the pillar moved.

The expression *lyftedoras brǣc* is commented on by G. Neckel ("Under edoras," *Beitr 41*[1916], 163–70) in the course of a semantic investigation of the obscure word *edor* 'fence, barrier.' After discussing the word *edorbryce* 'fence-breaking,' he says: "Entsprechend ist in der Exodus v. 251 davon die rede, dass die feuersäule die *lyft-edoras* 'bricht' (*brǣc*) : dem dichter schwebt das himmelsgehöft vor, in das die flamme wie ein räuber einbricht" (p. 166). Mürkens (p. 115) apparently takes the word to mean 'air-doors' and would read *lyfte doras* (so also Holthausen in G-K, p. 888).

252. *hildecalla.* The second element of this compound suggests strongly the existence of a native OE **callian,* or **ceallian,* probably very rare or restricted to poetic use. Cf.

ongan ceallian þā ofer cald wæter, Maldon 91, which is usually taken to be the first appearance of ON *kalla* in OE. In his note on this line in his edition of *Maldon*, Gordon defends the word *ceallian* as native OE.

253. *bēohata.* No satisfactory explanation or emendation of this word has been offered. The second element may be either *hāta* 'promiser' or *hata* 'hater'; for the first element, *bēah, bēot, bi-,* and *bod* have been proposed. Krapp favors the last of these suggestions, *(ge)bod,* as the most likely in view of the parallel with *hildecalla* but cannot explain the compound as a whole. There is a remote possibility that we have in the MS reading a complimentary epic epithet of some kind, 'bee-hater'; cf. 'bee-wolf' or 'bear,' the most popular of the etymologies proposed for the name Beowulf. Another possibility, and a good parallel to *hildecalla,* would be *beaduhāta.*

253b. 'The raising of the shield was a sign that an announcement was to be made' (Gordon's note on *Maldon 42, bord hafenode.*)

255. *monige.* Cosijn (*Beitr 20:*101) translates 'die volksmengen.' Cf. *hē tō mænegum sprǣc* 520.

256. *rīces hyrde.* Moses. A common expression for a king or prince. Cf. *Beow.* 2027, 3080.

259-98. The Speech of Moses. Exod. 14:13-14: "Et ait Moyses ad populum: Nolite timere: state, et videte magnalia Domini, quae facturus est hodie: Ægyptios enim, quos nunc videtis, nequaquam ultra videbitis usque in sempiternum. [14] Dominus pugnabit pro vobis, et vos tacebitis." Yet the speech as given in the poem bears as much, if not more, resemblance to Deut. 20:1-4: "Si exieris ad bellum contra hostes tuos, et videris equitatus et currus, et majorem quam tu habeas adversarii exercitus multitudinem, non timebis eos: quia Dominus Deus tuus tecum est, qui eduxit te de terra Ægypti. [2] Appropinquante autem jam proelio, stabit sacerdos ante aciem, et sic loquetur ad populum: [3] Audi, Israel, vos hodie contra inimicos vestros pugnam committitis, non pertimescat cor vestrum, nolite metuere, nolite cedere, nec formidetis eos; [4] Quia Dominus Deus vester in medio vestri est, et pro vobis contra adversarios dimicabit, ut eruat vos de periculo."

259b. *þēah þe Faraon brōhte.* This half-line is either hypermetric, an improbability since it would then stand alone in an otherwise normal passage, or else metrically most unusual. The latter must be the case here. Certainly it is difficult to assume any corruption, the passage being perfectly intelligible.

262. *þurh mīne hand.* Exod. 14:16, the Lord to Moses: "Tu autem eleva virgam tuam, et extende manum tuam super mare, et divide illud. . . ." Cf. *Beow.* 557-8: *heaþorǣs fornam mihtig meredēor þurh mīne hand.* The expression *þurh mīne hand* certainly seems to have more justification in the *Exodus* passage (cf. Note, 280).

265. *ægnian.* Perhaps the best suggestion for the emendation of this word is that of Kock (*JJJ* 26), namely, *ængian* (i.e. *engan*) 'oppress.' One would expect in the context a meaning like 'oppress, torment, persecute.' Less likely are the words with the general meaning 'terrify' (*ōgnian, egian, eglan*) which have been suggested.

266. *Ne willað.* This has been taken as a reflection of the Lat. *nolite* and is apparently merely a negative imperative, 'do not.' It is one of the few clear examples of Latinisms in the poem. Cf. 206-7.

266 f. The expression *dēade fēðan,* in the sense of 'as good as dead,' is the only example in this speech of the poet's usual bold style. The speeches in the poem are markedly more conventional in language than the ordinary narrative. Cf. Exod. 14:13, quoted in Note, 259-98.

269. *ic on beteran rǣd.* 'I give you better counsel.' The word *on* is from the verb *unnan* 'grant, bestow.'

271. *bidde.* Probably a second person plural (see Note, 124). Sedgefield would supply *ic* with *bidde,* but the change to the first person would be awkward here. Kluge (n.) suggests *bidden*(?).

277. *lifigendra lēoð.* 'The song of the living,' i.e., of the Israelites. This suggestion of Bright's does away with the repetition of *lēod* in both half-lines which is incurred by the usual emendation of MS *þeod* to *lēod.* The same speech is later referred to as *lēofes lēoþ* in 308. The Israelites are "living" especially in sharp contrast to the *dēade fēðan* 266, the Egyptians. One might also emend *lifigendra* to *lifigendre* (accusative singular neuter comparative) and read 'a more living [i.e., more inspiriting] song,' thereby sug-

.gesting a contrast between the first half of Moses' speech and the second, in which he offers positive action. Such a reading is perhaps too subtle, however. The proposals of Gollancz (p. lxxi) and Blackburn, *þēodne* and *þēoden* respectively, are to be rejected on grounds of meter.

278. It is best to omit the word *tō* altogether, since it cannot be made to fit into the meter properly and is not needed for the sense. Bright (*MLN 27*:17) suggests that its presence may be explained by the scribe's hesitancy between *tō* and *on*, both of which are used with *lōcian* (cf., for example, *þē þū hēr tō lōcast, Beow.* 1654). Blackburn wonders if it is an echo of *tō* in the preceding line. Sedgefield, though retaining *tō* in his text, remarks in his note that it is unnecessary.

279. *fǣrwundra sum.* 'A (certain) sudden miracle.' Cf. 357.

280 ff. Exod. 14:21–22: "Cumque extendisset Moyses manum super mare, abstulit illud Dominus flante vento vehementi et urente tota nocte, et vertit in siccum: divisaque est aqua. [22] Et ingressi sunt filii Israel per medium sicci maris: erat enim aqua quasi murus a dextra eorum et laeva." It is strange that the poet chooses to have Moses describe such a striking event, particularly since he departs from the biblical source by so doing. This passage was selected for censure by Emile Legouis in his generally unfavorable discussion of the poem. After criticizing the lack of artistic sense evident in having Moses describe the parting of the sea, he remarks: "Thus the great wizard, whose silent gesture had worked the miracle, is changed into an artless gossip whom the miracle seems to amaze as much as it does his people" (*A History of English Literature,* tr. Helen Douglas Irvine [New York, Macmillan, 1929], p. 40). Craigie ("Interpolations and Omissions in Anglo-Saxon Poetic Texts," *Philologica 2*:8) goes so far as to see evidence of an actual omission in the text: "The incident [opening of Red Sea] cannot reasonably be supposed to have been omitted by the poet, and its absence must be due to the loss of a portion of the text." He supposes the omission to have occurred after 275.

280. *and þēos swīðre hand.* The hand of Moses is given special mention in the summary of Moses' career found in Deut. 34:10–12: "Et non surrexit ultra propheta in Israel sicut Moyses, quem nosset Dominus facie ad faciem, [11] In omnibus signis atque portentis quae misit per eum, ut faceret in terra Ægypti Pharaoni, et omnibus servis ejus, universaeque terrae illius, [12] Et cunctam manum robustam, magnaque mirabilia, quae fecit Moyses coram universo Israel." And in Isa. 63:12 we find: "Qui eduxit ad dexteram Moysen brachio majestatis suae, qui scidit aquas ante eos . . ."

281. *grēne tācne.* This is an acceptable reading, although the evidence of the Vulg. *virga* has suggested to most editors the emendation to *tāne* 'twig, branch.'

283. *wæter on wealfæsten.* The corruption of *on* to *ond* is easily understandable. While one may omit the *ond* altogether and take *wæter* as subject and *wealfæsten* as object of *wyrceð*, it seems somewhat better to read *on*. Then *ȳð* becomes subject of *wyrceð;* 'the wave builds the water into a fortress-wall.'

283–8. This description of the dry sea bottom is reminiscent of II Samuel 22 (Vulg. II Regum 22):16: "Et apparuerunt effusiones maris, et revelata sunt fundamenta orbis, ab increpatione Domini, ab inspiratione spiritus furoris ejus." Ælfric in translating Exod. 14:21 adds a reference to a "street" which is not in the Vulgate: ". . . and þæt wæter wearð on twā gedǣled [divisa est aqua] and læg ān drīge strǣt ðurh ðā sǣ (added by Ælfric)" (*OE Heptateuch,* EETS O.S. 160, 250).

287. *fāge feldas.* Sedgefield translates: 'the variegated (sea-)floor'; Blackburn, 'shining, bright, referring to the white sand of the sea-bottom.'

287–8. What the poet means here is evidently something like 'the fields which waves have always covered up to this point in time.' *Forð heonon,* however, usually means 'henceforth, from this time forward'; and expressions with *ēce,* such as *in ēcnesse, in ēce tīd,* ordinarily look forward to the future as well. Cf. the somewhat similar use of *forð* in 404.

288. The addition of *tīd* makes the line metrically complete.

289–90. 'The south wind, the blast of the bath-way, destroyed the bound sea-bottoms.' By thus following the older punctuation of Thorpe and Bouterwek, one can provide an object for *fornam.* The *sǣgrundas* are presumably "bound" in the sense of being seemingly permanent, or perhaps it is suggested that they are now "bound" in the sense of being helpless or controlled by something else. *Sǣgrundas* here may mean 'depths of the sea' rather than the actual bottom of the sea. Blackburn takes *bæðweges blǣst* to be 'blowing of the sea,' i.e., waves of the sea, the stormy waters, object of *fornam*. But this is stretching the meaning of *blǣst*, which is most naturally taken as parallel with *sūðwind*. *Blǣst* is found elsewhere in OE only in the compound *blǣst-belg* 'bellows' (BTS) and as a mistaken gloss for *carbassa* 'sails,' *blǣstas* (H. D. Meritt, *Old English Glosses*, [New York, 1945], 34:270). The Vulg. equivalent of *sūðwind* is merely "flante vento vehementi et urente" (Exod. 14:21). In view of the poet's previous mention of the torrid southern regions in speaking of the Ethiopians, it is hardly surprising that he used the word *sūðwind*. But even this detail may be found in legend. Cf. Philo Judaeus, *De Vita Mosis* 1.176 (tr. F. H. Colson, Loeb Classical Library edition [London, 1935], *6, 367*) : "But at sunset a south wind of tremendous violence arose, and, as it rushed down, the sea under it was driven back . . ."

290b. *brim is āreafod*. 'The sea is parted.' (Vulg. "divisa est aqua"?)

291a. *sand sǣcir spāw*. The reading *spāw* for MS *span* gives a meaning, though not a very clear one, to the phrase 'the sea's retreat spewed sand.' Cf. *holm heolfre spāw* 450. But this line may be more corrupt than it appears. *Sǣcir* occurs only here and is perhaps too confidently defined in the dictionaries (G-K : 'refluxus maris'; B-T : 'retreat of the sea'). Metrically the line is apparently a D-type (Sievers' D4) like 450a just cited ; but if *cir* is really *cierr*, it is somewhat too heavy a syllable for that position. Sedgefield, who points out this fact, makes a violent reconstruction to *sandsǣ āspranc* 'the sandy sea has sprung apart.' But *sandsǣ* is certainly an unlikely sounding compound.

293. *eorlas ǣrglade*. A vocative : 'long-fortunate warriors.' Cf. *æðeling ǣrgōd* in Beowulf. Most commentators have translated the phrase as 'bronze-bright warriors.' Cosijn (*Beitr 20*:101) regards *ǣrglade* as an adverb(?) referring to *miltse*. W. F. Bryan (*MP 28*:159–60) thinks the word means 'anciently kind, formerly kind' and refers to *miltse*. But both these readings are awkward.

304. *āndægne fyrst*. Moore (pp. 87, 107) regards the statement that the wall of waters stood for a day as a significant addition and believes that "it is not of the sort that we should expect the poet to invent." But it is doubtful whether this represents an actual addition at all. There is no statement in the Bible as to the length of time the walls stood. The poet is perhaps merely using the phrase loosely to indicate that the action took place within the space of one day, and one might well imagine that the crossing of the Israelites would take up a good part of it.

305. A half-line is clearly missing here. A simple explanation for its omission might lie in the fact that the preceding five half-lines had vocalic alliteration ; a scribe carrying the alliteration in his head while writing, or even when rereading, would not easily notice the omission of another half-line with similar alliteration. The usual reading supplied by the editors is some variant of Grein's *ȳða weall*. The missing phrase should contain a subject for *hēold*, a subject which might be an epithet of God as well as of the wall of water—perhaps a phrase like that suggested by Grein (*Germ 10*:418), *hīe ēce drihten. Him se Alwalda* would be possible.

307. *Nalles hīe gehyr[w]don*. 'In no way did they scorn.' The emendation is for the reader's convenience. Actually *hige* is a form of *hīe, hī; gehyrdon* is a form of *gehyrwdon*. See Sievers-Brunner §408 for the form of *gehyrwan*. Cf. *Judgment Day I* (Exeter Book), 70 : *þonne hē gehyrweð ful oft hālge lāre*.

308. *lǣste nēar*. It is not quite clear what this phrase means here ; it may refer to the song which is 'nearer to completion' (so Johnson in his translation). Kennedy translates 'as the time for deeds drew near, when the words of their well-loved lord were ended, and the voice of his eloquence was still.'

309. *sances*. For *sanges*. According to Sievers-Brunner §215, such forms are frequent in Northumbrian, but they are also found in other dialects at various periods.

310 ff. The Order of the Tribes.—The first three tribes to cross the sea are mentioned by name, and it is clear that the poet intended a definite order. There is no mention of individual tribes in the account in Exodus. It is certain that the poet had some authority in legend or commentary for his version of the crossing. Holthausen (*Archiv 115*:162–3) cited a passage from Peter Comestor (twelfth century) in the *Historia Scholastica*, Exod. 31 (*PL 198*:1158) : "Et advocans Moyses singulas tribus secundum ordinem nativitatis suae hortabatur eos, ut ipsum praeeuntem sequerentur. Cumque timuissent intrare Ruben, Simeon et Levi, Judas primus aggressus est iter post eum, unde et ibi

meruit regnum." Comestor's story agrees with this poem more closely than any of the other versions in either Jewish legend (where the tribes usually are said to have marched across simultaneously in twelve paths through the sea) or in Latin versions of the same. In Comestor's version Judah goes first, and while it is not said who followed him, the order of names—Ruben, Simeon—agrees with this poem. No version earlier than Comestor's has been discovered. There is, however, some evidence in the Bible which might have served as the basis for the order. Judah, being the most powerful and prominent tribe in later history, might have been expected to take precedence. In Num. 2:9 in a discussion of the arrangement of the camp, Judah with Issachar and Zebulun is apparently in command of one section: "Universi qui in castris Judae enumerati sunt, fuerunt centum octoginta sex millia quadringenti: et per turmas suas primi egredientur." Reuben is in command of the second section, including Simeon and Gad, and his tribe is to set out in second place (Num. 2:16: "in secundo loco proficiscentur"). In this arrangement, however, the third tribe, Simeon, is not in the proper position.

313. *on ōnette.* 'Hastened on' (the unknown path). Little can be made of the MS reading *an on orette;* it seems necessary to omit the *an* entirely. The reading *on ōrette* ('in battle'?; cf. *Widsith* 41) does not seem particularly appropriate.

316. *gesǣlde.* The line may be translated 'after the glory of victorious deeds fell to his [Judah's] lot.' Here *gesǣlde* is taken as from *gesǣlan* (cf. *Beow.* 1249-50 for a somewhat similar use). There remains, on the other hand, a suspicion that the word should be *gesealde* (cf. God's gifts in 16 and 20). Blackburn lists it, with question mark, under both *gesǣlan* and *gesellan* in his Glossary; Kennedy translates 'grant.'

317-18. Mürkens (p. 74) refers to Gen. 49:8, a passage which contains Jacob's dying prophecy concerning Judah ("Juda, te laudabunt fratres tui: manus tua in cervicibus inimicorum tuorum, adorabunt te filii patris tui," etc.). The supremacy of Judah is demonstrated everywhere in the later historical books.

321. *lēon.* The lion of Judah. Mentioned in Gen. 49:9 and in Rev. 5:5: "ecce vicit leo de tribu Juda."

322. *drihtfolca mǣst* must be taken as parallel with the unexpressed subject of *hǣfdon* 319 and refers to the tribe of Judah.

323-326a. 'They would not long endure humiliation from any people, so long as their leader lived, when they lifted their spears for battle.' *Herewīsan* refers to Moses, as Bright (*MLN* 27:17) observes. He goes on to say: "The poet is conceiving the action to be in the spirit of the *comitatus,* and the *herewīsa,* who might be supposed to be the chief of Judah, is certainly Moses, in accordance with the prevailing note of the poem." Cosijn (*Beitr 20:102*) takes *herewīsan* as a reference to the lion standard. The phrase *be him lifigendum* is understood by Blackburn to refer to the men of Judah ('while they were alive') and so Kennedy translates. But Bright points out that the subject of an absolute clause of this sort cannot be the subject of the verb of the sentence.

327. *hǣgsteald mōdige.* In form, *hǣgsteald* is singular and *mōdige* is plural. Cosijn's reading, *hǣgstealdas mōdge,* is logical but not metrically acceptable. Perhaps *hǣgsteald mōdig* should be read, but the parallel phrase *wīgend unforhte* in the next line is plural.

328. *wǣlslihtes. Wǣlslihtes* seems to be nominative plural here. Cf. *forðwegas* for *forðweges* 248. This explanation is suggested by Cosijn (*Beitr 20:102*). Bright (*MLN 27:17*) takes *wǣlslihtes* as genitive dependent on *unforhte;* Sedgefield takes it as dependent on *mōdige.*

328b. See Note, 180b.

330. Moore (p. 87) includes among "organic additions" to the poem the statement here that there was fighting where Judah went. On p. 107 he says that this addition hints at battle between Israelites and Egyptians. But there is no reason for taking this passage as an actual addition. The addition was made previously, in a sense, when Judah was introduced by name into the scene of the crossing. The martial description of the Egyptian army (155 ff.) is another example of legitimate expansion on the theme of an army on the march. It might well be said that this passage suggests a battle between the two enemies, but the whole atmosphere of the poem hints at that. Furthermore, one could easily take the passage as referring to future battles in which the tribe of Judah played a prominent role, the battles mentioned in 20-2, the conquest of Canaan. Or perhaps the courage which Judah displays in entering the sea first can be expressed by the poet only in terms of warfare.

331. *flota.* There is no particular reason for calling Reuben a sailor; this is a fresh appearance of the nautical imagery. Cf. *sǣwīcingas* 333 and Note, 81.

333. *sǣwīcingas.* This is one of the earliest occurrences of the word *wīcing* in OE. It appears in *Widsith* 47 and 59 but is there usually regarded as a proper noun. Sedgefield points out that the first recorded instance of *wīcing* ('pirate') is in the AS Chronicle, A.D. 879, and believes that the occurrence of *sǣwīcingas* here "makes us pause before admitting, with most scholars, an early date for the poem." The poem cannot be considered later than the traditional date on the evidence of one word, however; and it is unlikely that this word was added by any late interpolators, since it is typical of the poet's preoccupation with nautical figures of speech.

335–9. For the basic account of Reuben's offense see Gen. 49:3–4: "Ruben primogenitus meus, tu fortitudo mea, et principium doloris mei: prior in donis, major in imperio. [4] Effusus es sicut aqua, non crescas: quia ascendisti cubile patris tui, et maculasti stratum ejus." But the passage most closely agreeing with the version in this poem is I Chron. 5:1–2: "Filii quoque Ruben primogeniti Israel (Ipse quippe fuit primogenitus ejus: sed cum violasset thorum patris sui, data sunt primogenita ejus filiis Joseph filii Israel, et non est ille reputatus in primogenitum. [2] Porro Judas, qui erat fortissimus inter fratres suos, de stirpe ejus principes germinati sunt." Here also the supremacy of Judah is asserted. Gen. 35:22 tells of Reuben's sin in lying with his father's concubine.

335b–339a. 'He destroyed his leadership with sins, so that he marched in the rear behind the beloved one [Judah? or more likely Moses]. From him his own brother had taken the right of the first-born in the nation, his wealth and station.'

339. Sievers (*Beitr 10:*195–6) cites this line as an example of alliteration between *j* and *ea.* He cites also 190, where he reads *inge* (i.e. *ginge*) *men,* and 33, where he reads *iū* (i.e. *gēo*) *gēre.* All this he attributes to Kentish influence or origin. But the last two lines, based on emendations, are very poor examples. Grein (*Germ 10:*418) reads *geearu* (with the same meaning) here, and Blackburn questioningly supports such an interpretation. There is little evidence for a word *earu,* however. It is more likely that the line has been corrupted at some time than that this represents the sole instance of "Kentish" alliteration.

343. *gūðcyste onþrang.* 'Pressed forward in a war-band.' Cosijn (*Beitr 20:*102), citing *Guth.* 896, *hloþum þringan,* would read *gūðcyston* (i.e. *gūðcystum*) *þrang.* This may be a more likely reading, but some sense can be made of the MS form.

345a. *ofer gārsecge.* Krapp suggests that the MS *garseges* may have been a scribal anticipation of the ending of *Godes.*

346. *meretorht.* The chief objection to the MS *mǣretorht* is the fact that no compounds exist with *mǣre* as the first element, whereas there are many with *mere,* including *meretorht* (*Meters* 13:61).

347–351a. 'Then there one host of people marched after another, in ironclad armies (a single man, greatest in power, guided [them], for which he became famous), forth on their ways, the nation following the clouds, tribe following tribe.' One might perhaps expect that *mægenþrymmum* referred to the host, but since *wīsian* takes the dative such a construction would hardly be possible. *Mǣst* would then be left out of the picture entirely. Cf. *mægenþrymma mǣst* 583.

350. *folc æfter wolcnum.* While it may be thought tempting to change *wolcnum* to *folcum* or *folce,* the MS reading makes sense when we assume the poet to be referring to the pillar of cloud. It will be borne in mind that it was a *nubes tenebrosa* which separated the combatants the previous night (205 ff.; Exod. 14:20). Metrically, *folcum* or *folce* would of course result in double alliteration in the second half-line, an impossible construction.

352. *mægburga riht.* 'The right of the tribes,' either the rights to which each tribe was entitled or, more exactly, the position each tribe was to take. Num. 2 is indicated by Konrath (*ESt. 12:*138–9) as the probable source of this detail. See, for example, Num. 2:34: "Feceruntque filii Israel juxta omnia quae mandaverat Dominus. Castrametati sunt per turmas suas, et profecti per familias ac domos patrum suorum."

353. *eorla æðelo.* See the preceding Note; the phrase seems to mean the ancestry and social status of individual warriors. Ebert (*Anglia 5:*409), who believed that the sen-

tence referred to the right or claim of the Israelites to the Promised Land, emended to *eorla ǽðel* (i.e. *ēðel*) 'der männer heimat.'

353b. *Him wæs ān fæder.* It seems very probable that the poet had in mind here the traditional etymological interpretation of the name Abraham. See Gen. 17:4–5: "Dixitque ei Deus: Ego sum, et pactum meum tecum, erisque pater multarum gentium. [5] Nec ultra vocabitur nomen tuum Abram; sed appellaberis Abraham; quia patrem multarum gentium constitui te." The name is explained by Jerome as meaning "pater videns populum" (*Onomastica Sacra,* [ed. P. de Lagarde, Göttingen, 1870], p. 3) or "pater videns multitudinem" (p. 77). In any case it is certainly Abraham and not Jacob who is meant here, as is clear from the following lines.

354. *landriht gepah.* Perhaps the literal translation is most suitable here: 'he received the right to the land.' God's promise of the land of Canaan to Abraham is found in several places in the book of Genesis (17:8, 15:18, etc.).

358. *onriht.* Onriht is found as an adjective but not as a noun. Its meaning is usually 'proper, right.' Johnson translates *onriht Godes* as 'God's peculiar people,' and so B-T and Blackburn. It seems to be an adjective, modifying *cyn.*

359–61. 'So the ancients tell in their cunning, those who have best known the tribal lineage, the origin of men and the descent of each.' Surely this is a reference to the detailed and numerous genealogies in the Pentateuch, as usual adapted to a prominent feature in Anglo-Saxon tradition.

362–446. This section, the so-called interpolation, is omitted entirely from the editions of Kluge and Sedgefield and from the translation of Gordon. By those who have regarded it as a separate poem or fragment of a poem, it has been given various titles: "Exodus B" (Balg, *Der Dichter Cædmon und seine Werke* and Ziegler, *Der poetische Sprachgebrauch in den sogen. Cædmonschen Dichtungen*); "Isaaks Opferung" (Binz, *AnglBeibl* 14:357); "Noah und andere Patriarchen" (Brandl). See full discussion of the problem in the Introduction.

362. *Nīwe flōdas.* 'New floods,' i.e., new to the world, strange, never seen before. It seems unlikely that the poet is comparing the deluge with the "floods" which overwhelm the Egyptians in the Red Sea, since he has not yet mentioned them. But there may well be a comparison implied between Noah's voyage and the "voyage" of the Israelites over dry land. (See Note, 81.)

Reading the words *ofer lāð* as two words rather than one makes the line better metrically. Does the emphasis on *ofer* suggest an antithesis, since the Israelites are travelling *under* the "floods"?

364. *drenceflōda.* Cf. *Gen.* 1398, *se drenceflōd.*

366. *trēowa.* Probably 'covenant, promise' here rather than 'faith.' Cf. the meaning of *trēowa* 426. The Noahic Covenant is found in Gen. 6:18, 9:9–17.

369–374a. 'For the saving of lives of all the race of earth, the wise seafarer had counted out everlasting survivors, a first generation of each, father and mother of all those that bear offspring, more diverse than men know.'

373. *missenlīcra.* This emendation, suggested in B-T *s.v. mismicel,* is here adopted since it is comprehensible. The MS reading *mismicelra* is quite obscure. A comparative form seems required here; if the word contains *micel* as its second element, the comparative should be *māre.* As emended, the passage may be translated 'of many kinds when reckoned up, more so than men know' (B-T).

377 ff. Abraham's father is the ninth from Noah. Cf. Gen. 11:10–27: Noe, Sem (1), Arphaxad (2), Sale (3), Heber (4), Phaleg (5), Reu (6), Sarug (7), Nachor (8), Thare (9). Thare (A.V. Terah) is the father of Abram, Nachor, and Aran.

380–1. *naman nīwan.* The change of his name from Abram to Abraham. The relevant passage is quoted in Note, 353b.

382–3. Cf. Gen. 17:6: "Faciamque te crescere vehementissime, et ponam te in gentibus, regesque ex te egredientur."

383b. *Hē on wræce lifde.* 'In exile.' Gen. 12:1: "Dixit autem Dominus ad Abram: egredere de terra tua, et de cognatione tua, et de domo patris tui, et veni in terram, quam monstrabo tibi." The reference may be to the fact that Abraham here was ordered to leave his home in Ur of the Chaldees or perhaps more generally to the wanderings which extended over most of his life.

384–446. The Offering of Isaac. The story is found in Gen. 22. With the version here may be compared the account in *Gen. A* 2846–936. There are few striking similarities in language; the version in *Gen. A* is longer and much closer to the original. The *Exodus* version is on the whole much more intensely focused on the symbolic significance of the incident. The place of sacrifice (Mt. Moriah) is identified and connected with Solomon's temple; all extraneous characters (e.g., Abraham's servants) and events (e.g., the Lord's speeches before the offering) are omitted entirely; and the speech of the Lord at the end is expanded and emphasized more strongly than in *Gen. A*.

386. *on Sēone beorh.* 'On Mt. Zion.' Mürkens reads *onsēone beorh,* which he regards as having its source in the phrase "in terram visionis" (Gen. 22:2), but the alliteration precludes such a reading. There are a good many occurrences of the word *Sion, Seon* elsewhere; see an article by Pamela Gradon, "A Contribution to Old English Lexicography," *Studia Neophilologica, 20* (1947–48), 199–202, where the forms are collected.

387–8. The phrase *wuldor gesāwon* is taken as parenthetical; *wǣre* and *hēahtrēowe* are parallel. See Kock JJJ 16.

389–96. Mount Moriah. The identification of the hill on which Isaac was to be sacrificed with the mountain on which Solomon built the temple is nowhere made directly in the Vulgate. As Moore (p. 101) pointed out, the most probable source of the information is in Josephus (*Jewish Antiquities* I, 226). Jerome (*Quaestiones in Genesim, PL 23:969–70*) identifies the two places: "Aiunt ergo Hebraei hunc montem esse in quo postea templum conditum est in area Ornae Jebusaei, sicut et in Paralipomenis scriptum est: Et coeperunt aedificare templum in mense secundo, in secunda die mensis in monte Moria." The reference which Jerome makes here is to II Chron. 3:1–2 (which appears in a slightly different form in the Vulgate). The identification is also to be found in Jewish legend; cf. Ginzberg, *Legends of the Jews, I,* 285.

391. *tempel Gode.* A metrical variation which appears elsewhere. (Perhaps the *-el* was given intermediate stress in *tempel.*) See Pope, *The Rhythm of Beowulf,* p. 333 (§98). Blackburn reads *tempel gōde* 'the good temple,' but *tempel* is neuter.

393. For an account of Solomon's extraordinary reputation in the Middle Ages, see R. J. Menner's Introduction to his edition of *The Poetical Dialogues of Solomon and Saturn* (New York, 1941).

399. It seems best to repunctuate so that *ādfȳr onbran* is taken with *fyrst ferhðbana* and 399b is regarded as a parenthetical comment. Then the passage would read 'At first the (would-be) murderer kindled the funeral pyre (he was not the more doomed because of that!)' In other words, Abraham is here called a *ferhðbana;* the parenthetical remark reassures us that, although this had the appearance of murder, it was not, and Abraham was not 'doomed' or damned for it. Such a reading preserves some sense and does not require emendation. Perhaps a clearer reading would be obtained if one read *fyrmest* for *fyrst* and *fāgra* for *fǣgra;* one would then translate 'The foremost of the slayers kindled the funeral pyre—(he was not the more criminal for that).' If one takes 399 to be a complete sentence, however, as most of the editors do, it is almost impossible to make an acceptable reading out of it. Blackburn translates 399 as 'the first murderer (Cain) was not more doomed (i.e., more threatened with death) than was Isaac.' He offers as evidence in support of this Gen. 4:14, where mention is made of Cain's fear of death ("omnis igitur qui invenerit me, occidet me"). Krapp doubts, however, that *fyrst* can here be taken as an adjective in the sense 'first.' He points out that this is the only OE occurrence of *fyrst* as adjective in the *OED,* the next instance being for the year 1220. He, with Bright and Thomas, reads *fǣgenra* for *fāgra,* translating 'At the first the life-destroyer was not the more joyful.' Cosijn takes *ferhðbana* to refer to the devil, paraphrasing 'Satan brauchte sich nicht zu freuen, denn Abraham blieb Gott gehorsam.' Perhaps one could emend *fyrst* to *fyrht* or *forht* ('the frightened killer').

401. *beorna. Bearna* would probably make better sense here, especially with *sunu* in the following line. Blackburn suggests that this is a Northumbrian form, but see *Seasons for Fasting (Anglo-Saxon Poetic Records, 6* [New York, 1942], ed. E. V. K. Dobbie) which has *beorn* for *bearn* in 68 and 178 and *weord* for *weard* in 153. But there is a chance that *beorna sēlost* is correct, since Isaac is the *only* son, as we are told in the following lines.

404–5. '. . . the comfort of his life, which he had awaited so long, his long-enduring hope, as a bequest to the people.' 'Comfort' and 'hope' refer to Isaac, and the passage emphasizes the pathos of Abraham's situation. Cf. a similar use of *forð* in referring to past time in 287; the similarity may be counted as some evidence for the unity of the poem.

406. *þæt*. 'This, namely'; refers forward to the phrase in 409–10.

408. *grymetode*. A word used ordinarily of the roaring of animals; here apparently an exceptionally vivid description of the harsh sound of the sword being drawn from its sheath.

409–10. '. . . (showed) that he did not hold his [Isaac's] life more dear than obeying the King of Heaven.' The construction is somewhat elliptical; *þæt* should be supplied in sense after *þonne*. *Līfdagas* merely means 'life'; cf. *Beow.* 793.

411. A half-line is missing, here supplied from *Gen.* 2832a: *Đā Ābraham*. In a sequence of what must have been six consecutive half-lines with vocalic alliteration, only five appear. Cf. 305 for what is probably a similar omission. The missing half-line may have contained the name *Ābraham* and another word, as both Blackburn (*Ābraham sweorde*) and Krapp (*Ābraham þā*) suggest. Grein and Wülker had placed the words from *up* to *sinne* in a single (hypermetric) line, but Pope (*The Rhythm of Beowulf*, p. 103) does not accept it as hypermetric but as the remnant of two normal verses.

413. *ecgum rēodan*. 'Kill with sword'? (*rēodan* 'to redden with blood, kill') or 'with red sword'? For the common reading *rēod* for *rēad*, see B-T. If the MS reading were preserved, one might read *ēagum rēodan* 'with red (weeping) eyes,' but the parallel *ecgum—mid mēce* seems too obvious.

414. *Metod*. All editors but Wülker change MS *God* to *Metod* to secure alliteration in the line. Wülker observes that here we have *doppelreim*, an unlikely possibility in this MS.

417 ff. Gen. 22: 11–12: "Et ecce Angelus Domini de coelo clamavit, dicens, Abraham, Abraham. Qui respondit: Adsum. [12] Dixitque ei: Non extendas manum tuam super puerum, neque facias illi quidquam: nunc cognovi quod times Deum, et non pepercisti unigenito filio tuo propter me." In the Bible, the angel makes two speeches; the poet has combined and expanded them.

423b. The retention of *freoðo* gives a reading which is unsatisfactory metrically. The corruption of *frēode* to *freoðo* is easily imaginable, and the sentence is made clearer by the addition of *tō*.

426. *Hū*. Here almost in the sense of 'why.'

427–31. 'Heaven and earth cannot overturn His glory's word(s?), too broad and wide for the regions of earth, the circuit of the world and high heaven, the abyss of the sea and this mournful air to embrace.' Based on Toller's translation (BTS *s.v. behwylfan*) as amplified by Bright (*MLN 27*:18). Bright suggests the meaning 'overturn, depose, bring to naught' for *behwylfan*, the meanings usually assigned to *āhwylfan*, rather than 'cover,' as Toller has it. Bright also proposes a number of biblical passages similar to this one which the poet may have had in mind; see, for example, Isa. 40:8: "Exsiccatum est foenum, et cecidit flos: Verbum autem Domini nostri manet in aeternum;" and Luke 21:33: "Coelum et terra transibunt; verba autem mea non transibunt." (Cf. also Isa. 51:6, Ps. 102:25–7, etc.) "The singular verb *mæg* 427 has *heofon* and *eorðe* as subject as two closely coordinated ideas" (Krapp, n.). *Mæge* 429 is plural; see Sievers-Brunner §425.

431. *gēomre lyft*. Cosijn (*Beitr 20*:104) suggests *eormenlyft*, citing Sievers (*Beitr 10*:195) as authority for the alliteration. But see Note, 339. The phrase *gēomre lyft* is puzzling in this context; there does not seem to be any scriptural basis for it. Perhaps *gēape lyft* should be read here.

432–46. Gen. 22:15–18: "Vocavit autem Angelus Domini Abraham secundo de coelo, dicens: [16] Per memetipsum juravi, dicit Dominus: quia fecisti hanc rem, et non pepercisti filio tuo unigenito propter me: [17] Benedicam tibi, et multiplicabo semen tuum sicut stellas coeli, et velut arenam quae est in littore maris; possidebit semen tuum portas inimicorum suorum. [18] Et BENEDICENTUR in semine tuo omnes gentes terrae, quia obedisti voci meae."

432. *þē āð swereð*. Kock (JJJ 27) in proposing *þē* for the MS *ne* cites *Beow.* 472, *hē mē āþas swōr*. Since a change is obviously needed here, it is probable that *þē* makes a better reading than the usual emendation *hē*. Cf. *þīnes* 435.

436–7. Cf. 83–4. The parallel in phrasing adds some evidence to the case for the unity of the poem. Cf. the other parallels cited in the Introduction in the course of the discussion of the "interpolation," p. 9.

439–42. The poet adds an idea from Gen. 13:16: "Faciamque semen tuum sicut pulverem terrae: si quis potest hominum numerare pulverem terrae, semen quoque tuum numerare poterit."

443. *be sǣm twēonum.* This phrase occurs also in 530. Mürkens (pp. 76–7) cites as source for the second occurrence of this phrase Exod. 23:31: "Ponam autem terminos tuos a Mari rubro usque ad Mare Palaestinorum, et a deserto usque ad fluvium . . ." A more detailed definition of boundaries is found in Num. 34:5–12: "Ibitque per gyrum terminus ab Asemona usque ad torrentem Ægypti, et maris magni littore finietur. [6] Plaga autem occidentalis a mari magno incipiet, et ipso fine claudetur . . . [12] Et tendent usque ad Jordanem, et ad ultimum salsissimo claudentur mari. Hanc habebitis terram per fines suos in circuitu." Klaeber (*MLN 33:*221n.), after mentioning the passage cited by Mürkens, goes on to say: "There is a strong temptation to trace back to these *Exodus* passages the famous phrase *be sǣm twēonum* . . . which also occurs *Beow.* 858, 1297, 1685, 1956, *Guth.* 237 . . . 1333, *Par.Ps.* 71.8 (—a mari usque ad mare)." The usual interpretation of the expression, however, is that given by Rau (*Germanische Altertümer in der ags. Exodus,* p. 17), who explains it as a phrase originating in the peninsular continental home of the Anglo-Saxons between the North Sea and the Baltic. The question of its origin cannot be definitely answered, but its widespread occurrence points to the probability that it was a native expression rather than a borrowed phrase. If we accept it as traditional, we have here an astonishing example of the skill with which the poet managed to apply such native phrases accurately to a new context.

444. Perhaps a more specific application of the phrase "possidebit semen tuum portas inimicorum suorum" (Gen. 22:18, quoted in Note, 432–46).

ingeðēode. The MS reading *incaðēode* is preserved by Blackburn, who translates it in his Glossary 'hostile nation,' and by Gollancz (p. lxxiii), who translates it 'culprit folk.' But see Note, 142.

446. The word *sēlost* ends p. 163, which is about three-quarters filled. After it is placed a check-like punctuation mark. See Introduction, p. 10, for an account of the MS gap which follows. Presumably the missing section contained a description of the completion of the crossing, the pursuit into the sea by the Egyptians, and the beginning of the debacle in the midst of which we find the Egyptians at 447, where the text recommences. There is no reason to believe that the Abraham episode is not essentially complete as we have it. The matter with which it was primarily concerned, God's promise to the Israelites of the Land of Canaan, has been fully covered.

447. *Folc.* The Egyptians.

449. *beorhhliðu.* These must be the hills along the shore, but they have been understood as the waves themselves. Gordon translates 'the mountainous waters were bedewed with blood.'

453. *forhtigende.* The original form, as the meter shows, was probably *forhtende,* the Anglian form. Cf. Sievers-Brunner §412 An. 10 and Sievers, *Beitr 10:*482.

456. *atol ȳða gewealc.* Cf. *Beow.* 848, *atol ȳða geswing.*

457b–458a. 'But fate closed off (their retreat) from behind with a wave.' The Egyptians turn to escape the way they came but find that the waters have closed in there as well.

462–463b. By placing *lyft up geswearc* in parentheses and thus not connecting it directly with the following *fǣgum stæfnum,* one is able to avoid the extraordinary reading 'the air grew darkened with doomed voices.' Yet it is by no means certain that this is not what the poet intended; if so, it would surely be one of his boldest rhetorical flourishes. *Cyrman* does not seem to be used transitively; otherwise, it would be tempting to to take *herewōpa mǣst* as object of *cyrmdon.*

463b. *flōd blōd gewōd.* 'Blood pervaded the waters.' An outstanding example of internal rime.

466. *cyre swiðrode.* The ordinary meaning of the word *cyre,* 'choice,' is with difficulty brought into this context. The only intelligible reading would be 'their choice grew less,' i.e., the Egyptians no longer had any choice (or chance of escape). Perhaps one might

emend *cyningas* to *cyninga* and read 'the choice of the kings grew less.' The verb itself may be either *swiðrian* 'grow strong' or *swiðrian* (i.e. *sweðrian*) 'withdraw, fail, weaken.' The emendations *cyrr* (to be connected with *sæcir* 291?) and *cyrm* are both possible; *cyrm* is perhaps to be preferred.

467. This line has no alliteration as it stands in the MS. The substitution of a synonym by a scribe is a not uncommon occurrence. The text shows evidence for the next 40 lines of extensive and, in some cases, quite inexplicable corruption.

470. *forðganges nep.* This phrase baffles explanation. While the word *nep* seems to be genuine, neither of the two explanations of it which have been offered is really satisfactory. There is a word found in the glosses, *nēp* or *nēpflōd*, which is identical with or related to Modern English *neap* and may mean 'tide' (see *OED, s.v.* NEAP a. & sb. 2). Thomas (*MLR 12:*345) cites Icelandic *hneppr* 'scant' in proposing an OE adjective *nep* 'lacking.' Johnson, following the first interpretation, translates 470b–471a 'their tide of advance was cunningly fettered'; Kennedy, following the latter, translates 'with no chance of escape, bound by their war-gear.' The immediate context of the phrase is itself so suspicious and ambiguous that it offers little help, and the bold style of this particular passage may well admit some extraordinary expressions. Here *nep* is taken provisionally as meaning 'deprived of,' parallel with *fæste gefeterod* and *searwum āsæled.* Of the emendations, that of Bright (and Krapp) is perhaps the most reasonable; *nep* is changed to *weg* and the sentence is translated 'their way out was beset by fatal snares.'

471a. The fact that no general agreement has been reached on the significance of *searwum āsæled* renders even more difficult the explanation of the preceding phrase. *Searwum* could mean either 'by trickery or cunning' or 'by their war-gear or armor.' Conceivably either reading could be justified by the Bible. In the first instance, it might be felt that the Egyptians were trapped by cunning. perhaps a reference to Moses' magic powers. In the second, as is suggested by Hofer (*Anglia 7:*387), the idea that the Egyptians were entangled in their own accouterments could have come ultimately from the phrase "subvertit rotas curruum" in Exod. 14:25. Since there has been no reference (except possibly in *gyrdwīte* 15) to Moses as a magician, the latter possibility seems more likely.

471b. *sand bāsnodon.* The emendation of MS *barenodon* to *bāsnodon* seems almost inevitable in view of the following clause with *hwonne:* 'the sands awaited (or waited) . . . until. . . .' But even this emendation does little to clear up the following passage. Possibly *barenodon* represents some corruption of *bærnan* or an equivalent: 'the sands were hot and dry until the ever-cold sea,' etc.

472a. *witodre wyrde.* The statement of Klaeber (*ESt. 41:*110) that *witod* is never applied to a person seems to force the emendation of MS *fyrde* to *wyrde.* Just how this phrase fits into the pattern is still not quite clear. Presumably 'the sands waited for the appointed destiny' (so Johnson and Kennedy translate).

474a. *æflāstum gewuna.* 'Now accustomed to wandering (off the track)'? A peculiar phrase at best, but perhaps an attempt to describe or even personify the sea. The following *nacud nȳdboda* bears this out. Perhaps the image is one of an outlaw or exile returning for revenge, a type common enough in heroic tradition. Cosijn's brave attempt, *æflāst-ungewuna,* is unfortunately unmetrical; he translates 'der noch nie hinweggeströmt war.'

476. *genēoþ.* If this represents an actual preterite, with the infinitive suggested by G-K (*genēopan* or *genōpan*), this is the only place where it occurs and its meaning is only to be guessed from the context. A meaning like 'overwhelm' would be appropriate here. The difficulty with Sedgefield's suggested *gehwēoþ* here is that one expects a stronger word than 'menaced.' (See Glossary.)

479. *sæmanna sīð.* Probably 'the course of the seamen,' i.e., the Israelites, since the Egyptians are nowhere else called 'seamen' but rather 'land-men.' (See Note, 81).

480. *mōdge rȳmde.* The MS and many of the editors read *mōd gerȳmde.* Blackburn translates 'loosed its fury' (but *Metod* is clearly the subject). *Gerȳman* does not seem to be used elsewhere in the sense of 'give vent to (an emotion).' Reading *mōdge rȳmde,* one may translate 'swept away the valorous.' It is possible that this refers to the Israelites, who were removed to safety. By indicating a comma after *rȳmde,* one may understand the sentence as meaning that the sea (had) threatened the march of the seamen until the

true Lord removed the warriors. Then the subject of the two verbs in 481 would be *brim*. It should be borne in mind, however, that *mōdige* has already been used of the Egyptians in 465.

483a. *lagu land gefēol.* 'Water fell on land.' *Gefeallan* is a transitive verb. Cf. 492(?).

485b–490a. Perhaps the most obscure passage in the poem. A translation of the most tentative kind: 'when the Mighty One struck with holy hand the proud people, the God of heaven, Guardian of the protecting column. They could not restrain the path of the helping (waves?), the rage of the sea, but He [or it?] destroyed many with screaming terror.'

486b–487a. *heofonrīces [God], Weard wērbēamas.* This reading was suggested by Blackburn. It is clear that a syllable is missing somewhere in 486 or 487, since *wer beamas,* set off by dots in the MS, has only three syllables. In view of the meaning of *bēam* as 'pillar' elsewhere in the poem, it seems best to take it here as meaning that, and the compound *wērbēam* as being for *wērbēam* 'protecting pillar.' For the genitive singular in *-as,* cf. *forðwegas* 248. Thus *Weard wērbēamas* 'guardian of the protecting pillar' would be a reference to God, *se Mihtiga.* Thomas (*MLR 12:345*) reads *on wērbēamas* in 487a but takes the *wērbēamas* to be the protecting columns of water, perhaps thereby forcing the meaning of *bēam* in this poem. As for other interpretations, that of Dietrich and Grein should be mentioned; they regard the compound *werbēam* as meaning 'Mannbaum' or 'baumstarker Mann,' a kind of kenning for warrior, and cite ON parallels (e.g., *egg-viðr, geir-viðr*). But such a compound would be extraordinary in OE. Sedgefield defines *werbēamas* as 'flood-gates, weir-bars.' Perhaps the most natural of more drastic emendations is the *wērge beornas* suggested by G-K.

488b. *helpendra pað.* This obscure expression may make the best sense if taken as meaning 'path of the helpers,' that is, presumably, the path of the waves which are assisting the Almighty. This is Bright's interpretation. But this is admittedly unsatisfactory; *helpendra pað* and *merestrēames mōd,* apparently in apposition, make a dubious pair at best. Blackburn takes *pað* as meaning 'onset, course' and the 'helpers' as being the "protecting walls of water." This interpretation is followed by Kennedy and Gordon in their translations. Yet *pað* certainly does not ordinarily mean 'onset,' and the function of the walls of water at this stage can hardly be called one of helping. There is the possibility that the juxtaposition of *hel* and *pað* suggests something like 'path to hell,' recalling the description of the death of the first-born earlier in the poem. Holthausen (G-K, p. 885) in fact suggested *helwarena pað.* Many of the other emendations have been suggested on the analogy of such OE kennings for sea as *hronrād* 'whale-road.' None of the suggested words are very firmly supported, however; the best may be Holthausen's *hwelpendra pað* 'path of the seabirds.' (Perhaps, if this were accepted, it would be advisable to read *bæð* for *pað;* cf. *Beow.* 1861, *ofer ganotes bæð*).

491a. *up ātēah, on slēap.* Somewhat irregular metrically, but apparently an A-line with double alliteration, corresponding most closely to Sievers' type A2ab; cf. *Beow.* 1650a, *wlitesēon wrǣtlīc.* This verse is more heavily burdened than the one in *Beowulf.* Sedgefield suggests reading *tēah* for *ātēah.*

492a. *wēollon wælbenna.* 'Wounds gushed [bled].' The first element in the compound *wælbenn* is probably *wæl* 'slaughter.' But B-T reads *wǣl-benn* 'a wound inflicted by the sea,' taking the first element as *wǣl* 'deep water of the sea.' Sisam (*MLN 32:*48) questions the second element in the usual sense of 'wound'; he reads *wælbend,* translating 'the death-bonds (i.e., the enveloping waves) seethed' (cf. *Beow.* 1936, *wælbende*). But such an emendation seems unnecessary. Certainly the mention of wounds is not unusual in view of the frequent mention of blood elsewhere in this description.

492b. *wītrod.* On the interpretation given this word depends the meaning of the following lines. Since *gefeallan* is probably transitive here, as in 483, *wītrod* may be either subject or object of *gefēol.* The expression *handweorc Godes* is probably a reference to the wall(s) of water, in view of the following adjective *fāmigbosma;* there is a possibility that some sort of weapon like the *alde mēce* of 495 is meant. Thus it seems fairly certain that *wītrod* is what is fallen on, the object of the sentence. But what the elements of the compound are remains obscure. Probably it is a form of *wīg-trod* 'the marching army' or 'war expedition.' The other suggested forms include *wit-rad, wīgrād,* and *wiþertrod.* Sedgefield, on the other hand, reads *wīg-rōd* 'the war-pole' and further explains that it is "the pole or mast, the *seglrōd* of 83, which . . . now descends from heaven with terrific force and breaks down the sea-wall." He of course takes it to be subject of *gefēol*.

494. *Fāmigbosma* is scarcely to be taken as an epithet of God. It apparently modifies *handweorc* and refers to the walls of water now falling. The emendation of MS *flōd-wearde slōh* to *flōdweard geslōh* and the full stop after *fāmigbosma* are based on a suggestion of Cosijn (*Beitr 20:105*). The dictionaries take *flōdweard* as a feminine noun; Blackburn translates it 'flood-keeping . . . the waves that held back the sea.' But to read *flōdweard* 'guardian of the flood' not only provides a more likely compound but also gives us a proper agent to wield the ancient sword of the next line.

498. *flōdblāc*. A vivid adjective, which one may suspect was coined by the poet. Translate 'pale with fear of the flood.'

499. The most likely explanation of the difficulty in this passage is that a line has fallen out after 499, since there is no verb in the passage as it stands. Such a line might have contained a verb with the meaning 'fall' and perhaps a phrase parallel to *brūn yppinge* and *mōdwǣga mǣst*. The passage would then read 'when on their backs (or shoulders) the *brūn yppinge* (had fallen . . .), greatest of raging waves.' A change of *hīe* to *him* would probably be necessary. One is tempted to preserve *on bōgum* partly because it makes sense (cf. *mēara bōgum* 171) and partly because it presents no metrical difficulties. The emendations of the commentators, in attempting to supply a verb, are *onbugon, on bugon*, and *on buge*. The first form would give the rare short A3 metrical type; the second and third would give a highly improbable C-line with transverse alliteration (ABBA). It should be noted that Mürkens (who reads *on bugon*) reverses the position of the words in the second half-line, reading *ypping brūnne*, a change which would at least provide a better metrical pattern. The meaning of the word *ypping* is not clear. If related to *up*, it may mean 'elevation'; if to *open*, 'manifestation.' In any case it is fairly clear from the context that it refers to the waves or walls of water falling on the Egyptians. It is probably plural; the possibility of elision (*brūn' yppinge*) was suggested by Thomas (*MLR 12:345*), and Dietrich reads *brūne*. *Brūn* is used elsewhere in describing the sea (cf., for example, *brūne ȳða, An.* 519). In connection with *ypping*, cf. *ypplen* 'summit,' *Seasons for Fasting* 130.

501a. *d[ē]aþe gedre[n]cte*. This emendation by Sedgefield is not wholly satisfactory but makes some sense. The usual meaning of *gedreccan*, 'torment, vex,' seems less likely here than the meaning 'drown'; the poet is summarizing the whole event rather than describing the process. A recent ingenious attempt by Else von Schaubert (*Philologica: The Malone Anniversary Studies* [Baltimore, 1949], pp. 41-2), to preserve the MS reading should be noted. She would read *ðā þege drecte* 'als diese durch Trinken geplagt wurden,' taking the phrase as a participial construction in the nominative, with *þege* as instrumental of *þegu* 'taking of drink, drinking' (cf. *bēorþegu, wīnþegu*, especially the former, used of a flood in *An.* 1533). The chief objection to such a reading is on metrical grounds; it would give a C-line with the alliteration on the second stress. Her proposed scansion with heavy primary accent on *ðā* and secondary accent on *þege* is unlikely.

503. The addition of *grund* seems obviously necessary here, since there is no alliterating word.

504. *mereflōdes Weard*. The Lord. Blackburn takes *weard* to mean the wall of water, and so Gordon in his translation. But the contest here is between Pharaoh (*Godes andsaca;* cf. Note, 15) and the Lord.

505. *heorufæðmum*. Was the scribe unfamiliar with the poetic element *heoro* (*heoru*)? Cf. *heora wulfas* for *heoruwulfas* 181. No compounds with this element appear in either *Genesis* or *Daniel*.

508 ff. An elaboration of the idea already mentioned in 456-7. Both are based on Exod. 14:28: "nec unus quidem superfuit ex eis."

509. *ungrundes*. 'Bottomless, measureless.' B-T cites the similar ON *u-grunnr, ugrynnr*.

510. *heora*. Blackburn points out that the same scribe has written other genitive plurals in *-o* (*Gen.* 1270, 1866).

514a. The half-line is metrically too short. It is unlikely that any important or essential words have been lost. Grein's reading *spilde spelbodan* (better: *spelbodan spilde?*) is somewhat anticlimactic following the strong image in *geswealh*.

514b. The phrase *sē ðe spēd āhte* should be taken with *āgēat gylp wera* as a single sentence (so Krapp). Most editors and translators, placing a comma before *sē ðe*, take it as referring directly to *meredēað*. But the following line seems to indicate a deliberate emphasis on the contest between God and the Egyptians, and God may be understood as the subject here.

516–90. The rearrangement of the text here is discussed in the Introduction, pp. 11–12.

523. *ūs on*. The MS reading *ufon* is incomprehensible, although Blackburn preserves it, translating 'from his home in the heavens (lit. from above).'

529–30. Mürkens (p. 76–7) cites Exod. 23:31: "Ponam autem terminos tuos a Mari rubro usque ad Mare Palaestinorum, et a deserto usque ad fluvium: tradam in manibus vestris habitatores terrae, et ejiciam eos de conspectu vestro."

537. The line seems to have lost a word or two, perhaps something like *ongunnon þā*. Most editors emend *gefēon* to *gefēgon* and make a normal half-line. But a normal half-line in a five-line hypermetric series is suspicious, as Pope (*The Rhythm of Beowulf*, p. 103) has pointed out. With the possible exception of 540a, the rest of the following hypermetric lines are regular.

540a. As this half-line stands, it breaks down into two normal half-lines (and is so printed by Blackburn in his text). Sievers (*Beitr 12*:476) and Pope (p. 149) have suggested reversing the order of words to read *brimu ealle him blōdige þūhton* to regularize the meter. Pope adds: "There remains a chance, however, that the MS. is correct, and that this irregularity, which involves a real precedence of the secondary over the primary accent, is to be explained as a startling instance of a general tendency on the part of the long 4–4 measure to split into two 2–4 measures."

541b. The alliterating word is missing in this half-line; the word *herge*, supplied by Grein, is satisfactory.

542–6. This is a description of the Song of Moses (Exod. 15). The reference to the women seems to be based ultimately on Exod. 15:20: "Sumpsit ergo Maria prophetissa, soror Aaron, tympanum in manu sua: egressaeque sunt omnes mulieres post eam cum tympanis et choris." See also Philo Judaeus (*De Vita Mosis* I, 180), who tells us that after the crossing the Hebrews had two choirs, one of men and one of women, on the beach, presided over by Moses and his sister respectively.

547 ff. The tradition that the Israelites gained possession of weapons and treasure which were cast up on the shore of the Red Sea after the drowning of the Egyptians is fairly widespread although not actually to be found in the book of Exodus. As Holthausen (*Archiv 115*:162) first pointed out, it is to be found in Josephus (*Jewish Antiquities* II. 349), in Peter Comestor (*PL 198*:1158: ". . . et tulit Israel arma mortuorum"), and elsewhere. The collections of Jewish legends give the fullest account. Ginzberg in *The Legends of the Jews* observes: "On their leaving the land only the private wealth of the Egyptians was in their hands, but when they arrived at the Red Sea they came into possession of the public treasure" (*2*, 371); and further, "The sea cast up many jewels, pearls, and other treasures that had belonged to the Egyptians, drowned in its waves" (*3*, 37). What the actual Latin source was from which the poet was likely to have obtained it cannot be determined.

547. *Ēbrisc mēowle*. What must be meant, to judge from the following lines, is the Hebrew women who are here adorning themselves with the spoils of war. They have just been mentioned in the preceding passage as singing the song of triumph. The MS reading *afrisc* is almost impossible to retain. The Hebrews could scarcely be called Africans (although Klaeber, *ESt. 41*:111, would take *afrisc* as expressing an accidental relation, i.e., the Hebrews in Africa being called Africans). Nor would the word, properly speaking, refer to the Egyptians, since among classical and medieval geographers as a rule the term "African" was reserved for Libyans and Mauretanians. Pliny (*Nat. Hist.* v.9.47) includes Egypt in Asia; in v.9.48, he says that the inhabited country next to Africa is Egypt. Thus the emendation *ēbrisc* suggests itself quite naturally. Presumably the sequence was **ebrisc* to **efrisc* to *afrisc* in the history of the MS. For the confusion of *f* and *b* in such biblical loanwords, cf. *Coreffes* for Vulg. Choreb 'Horeb,' *Sol. and Sat.* 185, and *Coferflōd* for the river Chebar (Vulg. Chobar), *Sol. and Sat.* 20. The emendation of Blackburn and Krapp, who keep *afrisc*, of *mēowle* to *nēowle* (Krapp translates 'Then an African [Egyptian] was easily found prostrate on the shore of the sea, adorned with gold') is not necessary. Gollancz (p. lxxv) would read *ēbrisc nēowle* 'the Hebrew prostrate in prayer.'

549. 'With the hand they lifted neck-ornaments.' Cosijn (*Beitr 20:*106) suggests this reading, citing in support of this interpretation of *halswurðung* the word *brēostwurðung Beow.* 2504. Cf. also *healsbēag* in *Beowulf.* The older interpretation of *halswurðung* is really much less likely. B-T defines 'a celebration because of safety'; Gordon translates 'they raised their hands in thanksgiving for safety.'

552-3. The Israelites are the *sǣlāfe;* the phrase *on ȳðlāfe* means 'on the shore.' The sentence may be translated 'the survivors began to divide according to the standards [i.e., according to the tribes] the ancient treasures on the shore . . .' It would be possible, on the other hand, to take *sǣlāfe* as appositive to *mādmas,* with the meaning 'booty cast ashore' (so Blackburn, Sedgefield, Krapp).

554b. The MS reading *heo on riht sceo* is obviously faulty. Translate (reading *sceōdon* from *sceādan*) 'they divided justly the gold and precious cloth,' etc.

555. *Iōsepes gestrēon.* The fabulous wealth which Joseph had accumulated (which may have been dwelt on at some length in the passage missing after 141) came into the possession of the Egyptian Pharaoh after Joseph died. Ginzberg (*Legends of the Jews, 2,* 125) says on this subject: "The wealth of the whole world flowed into Egypt at that time, and it remained there until the exodus of the Israelites. They took it along, leaving Egypt like a net without fish." There is some confusion as to when the Israelites obtained this treasure, however. They are sometimes said to have taken it with them when they "spoiled the Egyptians" before leaving; yet the passage from Ginzberg already quoted in Note, 547 ff. suggests that they obtained the bulk of it in the sea.

558-64. A passage of the greatest obscurity, but perhaps typical of the poet's cryptic and allusive style. The chief difficulties are these: (1) The impression is certainly created here that Moses spoke *ēce rǣdas*—apparently laws or counsel of some kind—to the Israelites immediately after the crossing, on the shore of the sea (*on merehwearfe*); (2) the meaning of *dægweorc* (so MS) 561 is not clear. It is apparently some sort of title to the collection of laws which Moses has been given by God in the course of their wanderings. By far the simplest and most convincing explanation of these allusions is that offered by Cosijn (*Beitr 20:*105), reinforced by a few hints from Blackburn and Gollancz (p. lxxvii) and from Krapp (p. xxix n.). The reference here is to the whole book of Deuteronomy, which is, in effect, cast in the form of one long farewell speech by Moses. This contains the *ēce rǣdas,* the essential parts of the Law of Moses. Deut. 1:3 is cited by Cosijn: "Quadragesimo anno, undecimo mense, prima die mensis locutus est Moyses ad filios Israel omnia quae praeceperat illi Dominus ut diceret eis." This he offers as an explanation of the word *dægweorc,* 'das werk eines tages.' (But see Note, 561.) Deut. 1:1 is more interesting, since it gives the location of the final address as on the Red Sea: "Haec sunt verba, quae locutus est Moyses ad omnem Israel trans Jordanem in solitudine campestri, contra Mare rubrum, inter Pharan et Thophel et Laban et Haseroth, ubi auri est plurimum." (The last phrase is not found in the A.V., which reads ". . . Laban, and Hazeroth, and Dizahab." Has the poet here taken the phrase to refer to the treasure of the drowned Egyptians cast on the shore?) The *ēce rǣdas* have in the past been taken to refer to the Decalogue; it is quite true that the Ten Commandments are, for Christians, the most memorable part of Moses' law, but it should be noted that the Ten Commandments appear in chapter 5 of the book of Deuteronomy as well as in the book of Exodus. Moore (pp. 96n., 97n.) tries to make a case for the interpretation that the reference is actually to the Song of Moses here. He maintains that 565-7 suggest allegorical interpretation, which he regards as unsuitable for the Decalogue but as having been applied on a large scale to the "Cantemus Domino," the Song of Moses. His objection that the poet, who knew his Bible well, would not make such a blunder as to say that the Decalogue was given to Moses on the Red Sea is largely invalidated by the facts noted above.

561. *dægword.* Suggested by Gollancz (p. lxxvii) in place of the mysterious MS *dægweorc.* He conjectures that the poet intended to translate the Latin name of Chronicles, "Dierum Verba," which is a translation of the Hebrew name, Dibre Haiamim. But the Hebrew name for Deuteronomy, Elle Haddebarim, being somewhat similar to the Hebrew name for Chronicles, was often confused with it. He even suggests that the poet might actually have originally written "Debarim" (which was then presumably glossed as 'dægword' and the gloss was eventually taken into the text and corrupted to *dægweorc*). Since the reference seems clearly to be to Deuteronomy and the word *nemnað*

implies some sort of title, this interpretation, although it may seem farfetched, is at least preferable to the meaningless *dægweorc*.

563. *dōma gehwilcne*. Cosijn (*Beitr 20*:105) cites Deut. 6:1: "Haec sunt praecepta, et ceremoniae, atque judicia, quae mandavit Dominus Deus vester ut docerem vos, et faciatis ea in terra, ad quam transgredimini possidendam."

565-8. 'If the interpreter of life, bright in the bosom, the guardian of the body, wishes to unlock ample benefits with the keys of the spirit, the mystery will be explained, wisdom will go forth.' 'The interpreter of life' is the intellect which inhabits the body; it has the power to bring meaning out of the scriptures. This passage is, as Moore (p. 96n.) suggests, clearly a reference to the universal medieval distinction between the letter and the spirit. The learned Christian is able to interpret any part of scripture in order to bring to light the spirit, the allegorical or symbolical meaning.

567. *ginfæstan gōd*. 'Ample benefits.' That *ginfæsten* should have been written for *ginfæstan* would not be unusual in this MS (see Note, 248).

568. Krapp puts a stop after *cǣgon* and begins a new sentence with *rūn*. The phrase *gif onlūcan wile* he attaches to the end of the sentence beginning at 561b. This may have been suggested by the fact that *rūn* begins with a small capital in the MS, but it seems a less coherent reading.

572 ff. This seems to represent an attempt (whether by the poet himself cannot be proved) to connect the concluding homiletic passage with the rest of the poem and especially the reference in the beginning of the poem to the laws of Moses. On the whole, the best evidence for the genuineness of this conclusion is the cross reference to the beginning of the poem. It would be difficult to believe that the "proem" was also an interpolation. The "better" advice which scholars can show us is the Christian doctrine, which presumably they can find foreshadowed throughout the O.T.

574. *līfwynna*. This emendation is probably necessary, since the only other occurrence of *lyftwynn* is in *Beow.* 3043 where it describes the dragon's joy in flying.

576. *ēðellēase*. The poet may be attempting to draw a comparison between man's condition on earth and the homeless wanderings of the Israelites described in the body of the poem (cf. *ēðellēasum* 139). As they sought the Promised Land, so we seek heaven.

581-2. 'So now arch-thieves share the kingdom (or rule?), old age and early death.' They are thieves in that they rob men of life. This is the reading suggested by Klaeber (*Archiv 113*:147). For *dǣlan* in this sense of 'share (power, property)' see *Gen.* 26-7, 2789. The older interpretation of the passage may be seen in Gordon's translation: 'Whether now great sinners have as their lot old age or early death . . .'

GLOSSARY

IN the order of words, æ is treated as though it were *ae;* ð (þ) follows *t.* Nouns and adjectives in *ge-* are under *g,* but the *ge-* prefix is disregarded in the case of verbs. Roman numerals indicate the classes of strong verbs; the other abbreviations for gender, declension, and conjugation (e.g., *as.* for accusative singular, *wk.1* for weak verb of the 1st class, *fi.* for feminine *i*-stem) are standard (see Klaeber's *Beowulf*).

The asterisk designates words found nowhere else in OE, on the evidence of the dictionaries.

Full capitals are used to indicate Modern English descendants of OE words where it is found useful to do so, but such archaic or obsolete modern forms as are found in the *OED* are not usually provided. Where the word in the text has been emended, the corresponding line number in the Glossary is italicized or else attention is called to the Note to that line. When a word has been supplied editorially the line number is put in square brackets.

The vowel quantities in the biblical proper names, e.g., *Ābraham, Ēgypta,* are indicated provisionally on the basis of the meter, but it is not possible to be certain of them in some cases.

Ābraham, m. Ābraham; ns. 380, 398, [411], 419; gs. Ābrahames 18, 273, 379. (Metrically dissyllabic; cf. Isra(h)el.)

ābrecan, IV. BREAK into, break; pp. npm. ābrocene 'shattered' 39.

ābregdan, III. move, withdraw, remove; pp. ābroden 269.

ābrēotan, II. destroy, kill; inf. 199.

ac, conj. but (after neg. clause); 243, 416, 443, 457, 489, 513.

ācol, adj. frightened, excited by fear; dpf. āclum 546.

*ādfȳr, n. funeral-fire, pyre; as. 398.

ādrencan, wk.1. drown; pp. ādrenced 459. (DRENCH)

ādrincan, III. be extinguished (of fire); pret. 3 sg. ādranc 77.

æfen, mn. EVENing; gp. æfen[n]a 108.

æfenlēoð, n. EVENing-song; ns. 201; as. 165.

*æflāst, m. wandering from a course?; dp. æflāstum 474.

æfter, adv. AFTER(wards), following, at that time; 105, 418.

æfter, conj. AFTER; 109.

æfter. prep. w. dat. 1. (temporal) AFTER; 5, 299, 532; 2. (spatial) spreading over, along, toward; 132, 212, 396, 511; AFTER, following; 195, 331, 340, 347, 350, 351; 3. æfter maðmum 'after (obtaining) the treasure' 143; cf. *Beow.* 2750.

æghwæðer, pron. subst. each (of two); nsm. 95.

æghwilc, pron. each (one), every (one); asm. æghwilcne 188; (as subst.) ns. 351.

*ægnian. wk.2. oppress? terrify?; inf. 265. (See Note.)

æht, fi. possession, power; as. 11.

*ælfaru, f. whole army?; ds. ælfere 66.

ænig, pron. ANY(one); nsm. 456, 509; gsf. ænigre 326.

ær, adv. ERE, before, previously; 28, 138, 141, 285, 458.

ærdæg, m. EARly part of the DAY, daybreak; ds. ærdæge 198.

*ærdēað, m. EARly DEATH; ns. 582.

æren, adj. made of brass, brazen; dpf. ærnum 216.

ærende, nja. (ERRAND), message; as. 561.

*ærglæd, adj. long-fortunate?; npm. ærglade 293. (See Note.)

æt, prep. w. dat. AT, in (time or place); 37, 128, 267, 467.

æt, m.(n.?) something to EAT, food; gs. ætes 165.

ætgædere, adv. toGETHER; 190, 214, 247.

Æthān, m. or n. Etham, on the route to the Red Sea; gs. Æthānes 66.

ætniman, IV, w. dat. take away (from); inf. 415.

æðele, adj.ja. noble, excellent; gsn. wk. æðelan 227.

æðelo, f. (noble) rank, descent, race; as. æðelo 339, 353; dp. æðelum 186.

āfæran, wk.1. terrify, make afraid; pp. āfæred 447.

āfæstnian, wk.2. strengthen, FASTEN, make firm; pp. āfæstnod 85.

āgan, prp. possess, have; inf. 317; pret. 3 sg. āhte 514; neg. pret. 3 pl. nāhton 210. (OWE)

āgen, adj. (one's) OWN; asn. āgen 419.

Āgend, mc. (owner), the Lord; ns. 295.

āgēotan, II. destroy, consume (lit. pour out); pret. 3 sg. āgēat 515.

āhebban, VI. raise, lift up, exalt; pret. 3 sg. āhōf 253; pp. āhafen 200.

āhlēapan, rd. LEAP forth, jump up; pret. 3 sg. āhlēop 252.

āhȳdan, wk.1. HIDE, conceal; inf. 115.

ālædan, wk.1. LEAD away; pret. 3 sg. ālædde 187.

aldor, m. chief, prince; ns. 12; as. 31; (of God) Lord; as. 270.

aldor, n. life; only in phrase tō aldre 'forever, always' 425.

ālesan, v. select, choose; pp. ālesen[e] 183, ālesen 228.

alh, m. temple; as. alh *392.*

Alwalda, wk. adj. as m. noun. the omnipotent one, the Lord; ns. 11.

alwihte, fi.pl. all creatures, all created things; gp. alwihta 421.

ālȳfan, wk.1. permit, allow, grant; pp. ālȳfed 44, 575.

ān, num. adj. & n. ONE; nsm. 353; gsn. ānes 305; (as noun) one person; nsm. 348; gpm. in phrases ānra gehwilc, gehwā 'each one' 187, 227; nsm. wk. 'alone' 440.

anbid, n. expectation; ns. 576.

and, conj. (always abbreviated 7–9) and; 1, 10, 13, etc. (33×).

āndæge, adj. lasting ONE DAY; asm. āndægne 304.

andrædan, rd. DREAD, fear; inf. 266.

andsaca, wk.m. denier, adversary, enemy (i.e. Devil); ns. 503; gs. (ap.?) andsaca[n] 15.

ānga, wk. adj. sole, ONly; asf. āngan 403.

*āngetrum, n. (a single) host, body of men; ns. 334.

ānmōd, adj. (ONE-MOOD), resolute, determined, bold; nsm. 203.

ānpæð, m. (ONE-PATH), narrow or lonely path; ap. ānpaðas 58.

*antþigð, f. prosperity; as. antþigða *145*. (See Note.)

āræman, wk.1. raise oneself, arise; pret. 3 sg. āræmde 411.

āræran, wk.1. (REAR), raise, erect; pret. 3 sg. ārærde 295; pp. ārǣred 320.

āre, wk.f. honor, glory; ds. āran 245.

*āreafian, wk.2. tear apart, separate?; pp. āreafod 290.

ārīsan, I. ARISE, rise; inf. 217; pret. 3 sg. ārās 100, 129, 299.

āsǣlan, wk.1. tie, bind; pp. āsǣled *471*.

āscippan, VI. create, originate; pret. 3 sg. āsceōp 381.

āstīgan, I. rise up, mount, ascend; pret. 3 sg. āstāh 107, 302, 451, 468.

āswebban, wk.1. put to sleep, kill, destroy; pret. 3 sg. āswefede 336.

āteon, II. move, climb; pret. 3 sg. āteah 491.

atol, adj. hideous, horrible, dire; nsm. 201, 456; asn. 165.

āð, m. OATH; as. 432.

āðswaru, f. OATH(-swearing); ds. āðsware 526.

āwa, adv. always; 425.

āwyrgan, wk.1. strangle, corrupt; pp. nsm. āwyrged 575.

*bælc, m. covering, canopy; is. bælce 73.

bǣlblyse, f. blaze of a fire; as. bǣlblyse 401.

bæðweg, m. BATH-WAY, sea; gs. bæðweges 290.

bald, adj. BOLD; nsm. 253.

bana, wk.m. killer, murderer; nsm. 39. (BANE)

bānhūs, n. BONE-HOUSE, body; gs. bānhūses 566.

bāsnian, wk.2. await, wait; pret. 3 pl. bāsnodon *471*.

be, prep. w. dat. BY, beside; 134; be sūðan 'to the south' 69; be (wæstmum) 'according to' 243; be 323, be him lifigendum 'while he lived' 324; be sǣm tweonum 'between the seas' 443, 530.

beacen, n. (BEACON), sign, signal; as. 320; gp. beacna 345; dip. beacnum 219.

*beadosearo, n. war-gear (armor? weapon?); ap. 540.

*beadumægen, n. battle-strength, army; gs. beadumægnes 329.

beag (beah), m. ring (token of wealth); ap. beagas 524.

*bealospel(l), n. (BALE-SPELL), tale of misfortune, bad news; gp. bealospella 511.

*bealuben(n), fjo. BALEful wound; ap.? bealubenne 238.

bealusīð, m. (BALEful) deadly journey, path to death; ds. bealusīðe 5.

beam, m. (BEAM), pillar, column; ns. 111, 535; np. beamas 94; gp. beama 249; ap. beamas ('rays of light') 121. (Cf. *OED* beam.)

bearhtm, m. noise, clamor; is. bearhtme 65.

bearm, m. bosom, lap; as. 375.

bearn, n. child, son (Scot. BAIRN); as. 415, 419; np. 28, 395.

bebeodan, II. order, command; pret. 3 sg. bebead 101, 215, 382, 563.

becuman, IV. COME, arrive; pret. 3 sg. becōm 46, becwōm 135, 344, 456; w. acc. 'befell' 447.

befæðman, wk.1. embrace, include; inf. 429.

befaran, VI. surround, entrap?; pp. npm. befarene 498.

befōn, rd. seize, encircle; pret. 3 sg. befeng 416.

beforan, prep. w. dat. BEFORE, in front of; 93.

behealdan, rd. I. HOLD, keep, preserve; pret. 3 sg. behēold 205; 2. BEHOLD, see, observe; pret. 3 sg. behēold 109.

behindan, adv. BEHIND; 457.

behwylfan, wk.I. overturn, destroy; inf. 427.

*bēlegsa, wk.m. flame-terror; is. bēlegsan 121.

belūcan, II. LOCK (up), enclose, shut up; pret. 3 sg. belēac 457; pp. npf. belocene 43.

bēodan, II. announce, advise; pret. 3 sg. bēad 352.

gebēodan, II. command, proclaim?; pret. 3 sg. geb[ē]ad 191.

*bēohata, wk.m. boaster?; ns. 253. (See Note.)

bēon. See eom.

beorh, m. hill, mountain; as. 386; dp. beorgum 132, 212, burgum 222.

beorhhlið, burhhlið, n. mountain-slope; np. beorhhliðu 449; ap. burhhleoðu 70.

beorht, adj. BRIGHT, gleaming, magnificent; nsm. 415, 566: asn. 219; supl. nsm. beorhtost 249.

*beorhtrodor, m. BRIGHT sky, heaven; as. 94.

beorn, m. man, hero, warrior; np. beornas 375; gp. beorna 401, 531.

bēorsele, mi. BEER-hall, festive hall; ap. bēorselas 531.

beran, IV. BEAR, carry, wear; inf. 219; pret. 3 pl. bǣron 59, 193, 332.

berēafian, wk.2. BEREAVE, rob; pp. berēafod 45.

*berēnian, wk.2. arrange, plan; pret. 3 pl. berēnedon 147.

berēofan, II, w. dat. deprive; pp. npm. berofene 36.

berstan, III. BURST, break (noisily), crash; pres. part. nsm. berstende 478; pret. 3 pl. burston 484.

bestēman, wk.I. make wet, soak, spatter; pp. bestēmed 449.

bētan, wk.I. restore, improve; pret. 3 pl. bēt[t]on 131.

betera. See gōd, adj.

beþeccan, wk.I. cover, conceal; pp. beþeaht 60.

bīdan, I. (BIDE), wait, await, remain; pret. 3 sg. bād 213, 300, 518; pret. 3 pl. bidon *249,* beodan 166.

gebīdan, I. await, endure, experience; pret. 3 sg. gebād 137, 404; pp. gebiden 238.

biddan, V. ask, pray (for); pres. opt. 2 pl. bidde 271.

bill, n. (BILL), sword; dp. billum 199.

*bilswæð, n. (BILL-SWATH), sword-track, wound; np. bilswaðu 329.

bindan, III. BIND, tie; pret. 3 sg. band 15.

blāc, adj. bright, shining; npm. blāce 111, 121.

blæc, adj. BLACK; dpn. blacum 212.

blǣd, m. power, success, glory; ns. 531, 588; as. 318.

*blǣst, m. (BLAST), blowing; ns. 290.

*bland, n. mixture, confusion; ns. 309.

geblandan, rd. mix, mingle; pp. geblanden 477.

blīcan, I. shine, glitter; pret. 3 pl. blicon 159.

blīðe, adj. BLITHE, joyful, glad; npm. (npf.?) 550.

blōd, n. BLOOD; ns. 463; ds. blōde 449.

*blōdegesa, m. BLOODY horror or terror; ds. blōdegesan 478.

blōdig, adj. BLOODY; npn. blōdige 329, 540.

bōcere, m. BOOK-man, learned man; np. bōceras 573.

bodigean, wk.2. announce; inf. 511. (BODE)

bōg, m. shoulder, back (of a horse); dp. bōgum 171, 499?. (BOUGH)

bord, n. (BOARD), shield; as. 253.

bordhrēoða, wk.m. shield ornament; ds. bordhrēoðan 236; np. bordhrēoðan 159; dp. bordhrēoðan 320.

bōt, f. reward, compensation; as. bōte 5, 550. (BOOT)

brād, adj. BROAD, spacious; asn. brāde 524.

brǣdan, wk.1. spread out; pitch (a tent)?; pret. 3 pl. brǣddon 132.

brecan, IV. BREAK, burst (through); pret. 3 sg. bræc 251.

bregdan, III. brandish, swing; strike (tents)?; pret. 3 pl. brudon 222.

brēost, nf. BREAST; dp. brēostum 269, 566.

brēostnet, nja. BREAST-NET, corselet; as. 236.

brim, n. sea, surf, waters; ns. 290, 478; np. brimu 540.

bringan, wk.1 (III). BRING; pret. 3 sg. brōhte 259.

*brōðorgyld, n. vengeance for BROTHERS; as. 199.

brūn, adj. BROWN; npf. brūn 499; apm. brūne 70.

bryttian, wk.2. make use of, enjoy; pres. 3 pl. bryttigað 376.

burh, fc. fortified place, city; as. 524; dp. burgum 511; ap. (sg. meaning) byrig 66. (BOROUGH, BURG[H])

burhhlið. See beorhhlið.

burhweard, m. defender of fort or city; ap. burhweardas 39.

gebycgan, wk.1. BUY, pay for; pret. opt. 3 pl. gebohte 151.

bȳme, wk.f. trumpet; ns. 132; np. bȳman 159; dp. bē[m]um 216; ap. bȳman 222.

byrnan, III. BURN; pres. part. nsm. byrnende 111, asm. byrnendne 73; pret. 3 sg. barn 115.

cǣg, f. KEY; dp. cǣgon 567.

camp, mn. battle, fight; is. campe 21.

Cananeas, pl. Canaanites; gp. Cananea 445, 523.

carlēas, adj. (CARE-LESS), free from sorrow; npn. wk. carlēasan 166.

cēne, adj.ja. brave, bold; gpm. cēnra 356; supl. asn. cēnost 322. (KEEN)

cennan, wk.1. give birth to, beget; pret. 3 sg. cende 356.

cēosan, II. CHOOSE, try; pret. 3 pl. curon 243.

cīgean, wk.1. call, summon; inf. 219.

*cinberg, f. chin-guard on helmet; as. cinberge 175.

*cist, f.? band of warriors, company; gp. cista 229, 230.

cnēoris(s), f. generation; dp. cnēorissum 3.

cnēo(w)māgas, m.pl. relatives, kinsmen; np. cnēowmāgas 185; gp. cnēomāga 21, cnēowmāga 318, 435.

*cnēowsibb, f. generation, race; as. cnēowsibbe 356.

cniht, m. boy, youth; as. 406. (KNIGHT)

corðor, n. troop, body of men; ds. corðre 191, 466.

cræft, m. power, cunning, CRAFT, skill; ns. 245; ds. cræfte 84, 437; dp. cræftum 30.

cringan, III. fall (in battle), die; pret. 3 pl. crungon 482.

cuman, IV. COME; pres. 3 sg. cym[e]ð 582; pret. 3 sg. cōm 508, cwōm 91, 202,
417; pret. 3 pl. cōmon 341; pret. opt. 3 sg. cōme 475.

cumbol, n. banner, standard; np. 175.

cunnan, prp. know, be able to; pres. 3 pl. cunnon 373, 436; pret. 3 sg. cūðe
351; pret. 3 pl. cūðon 28, 82.

cunnian, wk.2 w. gen. try, make trial of, tempt; pret. 3 sg. cunnode 421.

cūð, adj. known, well-known, famous; nsm. 191; gsn. cūðes 230.

cwealm, m. death; ds. cwealme 469.

cwēn, fi. (QUEEN), wife; dp. cwēnum 512.

*cwyldrōf, adj. bold in killing; npn. 166.

cyme, mi. coming, approach; as. 179.

cyn(n), nja. race, people, family, tribe; ns. cyn 29, 145, 310, cynn 351; gs.
cynnes 227, 435; ds. cynne 351; as. cyn 14, 265, 358, 523, cynn 198.

cynerīce, n. kingdom; ap. cynerīcu 318.

cyning, m. KING (frequently of God); ns. 9, 141, 175, 390, 421; np. cyningas
185, 191, 466.

cyre, m. choice; ns. 466. (See Note.)

cyrm, m. noise, shout; ns. 107.

cyrman, wk.1. cry, shout; pret. 3 pl. cyrmdon 462.

gecȳðan, wk.1. make known, announce, reveal; pret. 3 sg. gecȳðde 292, 406;
pp. gecȳðed 420.

dǣd, fi. DEED, action; dp. dǣdum 584.

*dǣdlēan, n. reward for DEEDS; as. 263.

*dǣdweorc, n. (DEED-WORK), deed, action; ds. dǣdweorce 543.

dæg, m. DAY; ns. 47, 584; ds. dæge 263; dp. dagum 97.

*dægsceadu, f. DAY-SHADOW?; gs. dægsceades (MS dægscealdes) 79. (See
Note.)

dægweorc, n. DAY('s) WORK; gs. dægweorces 315, 507; as. dægweorc 151.

dægwōma, m. rush of DAY, dawn; ns. 344.

*dægword, n. DAYS' WORDS?; as. (ap.?) dægword (MS dægweorc) 561.
(See Note.)

dǣlan, wk.1. DEAL, divide, share; pres. 3 pl. dǣlað 581; inf. 552.

gedǣlan, wk.1. divide, separate, break up; pp. gedǣled 76, 207.

Dāuid, m. David; gs. Dāuides 389.

dēad, adj. DEAD, dead man; gpm. dēadra 41; apm. dēade 266.

dēað, m. DEATH; ds. dēaðe 34, 448, *501*.

*deaðdrepe, m. DEATH-blow; is. 496.

*dēaðstede, m. place of DEATH; ds. 557.

dēawig, adj. DEWY; nsm. 344.

dēawigfeðera, adj. DEWY-FEATHERED; nsm. (npm.?) dēawigfeðere 163.

dēman, wk.1 w. dat. (DEEM), judge; pres. 3 sg. dēmeð 585.

dēofolgyld, n. (DEVIL-worship), idol; np. 47.

dēop, adj. DEEP (lit. and fig.), significant, solemn; nsn. 507; asn. 315, 561;
supl. asm. dēopestan 364.

dēop, n. DEEP; as. 281.

dēor, n. beast, wild animal; np. 166; gp. dēora 322. (DEER)

dēore, adj. DEAR, excellent; npm. 186.

dēormōd, adj. strong in heart, brave; gp. dēormōdra 97.

dōm, m. power, law, ordinance; ds. dōme 538; gp. dōma 563; ap. dōmas 2. (DOOM)

drēam, m. joy, happiness; ns. 574; ds. drēame 589. (DREAM)

gedrencan, wk.I. drown; pp. gedre[n]cte 501, gedrenced 34 (see Note).

drenceflōd, m. drowning-FLOOD, deluge; gp. dren[ce]flōda 364.

drēogan, II. endure, suffer; pret. 3 sg. drēah 49.

drēor, m. or n. blood, gore; ds. drēore 151.

drēosan, II. fall, perish; pret. 3 pl. druron 47.

gedrēosan, II. fall, perish; pret. 3 sg. gedrēas 500.

driht, f. crowd, host, army; np. drihte 496; gp. drihta 79.

Drihten, m. the Lord; ns. 8, 25, 91, 92, 262, 526, 563, 584; as. 543, 589.

drihtfolc, n. people, nation; gp. drihtfolca 34, 322, 557.

*drihtnē, m. corpse (killed in battle); dp. drihtnēum 163.

drȳge, adj. DRY; npm. 283.

drysmian, wk.2. grow dark, become gloomy; pret. 3 sg. drysmyde 40.

dugoð, f. band of retainers, host; ns. 41, 91, 501, 589; gs. dugeðe 183, duguðe 228.

ēac, prep. w. instr. besides, also; 245, 374, 381, 588; (swā) ēac [514].

ēaca, wk.n. increase, addition, reinforcement; as. ēcan 194.

ēad, adj. rich, happy; asn. ēade 186.

ēad, n. wealth, riches; as. 339.

ēadig, adj. blessed, happy; (as subst.) gpm. ēadigra 4; apm. ēadige 587.

eafera, wk.m. offspring, son; as. eaferan 412.

ēage, wk.n. EYE; dp. ēagan 179, ēagum 278.

eald, adj. OLD, ancient, time-honored; dsm. alde 495; asf. ealde 408; npm. ealde 'old men' 285, 359; dpn. ealdum 33; apm. ealde 553; comp. nsm. wk. yldra 'ELDER' 141.

ealdordōm, m. leadership, authority; as. 317, 335.

*eald[or]wērig, adj. fatally weary?; npm. eald[or]wērige 50. (See Note.)

eall, adj. ALL; nsf. 88, 214; nsn. 100, 299, 500; gsm. ealles 509; gsn. ealles 144; dsn. eallum 370; dsm. ealle 84, 437; npm. ealle 190, 249; npn. ealle 540; dpm. eallum 261; apm. ealle 440.

*eallwundor, n. (ALL-WONDER), great miracle; gp. eallwundra 546.

earm, adj. wretched, miserable; (as subst.) gp. earmra 576.

Ēbrisc, adj. Hebrew; nsf. 547 (MS afrisc).

ēce, adj.ja. eternal; nsm. 11, nsm. wk. ēcea 273; nsn. ēce 580; asf. ēce 288?, 370; apm. ēce 474, 558.

ecg, f. (EDGE), sword; ns. 408; dp. ecgum 413.

efne, adv. EVEN(ly), alike; 76.

*efngedǣlan, wk.I. divide EVENly, share alike; pret. 3 sg. efngedǣlde 95.

eft, adv. I. afterwards; 389; 2. back, again; 452, 508.

*eftwyrd, f. future fate? retribution?; ns. 582.

egesa, wk.m. terror, fear; np. egsan 136, egesan 201, 491.

egesfull, adj. terrible; nsm. 506.

Ēgypte, pl.adj. Egyptian; np. Ēgypte 452; gp. Ēgypta 50, 145, 501, Ēgipte 444; dp. Ēgyptum 506.

ellen, n. courage, valor; as. 218.

ende, mja. END; ds. 128, 267, 467.

enge, adj.ja. narrow; apm. 58.

engel, m. angel; ns. 205; gp. engla 380, 432, 526.

ēode. See gān.

eom, anv. AM, be; 3 sg. is 267, 268, 273, 290, 293, 380, 420, 521, 574; 3 pl. syndon 283, 297; opt. 1 pl. sȳn 571; wesan, v: be; pret. 3 sg. wæs 12, 19, 22, etc. (40✕); pret. 3 pl. wǣron 43, 60, 148, etc. (11✕); pret. opt. 3 sg. wǣre 378; bēon, anv.: BE; 3 sg. biδ 531, 568, 579, [588]; imper. 2 pl. bēoδ 259.

ēored, n. troop (of horsemen); as. 157.

eorl, m. nobleman, warrior, man; ns. 412; np. eorlas 293; gp. eorla 154, 261, 304, 353; ap. eorlas 216. (EARL)

eorp, adj. dark, swarthy; asn. 194.

eorδbūende, mc.pl. EARTH-dwellers, men; np. eorδbūende 84.

eorδcyn, n. EARTH-race, genus; ds. eorδcynne 370.

eorδcyning, m. (EARTH-KING), mighty king; gp. eorδcyninga 392.

eorδe, wk.f. EARTH; ns. 427; gs. eorδan 26, 430; ds. eorδan 441; as. eorδan 76, 403, 437.

ēower, poss. pron. YOUR; nsm. 531.

ēδel, m. native land, home; gs. ēδles 18.

ēδellēas, adj. homeless, lacking a country; dsm. ēδellēasum 139; npm. ēδellēase 576.

ēδelriht, n. RIGHT to a country; gs. ēδelrihtes 211.

ēδfynde, adj. easy to FIND, in great numbers; 547.

fācen, n. deceit, malice, fraud; ds. fācne 150.

fæder, mc. FATHER; ns. 353, 379, 415; gs. 446; as. 371; gp. fædera 29.

fæderæδelo, nja.pl. ancestry, pedigree; ap. 361.

fæderyncynn, n. race of foreFATHERS; ds. fæderyncynne 527.

fǣge, adj.ja. doomed to die, fated, as good as dead; nsm. 169; npm. 482; dpm. fǣgum 463; apm. fǣge 267; comp. nsm. fǣgra 399 (see Note).

fæger, adj. FAIR, beautiful; asm. fægerne 534.

fægre, adv. FAIRly, beautifully; 297.

fǣr, m. sudden disaster, panic?; as. 453. (FEAR)

*fǣrbryne, m. terrible burning; ds. 72.

fǣrspell, n. sudden terrifying news; ns. 135.

*fǣrwundor, n. sudden awe-inspiring WONDER; gp. fǣrwundra 279.

fæst, adj. FAST, firm, secure; nsm. 140; asf. fæste 423; asn. fæst 178, 579; dpm. fæstum 306.

fæste, adv. FAST, firmly; 407, 470, 498.

fæsten, nja. FASTness, fortress; gp. fæsten[n]a 56; as. fæsten 49 (or famine, FASTing? captivity? see Note).

fæδm, m. embrace, clutch, power; ds. fæδme 294, 569; dp. fæδmum 75, 306. (FATHOM)

fāg (fāh), adj. shining, bright, variegated; npm. fāge 287.

fāh, adj. hostile; nsm. 476, 584. (FOE)

fāmgian, wk.2. FOAM; pret. 3 sg. fāmgode 482.

*fāmigbosma, adj. FOAMY-BOSOMed; nsm.? 494.

fana, m. banner, standard; ns. 248. (VANE)

faran, VI. go, proceed, FARE; pres. 3 sg. færeð 282; pret. 3 sg. fōr 48, 330, 336, 347; pret. 3 pl. fōran 93, fōron 106.

Faraon, m. Pharaoh; ns. 259, 502; gs. Faraones 14, 32, Faraonis 156.

faru, f. march, expedition; as. fare 522.

gefeallan, rd. w. acc. FALL on; pret. 3 sg. gefēol 483, 492.

fela, n. indecl. much, many; 29; (with gp.) 10, 21, 24, 38, 49, 62, 546.

feld, m. FIELD; np. feldas 287.

feldhūs, n. (FIELD-HOUSE), tent; gp. feldhūsa 85; dp. feldhūsum 133, 223.

feng, mi. grasp, grip, (attack?); ns.? 246.

gefēon, V, w. dat. rejoice; inf. 537. (See Note.)

fēond, m. enemy; ns. 203; as. 32, 237; gp. fēonda 22, 294, 529, 538; dp. fēondum 64, 476.

feor, adv. FAR; 1, 381.

feorh, mn. life; gs. fēores 404, as. (ap.?) feorh 17, 538; living being; gp. fēora 361, 384; tō wīdan feore 'forever' 590.

*feorhgebeorh, n. protection for life, refuge; as. 369.

*feorhlēan, n. reward for life saved; as. 150.

fēorða, adj. FOURTH; nsn. fēorðe 133, 310.

fēran, wk.1. go; pres. part. asn. fērende 45.

gefēran, wk.1. go, travel; inf. 286.

*fērclam(m), m. sudden grip, clutch; ds. fērclamme 119.

ferhð, mn. mind, heart; ds. ferhðe 355; as. ferhð 119.

*ferhðbana, m. destroyer of life, murderer; ns. 399.

ferhðloca, m. enclosure of life, body; ap. ferhðlocan 267.

ferian, wk.1. carry; pret. 3 pl. feredon 375. (FERRY)

gefeterian, wk.2. chain, FETTER; pp. gefeterod 470.

fēða, wk.m. troop, tribe; ns. 312; ap. fēðan 225, 266.

*fēðegāst, m. warlike spirit?; ns. 476. (or fēðegest?; so BTS.; cf. Beow. 1976, El. 845).

fīftig, num. w. gen. FIFTY; 229.

findan, III. FIND; inf. 189, 454; pres. 3 pl. findað 562; pret. 3 pl. fundon 387.

fīras, mja.pl. men; gp. fīra 396.

flāh, adj. crafty, hostile; asm. flāne 237.

flēon, II. FLEE; pret. 3 sg. flēah 169; pret. 3 pl. flugon 203, 453.

flōd, m. FLOOD, body of flowing water; ns. 482; as. 463; ap. flōdas 362.

*flōdblāc, adj. FLOOD-pale, made pale by water; nsm. 498.

*flōdegsa, m. FLOOD-terror; ns. 447.

*flōdweard, m. guardian of the FLOOD; ns.? 494. (See Note.)

flōdweg, m. FLOOD-WAY; ds. flōdwege 106.

flota, m. sailor; ns. 331; np. flotan 133, 223.

folc, n. FOLK, nation, people, army; ns. 50 (or p.?), 106, 169, 350, 447, 534; ds. folce 88, 102; is. folce 56; as. folc 45, 72, 217; gp. folca 279, 340, 446; dp. folcum 502.

folccūð, adj. famous, known to people; nsm. 407.

*folcgetæl, n. number of the people; as. folcgetæl 229.

folcmægen, n. people's force, tribe; ns. 347.

folcriht, n. (FOLK-RIGHT), possessions, property; as. folcriht 22. (See Note.)

*folcswēot, m. multitude, host; gp. folcswēota 545.

*folctalu, f. FOLK-count, genealogy; ds. folctale 379.

folctoga, wk.m. leader of a people; ns. 14; ap. folctogan 254.

folde, wk.f. earth, ground; gs. foldan 369, 429; ds. foldan 396, 579.

folm, f. hand; dp. folmum 237, 396, 407.

for, prep. w. dat. beFORE, in front of; 252, 276, 314; FOR, because of; 235, 543.

foran, adv. beFORE, in front; 172.

forbærnan, wk.1. burn up; pret. opt. 3 sg. forbærnde 123; pp. forbærned 70.

foregenga, wk.m. FORErunner; ns. 120.

foreweall, m. FORE-WALL, bulwark; np. foreweallas 297.

forgifan, V. GIVE, grant; pret. 3 sg. forgeaf 11; pret. opt. 3 sg. forgēfe 153.

forgildan, III. repay, give back; pret. 3 sg. forgeald 315.

forgytan, V, w. gen. FORGET; pret. 3 pl. forgēton 144.

forhabban, wk.3. restrain, withhold; inf. 488.

forht, adj. afraid, timid; comp. npm. forhtran 259.

forhtian, wk.2. be afraid, fear; pres. part. npm. forhtigende 453.

forma, adj. first; nsm. 22. (Cf. FORMer.)

forniman, IV. take away, destroy; pret. 3 sg. fornam 289.

*forscūfan, II. drive away, repel; pret. 3 sg. forscēaf 204.

forstandan, VI, w. dat. (withSTAND), stand in the way of, obstruct; pret. 3 sg. forstōd 128.

forð, adv. FORTH, forward, away; 41, 103, 156, [340], 346, 529, 568; '(hence)forth' 287; 'go on' (of an action continued) 404.

forðām, forðon. 1. adv. therefore; forðon 187; forþon 200, 367; 2. conj. FOR, since; forðām 508.

forðgang, m. advance, progress; gs. forðganges 470.

*forðhere, m. marching or advancing army?; ds. forðherge 225.

forðon. See forðām.

forðweg, m. WAY FORTH, onward course; gs. forðwegas 248; as. forðweg 129; ap. forðwegas 32, 350.

Frēa, wk.m. the Lord; ns. 19 (Frêa), 274.

freca, wk.m. brave man, warrior; ap. frecan 217.

frēcne, adj.ja. terrible, dangerous; nsn. (or npn.?) frēcne 203.

frēcne, adv. terribly, severely, daringly; 38, 538.

fremman, wk.1. do, perform, commit; pret. 3 pl. fremedon 146.

frēobearn, n. FREE or noble son; np. frēobearn 446.

*frēobrōðor, m. own brother; ns. 338.

frēod, f. friendship; ds. frēode *423*.

freom. See from, adj.

frēomæg, m. relation, kinsman; dp. frēomāgum 355.

frēond, mc. FRIEND, lover; ns. 45; np. frēond 178.

freoðowær, f. peace treaty, covenant; as. freoðowære 306.

fretan, V. (EAT up), destroy; pret. 3 pl. frǣton 147.

gefrignan, III. learn, hear tell; pret. 1 sg. gefrægn 98, 285; pret. 3 pl. gefrūnon 360, 388; pp. gefrigen 1.

frōd, adj. old and wise; nsm. 355; nsn. 29.

frōfor, f. comfort, solace; ds. frōfre 88; as. frōfre 404.

from, adj. strong, bold, brave; nsm. freom 14, from 54.

from, prep. w. dat. FROM ; 378.

frumbearn, n. first-born, oldest child; gs. frumbearnes 338; gp. frumbearna 38.

*frumcnēow, n. first generation; as. 371.

frumcyn, nja. lineage, origin; as. frumcyn 361.

frumsceaft, fi.(mi.?) creation, creature; gp. frumsceafta 274.

ful, adj. w. gen. FULL; nsn. ful 451.

fullēst, m. aid, help; gp. fullēsta 522.

fyl, mi. fall; as. fyl *167*.

fūs, adj. eager to go, ready; nsm.? 129, 248; nsn. 103; npm. fūse 196.

gefyllan, wk.I. FELL, cut down, kill; pp. gefylled 38.

fȳr, n. FIRE; ns. 93, 579.

fyrd, f. army; ns. 54, 88, 223; ds. fyrde 331; as. fyrde 62, 254, fyrd 135, 156, 274.

*fyrdgetrum, n. war-band, company; ns. 103; as. *178*.

fyrdlēoð, n. war-song; as. 545.

fyrdwīc, n. military camp; ns. 129.

fȳren, adj. fiery; apm. fȳrene 120.

fyrmest, adv. foremost, first; 310.

fyrndagas, m.pl. DAYS of old; dp. fyrndagum 527.

fyrst, adv. at FIRST; 399. (See Note.)

fyrst, mi. space of time, period; ns. 267; ds. fyrste 189; as. 208, 304.

gefȳsan, wk.I. make ready, incite; pp. gefȳsed 54, 221.

galan, VI, sing, sound; pret. 3 pl. gōlan *545*.

gamol, adj. old, aged; npm. gamele 240.

gān, anv. GO, advance; pres. 3 sg. gǽð 568; pret. 3 sg. ēode 310, 335.

gār, m. spear; gs. gāres 240; np. gāras 158.

*gārbēam, m. spear(-shaft); gs. gārbēames 246.

gārberend, mc.pl. spear-BEARER, warrior; gp. gārberendra 231.

gārfaru, f. moving of spears, war-band; ds. gārfare 343.

*gārhēap, m. band armed with spears; ds. gārhēape 321.

gārsecg, mja. ocean, sea; ns. 490; gs. gārsecges 281, 431; ds. gārsecge *345*.

*gārwudu, m. spear(-WOOD); as. 325.

gāst, ma., mi. (GHOST), spirit, soul; ns. 169; gs. gāstes 96, 567; ap. gāstas 448, 587.

gearu, adj.wa. ready, alert; nsm. 339 (but does not alliterate; see Note).

gearwe, f.pl. gear, arms; ap. gearwe 59, 193.

gedriht, fi. band (of retainers), host; ns. 304.

gedrȳme, adj. joyful; supl. nsn. gedrȳmost 79.

gefrǽge, adj.ja. well-known, famous; supl. asn. gefrǽgost 394.

gefrǽge, nja. information from hearsay; is. in phrase mīne gefrǽge 'as I have heard' *368*.

gegrind, n. GRINDing together, clash; ns. 330.

gehwā, pron. w. gen. each (one); gsm. gehwǽs 361; gsn. gehwǽs *371;* dsm. gehwām 4, 6, 108, 209, 227 (see ān); asm. gehwone 529.

gehwilc, pron. w. gen. each (one); nsm. 187 (see ān); nsf. 230; gsn. geh[w]ylces 580; asm. gehwilcne 563; asn. gehwilc 374.

gehyld, ni. protection, custody; as. 382.

gelād, n. way, course; as. 58, 313?.

gelāð, adj. hostile, hateful; npm. gelāðe 206.

gemyndig, adj. MINDful of, obedient to; nsm. 516.

gēn, adv. yet, still; 249.

geofon, m. or n. sea, ocean; ns. 448; gs. geofones 548.

geoguð, f. YOUTH; ds. geoguðe 235.

gēomor, adj. sad, mournful; nsf. gēomre 431; apm. gēomre 448.

georne, adv. eagerly, firmly; 177.

gere, adv. entirely, very well; 291.

gēsne, adj. w. gen. deprived of, lacking; npm. gēsne 571.

gestrēon, n. treasure, wealth; as. gestrēon 555.

gesynto, f. health, success; gs. gesynto 272.

getenge, adj.ja. w. dat. close, pressing on; npm. getenge 148.

gewealc, n. rolling; ns. 456. (Cf. WALK.)

geweald, n. power, control, rule; as. 20, 383.

gewrit, n. writing, the Scriptures; dp. gewritum 562. (Cf. Holy WRIT.)

gewuna, adj. accustomed to; nsm. 474.

gif, conj. IF; w. ind. 242, 528, 565; w. opt. 52, 414.

gihðo, f. care, sorrow; dp. gihðum 577.

*gin, n. vastness, abyss; ns. 431.

ginfæst, adj. ample, liberal; apn. ginfæstan 567.

gnorn, adj. sad, sorrowful; comp. nsm. gnornra 455.

God, m. GOD; ns. 23, 71, 80, 152, 273, 292, 314, 380, 433, [486]; gs. Godes
15, 268, 345, 358, 493, 503, 536, 571; ds. Gode 12, 391; as. God 515.

gōd, adj. GOOD; comp. betera 'BETTER'; asm. beteran 269, 573; supl. sēlost;
nsf. 293; nsn. 446; asm. 401.

gōd, n. GOOD, benefit; ap. 567.

godweb, n. fine purple cloth; as. godweb 555.

gold, n. GOLD; ds. golde 548; as. gold 555.

grǣdig, adj. GREEDY, fierce; npm. grǣdige 162.

gram, adj. furious, hostile; npm. grame 144.

grēne, adj. GREEN; dsm. grēne 281; asm. grēnne 312.

grētan, wk.I. GREET, welcome; inf. 44; pret. 3 pl. grētton 181, 233.

grimhelm, m. mask-HELMet (with visor); as. 174; gp. grimhelma 330.

grund, m. (GROUND), bottom; as. grund 312, [503].

grymetian, wk.2. roar; pret. 3 sg. grymetode 408.

gryre, mi. terror, horror; ds. gryre 20; as (ds.?) gryre 490.

guma, wk.m. man; gp. gumena 174, 193.

gūð, f. war, battle; ns. 158; ds. gūðe 325.

*gūðcyst, f. war-band; ds.? gūðcyste 343.

gūðfremmend, mc.pl. fighter, warrior; gp. gūðfremmendra 231.

*Gūðmyrce, gūðmyrce?, m.pl. warlike border-dwellers? (or 'die kampf-
geübten Schwarzen'? Grein); ap. Gūðmyrce 59. (See Note.)

*gūðþrēat, m. war-band; ns. 193.

gūðweard, m. war-guard, leader; ns. 174.

gyfan, v. GIVE; inf. 263.

gyldan, III. pay, repay; inf. 150. (YIELD)

gylden, adj. golden; asm. gyldenne 321.

gyllan. wk.I. YELL; pres. part. asm. (dsm.?) gyllende 490.

gylp, n. boast, boasting; ns. 455; as. 515.

*gylpplega, m. PLAY involving boasting, battle; as. gylpplegan 240.

gȳman, wk.I. heed, pay attention to, keep; pret. 3 pl. gȳmdon 140.

*gyrdwīte, n. punishment with a rod; d(i)s. gyrdwīte 15.

gystsele, mi. GUEST-hall; as. 577.

gȳt, adv. YET, still; 235, 562.

habban, wk.3. HAVE, hold; inf. 218; pres. 3 sg. hafað 569; pret. 3 sg. hæfde
    120, 208, 366, 369; (as auxiliary 'have' w. pp.) pres. 3 sg. hafað 523;
    pres. I pl. hab[b]að I; pret. 3 sg. hæfde 30, 37, 75, 80, 183, 230, 535;
    pret. 3 pl. hæfdon 64, 197, 238, 319, 537.

hæft, m. captivity; ns. 551.

hægsteald, m. young man, warrior; np.? hægsteald 327. (See Note.)

hægstealdman, m. young man, warrior; np. hægstealdmen 192.

hæleð, mc. man, warrior, hero; np. hæleð 78, 376, 388; gp. hæleða 512; dp.
    hæleðum 7, 252, 394, 468; ap. hæleð 63.

hæs, f. command, beHEST; dp. hæsum 385.

*hæðbrōga, wk.m. heath-terror; ns. 118 (MS hæð; see Note).

hæwen, adj. blue, azure; nsf. hæwene 477.

hālig, adj. HOLY; nsm. 71; gsm. hāliges 96, 307, 385; dsm. wk. hālgan 74;
    dsf. hālige 560, dsf. wk. hālgan 257; asm. hāligne 392; asf. hālige 388,
    486, 528; asn. hālig 416; npm. hālige 89; apm. hālige 382, 536; apf.
    hālige 357, 366; supl. asn. hāligost 394.

*halswurðung, f. neck-ornament; ap. halswurðunge 549.

hām, m. HOME, dwelling; ds. hāme 457; as. hām (adverbial) 508; ap. hāmas
    454.

hand, fu. HAND; ns. 280; d(i)s. hand 275, handa 416, 549 (or ap.?); as.
    hand 262, 480, 486; np. handa 43.

handlēan, n. reward (given by HAND?); ns. 19.

handplega, m. HAND-PLAY, fighting; ns. 327.

handrōf, adj. strong-HANDed, good at fighting; gpm. handrōfra 247.

handweorc, n. HANDiWORK, work of (God's) hand; ns. 493.

hār, adj. HOARY, old; nsm.? 118; npm. hāre 181, 241.

hasu, adj. gray, tawny; npf. haswe 284.

hāt, adj. HOT; d(i)s. wk. hātan 122; dp. hātum 71.

hāt, n. heat; ds. hāte 78.

hātan, rd. order; pret. 3 sg. heht 63, 254, hēt 177.

gehātan, rd. promise; pret. 3 sg. gehēt 525.

*hātwende, adj. hot, burning; asm. hātwendne 74.

hē, hēo, hit, pers. pron. HE, she, IT, etc.; nsm. hē 12, 24, 30, etc. (29×);
    gsm. his 9, 17, 27, etc. (12×); dsm. him 10, 16, 24, 138, 183, 209, 314,
    316, 324 (or pl.?), 337, 340, 366, 380, 409, 415, 417; asm. hine 23, 180,
    414; asn. hit 538; np. hīe 29, 51, 59, etc. (22×), hēo 146, 554; gp.
    heora 55, 60, 218, 510, 540, hyra 131, 135, 199; dp. him 19, 69, 93,
    101, 117, 152, 154, 172, 206, 238, 242, 261, 319, 352, 353, 455, 540, 563;
    ap. hīe 52, 130.

hēaf, m.? lamentation, grief; ns. 35.

hēah, adj. HIGH, lofty, significant; nsn. hēah 19; supl. asn. hēahst 394.

hēah, adv. HIGH; 461, 468, 493 (these forms may be considered partly adjectival).

hēahfæder, m. (HIGH-FATHER), patriarch; gp. hēahfædera 357.

*hēahlond, n. HIGH LAND, mountain; as. hēahlond 385.

*hēahtrēow, f. HIGH or noble promise, covenant; as. hēahtrēowe 388.

*hēahþegnung, f. HIGH service; ds. hēahþegnunga 96.

hēahþungen, adj. noble; nsm. 560.

healdan, rd. HOLD, keep, possess; inf. 177; pres. 3 pl. healdȧð *577;* pret. 2 sg. hēolde 422; pret. 3 sg. hēold 306.

gehealdan, rd. HOLD, abide by; pres. 2 pl. gehealdȧð 528.

healf, f. (HALF), side; gp. healfa 209.

hēap, m. band, company, body of men; ds. hēape 192, 311; ap. hēapas 382, 536. (HEAP)

heard, adj. HARD, rough, severe; nsm. 327.

heaðorinc, m. warrior; np. heaðorincas 241.

heaðowylm, mi. (battle-surge), warlike feeling; np. heaðowylmas 148.

hebban, VI. (HEAVE), raise, lift; inf. 99; pret. 3 sg. hōf 276; pret. 3 pl. hōfon 301, 542, 549.

hēdan, wk.I, w. gen. (HEED), take care of (here virtually 'seize'); pret. 3 pl. hēddon 551.

hel(l), fjo. HELL; ds. helle 46.

helpend, m. HELPer?; gp. helpendra 488. (See Note.)

heofon, m. HEAVEN; ns. 46, 427; as. 73; dp. heofonum 376, 417, 441, 461, 493.

*heofonbēacen, n. HEAVEN-sign; ns. 107.

heofoncandel, f. HEAVEN-CANDLE; ns. 115.

*heofoncol, n. HEAVEN-COAL; dp. heofoncolum 71.

heofoncyning, m. HEAVEN-KING; ds. heofoncyninge 410.

heofonrīce, n. kingdom of HEAVEN; gs heofonrīces 486.

heofontorht, adj. HEAVEN-bright; nsn. 78.

heolfor, m. or n. blood, gore; ds. heolfre 450, 477.

heolstor, m. hiding place; as. 115.

heonon, adv. HENce, from this time on; 287.

*heorowulf, m. sword-WOLF, warrior; npm. heorowulfas *181.*

heorte, wk.f. HEART; ds. heortan 148.

*heorufæðm, m. deadly or hostile embrace; dp. heorufæðmum 505.

here, mja. army, crowd, host; ns. 247, 498, 518; gs. herges 13, 234, 457, heriges 107, 508; ds. herge [541]; np. hergas 46; dp. hergum 276; ap. hergas 260.

*hereblēað, adj. pale or afraid in battle; npm. hereblēaðe 454.

herebȳme, f. war-trumpet; ap. herebȳman 99.

*herecist, f. war-band, military unit; np. herecyste 301; ap. hereciste 177, 257.

*herefugol, m. bird that follows armies (eagle, vulture?); np. herefugolas 162.

hererēaf, n. spoil, plunder; gs. hererēafes 551.

herestrǣt, f. road for an army to march on; np. herestrǣta 284. (STREET) hereþrēat, m. band, troop; ds. hereþrēate 122; np. hereþrēatas 542.

herewīsa, wk.m. army leader; ds. herewīsan 323.

*herewōp, m. cry of an army; gp. herewōpa 461.

herian, wk.1. praise; pres. 3 pl. herigað 589; pret. 3 pl. heredon 543.

hettend, mc. enemy; np. 209.

hiht, mi. hope, trust; as. 405.

hild, fjo. battle, war; gs. hilde 162; ds. hilde 241; as. hilde 181, 505.

hild, m. protection, favor; as. 536.

*hildecalla, m. war-herald; ns. 252.

hildespel(1), n. tale of war, warlike speech; ds. hildespelle 541.

*hleahtorsmið, m. LAUGHTER-SMITH, one who causes laughter; dp. hleahtor-
    smiðum 43.

hlence, f. coat of mail; ap. hlencan 218.

hlēo, m.(n.)wa. cover, protection; ns. 79.

hlēoðor, n. (formal) speech; ns. 418.

hlīfian, wk.2. stand high, tower; pret. 3 pl. hlīfedon 89.

hlūd, adj. LOUD; nsm. 107; dsf. wk. hlūdan 518, dsf. hlūde 276; dpf. wk.
    hlūdan 99; apf. hlūde 542.

gehnǣgan, wk.1. subdue, conquer; pp. geh[n]ǣged 169.

hold, adj. loyal, gracious, kind; nsm. 19.

holm, m. sea; ns. 284, 450.

*holmig, adj. pertaining to the sea; dp. holmegum 118.

*holmweall, m. WALL formed by the sea; ns. 468.

hordweard, m. guardian of HOARD or treasure; gp. hordwearda 35, 512.

horn, mn. HORN, trumpet; ns. 192.

horsc, adj. quick (in mind), wise; nsm. 13.

hrā, hrǣ(w), n.(m.) corpse, body; dp. hrǣwum 41.

hraðe, adv. quickly; 502. (RATHER)

hrēam, m. cry, tumult; ns. 450.

hrēð, n. glory, triumph; ns. 316.

*hrēðan, wk.1. glory, triumph; pret. 3 pl. hrēðdon 541.

hreðer, m.n. breast, heart; ds. hreðre 366.

*hreðerglēaw, adj. wise, prudent; nsm. 13.

hrōf, m. ROOF, overhead covering; as. 298; ap. hrōfas 539.

hrōpan, rd. cry out, scream; pret. 3 pl. hrēopon *162*, 168.

hryre, mi. fall, death; ds. hryre 35; as. hryre 512.

hū, adv., conj. HOW; 426; w. ind. in dep. clause 25, 85, 89, 244, 280.

hund, num.n. HUNDred; ap. 232.

hwā, hwæt. 1. pron. interr., indef. WHO, WHAT; gsn. hwæs 'to what place'
    192; 2. interj. hwæt! (attention-calling exclamation: 'behold, listen!')
    1, 278.

hwæl. (See Note, 161.)

hwearfian, wk.2. advance, roll on; pret. 3 sg. hwearfode 158.

hwīlum, adv. at times, sometimes; 170. (WHILOM)

hwīt, adj. WHITE, gleaming; apf. hwīte 301.

hwonne, conj. WHEN, the time when; 250, 472.

hwōpan, rd. threaten; pret. 3 sg. hwēop 121, 448, 478.

hwylc, pron. (WHICH), anyone; nsm. 439.

hwyrft, mi. turning, motion (here 'way of escape') ; as. 210.
hycgan, wk.3. think, resolve; inf. 218.
hȳnðo, f. humiliation, injury; as. 323.
hȳran, wk.1. HEAR, obey; pret. opt. 3 sg. hȳrde 410; pret. opt. 3 pl. hȳrde 124.
gehȳran, wk.1. HEAR, listen, learn; pret. 3 pl. gehȳrdon 222, 255; pres. opt. 3 sg. gehȳre 7.
gehyrwan, wk.1. despise, speak ill of; pret. 3 pl. gehyr[w]don 307.
hyrde, mja. guardian, keeper; ns. 256. (HERD)

ic, pers. pron. I; ns. 98, 269, 280, 285, 291 ; np. wē 'WE'; 1, 571; dp. ūs *523*, *572*, *573*.
in, prep. (w. dat.) IN; 4, 94, 122, 200, 212, 244, 321, 424, 439, 527, 566; (w. acc.) into, to; 11, 234, 288, 296, 382, 401.
*ingeþēod, f. native people?; ap. ingeþēode (MS incaþeode) 444. (See Note.)
*ingefolc, n. native race; gp. ingefolca 142.
*ingēmend, mc. native rulers; np. ingēmen[d] 190. (See Note.)
*ingere, adv. entirely?; 33. (See Note.)
inlende, adj. native, indigenous; nsf. 136.
Iōsep(h), m. Joseph; gs. Iōsepes 555.
Īsaac, m. Isaac; as. Īsaac 398.
īsernhere, mja. army clad in IRON; dp. īsernhergum 348.
Isra(h)el, m. Israelite; gp. Israhela 91, 198, 265, Israela 358; dp. Israhelum 303, 558. (Metrically dissyllabic; cf. Ābraham.)
Iūdas, m. Judah; ns. 330.
Iūdisc, adj. belonging to the tribe of Judah; nsm. 312.

lǣdan, wk.1. LEAD, bring; pres. 3 sg. lǣdeð 522, 586; pret. 3 sg. lǣdde 54, 77; pret. 3 pl. lǣddon 194.
gelǣdan, wk.1. LEAD; pret. 3 sg. gelǣdde 62, 367, 384, 397; pp. gelǣded 535.
lǣne, adj.ja. transitory; nsm. 574; gsn. lǣnes 268.
lǣrig, m. border of a shield?; ns. 239. (See Note.)
lǣs. See lȳt.
*lǣst, f. fulfillment, performance?; ds. lǣste 308.
lǣstan, wk.1. do service, stand up (under strain), LAST; inf. 244.
gelǣstan, wk.1. carry out, fulfill; inf. 525.
lǣtan, rd. LET, allow; pret. opt. 3 sg. lēte 52, 414.
lāf, f. what is left; heirloom, (sword); as. lāfe 408; remnant, survivor(s); as. lāfe 370; ds. (tō) lāfe 405, 509.
lagu, mu. sea, water; ns. 483.
lagustrēam, m. (sea-STREAM), water(s); ap. lagustrēamas 367.
land, n. LAND; ns. 40; gs. landes 128; ds. lande 534; as. land 69 (p.?), 445, 483; np. land 60; ap. land 57.
landman, m. (LAND-MAN), inhabitant; gp. landmanna 179.
landriht, n. (LAND-RIGHT), right to the land; as. 354.
lang, adj. LONG; asm. langne 53; comp. apf. lengran 574.
lange, adv. LONG; 138, 324, 525; comp. leng 206, 264; supl. lengest 424.
langsum, adj. long-lasting, enduring; asm. langsumne 6, 405.

lār, f. instruction, counsel; ns. 268; as. lāre 307, 528; dp. lārum 390.

lāst, m. track; as. (on . . .) lāst 'after, behind' 167, 337.

lāstweard, m. follower, pursuer; as. lāstweard 'heir' 138, 400.

lātþēow, m. leader, guide; as. 104.

lāð, adj. hateful, hostile (as noun, 'enemy'); nsm. 40, 195; asm. lāðne 138; npm. lāðe 462; gpm. lāðra 57, 167; dpm. lāðum 195; dpn. lāðum 179.

*lāðsīð, m. hateful journey; ns.? 44.

lēan, n. reward, requital; ns. 507; as. lēan 315.

leng. See lange.

lēo, mf. lion; as. lēon *321*.

lēode, mip. people; np. lēode 90, 152, 445; gp. lēoda 12, 183, 228; dp. lēodum 277, 405; ap. lēode 44?, 70.

lēodfruma, wk.m. leader or founder of a people; ns. 354.

lēodgeard, m. territory; as. lēodgeard 57.

lēodhata, wk.m. persecutor of a people; ns. 40.

lēodmægen, n. (people's) army; gs. lēodmægnes 167, 195; ds. lēo[d]mægne 128.

*lēodscearu, f. people, nation; ds. lēodsceare 337.

lēodscipe, mi. nation, people; ds. lēodscipe 244.

*lēodwerod, n. army of a people; as. 77.

lēodwer, m. man of a nation; dp. lēodwerum 110.

lēof, adj. dear, beloved; nsm. 12, 354, 355; gsm. lēofes 53, 308, 337; comp. apm. lēofran 409; supl. nsn. lēofost 279, asn. lēofost 384.

lēoht, adj. (LIGHT), bright, shining; nsm. 251; nsn. 90.

lēoht, n. LIGHT; ns. 588.

lēoma, wk.m. light; np. lēoman 112.

lēoþ, n. song; ns. 308; as. lēoð *277* (MS þeod).

libban, lifgan, wk.3. LIVE; pret. 3 sg. lifde 383; pres. part. npm. lifigende 264; gpm. lifigendra 6, 277; dpm. lifigendum 324.

licgan, wk.3. LIE, lie dead; pret. 3 pl. lagon 458, 556.

*līcwund, f. (body-)WOUND; gs. līcwunde 239.

līf, n. LIFE; ns. 588; gs. līfes 5, 104, 268, 565; ds. līfe 537; as. līf 434.

līfdagas, m.pl. LIFE-DAYS; ap. līfdagas 409; dp. līfdagum 424.

Līffrēa, wk.m. Lord of LIFE; as. Līffrēan 271.

līfweg, m. LIFE-WAY; as. 104. (See Note.)

līfwynn, fi(jo.) LIFE-joy; ap. līfwynna (MS lyftwynna) *574*.

līg, mi. flame, fire; ds. līge 110, 122, 400.

*līgfȳr, n. flame, fire; as. 77.

lind, f. (LINDEN-)shield; gs. linde 239; dp. lindum 228, 251; ap. linde 301.

linnan, III. w. dat. give up, part from; pret. 3 pl. lunnon 497.

liss, fjo. kindness, mercy; gp. lissa 271 (or s.?), 588.

līðan, I. travel; pret. 3 sg. lāð 362.

līxan, wk.1. shine, glitter; inf. 157; pret. 3 pl. līxton 125, 175.

locc, m. LOCK (of hair); ap. loccas 120.

lōcian, wk.2. LOOK; pres. 2 pl. lōciað 278.

lust, m. w. gen. joy, desire (for); as. lust 53.

gelȳfan, wk.1. allow, grant; pp. gelȳfed 523.

lyft, mfi. air, sky; ns. 431, 462, 477, 483; as. 74.

*lyftedor, m. heavenly barrier, enclosure; ap. lyftedoras 251. (See Note.)
lyfthelm, m. air-HELMet, cloud; ds. lyfthelme 60.
*lyftwundor, n. air-WONDER; ns. 90.
lȳt, n. indecl. little; ns. 42; comp. lǣs (LESS), as adv.: þȳ lǣs 'LEST' 117.

mā, subst. n. MOre; 572; supl. mǣst (adv.) 'very much, best' 360.
mādmas. See māðum.
mǣg, m. kinsman, blood relative; gp. māga 17; dp. māgum 52.
mǣgburh, fc. tribe, family, group of kinsmen; as. 55; gp. mǣgburga 352; ap. mǣgburge 360.
mǣgen, n. I. strength, MAIN; ns. 242; gs. mǣgnes 67, 245; as. mǣgen 131; 2. army, military force; ns. 101, 210, 226, 300, 346, 459, 469, 500; gs. mǣgenes 215.
*mǣgenhēap, m. powerful band; dp. mǣgenhēapum 197. (G-K *s.v.* mǣgen-hæp 'kraftreich'; but cf. mǣgenþrēat.)
mǣgenrōf, adj. strong, powerful; nsm. 275.
mǣgenþrēat, m. powerful band; ap. mǣgenþrēatas 513.
mǣgenþrymm, m. might, power; gp. mǣgenþrymma 583; dp. mǣgenþrym-mum 349.
*mǣgenwīsa, m. leader of an army; ns. 521.
mǣgwine, mi. kinsman (and friend); dp. mǣgwinum 146, 314.
mǣre, adj.ja. famous, illustrious; nsm. 47, 102, 349; supl. asn. mǣrost 395.
mǣst. See micel, mā.
*mǣstrāp, m. MAST-ROPE, halyard; ap. mǣstrāpas 82.
maga, wk.m. son; as. magan 397, 414.
magan, prp. be able, can, MAY; pres. 3 sg. mæg 427; pres. opt. 3 sg. mæge 440; pres. opt. 3 pl. mæge 429; pret. 3 sg. mihte 189; pret. 3 pl. meahton 83, mihton 114, 206, 235, 488.
magorǣswa, wk.m. leader, prince; ns. *55*, 102, ds. magorǣswan *17*.
man(n), mc. MAN; gs. mannes 426; np. men 82, 373, 377; gp. manna 57, 143. 173, *334*, 356, 395, 517; ap. men 286.
mān, adj. criminal, wicked; dpf. mānum 149.
mānhūs, n. HOUSE of evil, hell; as. 578.
manig, adj. MANY; npm. monige 255; dpm. manegum 489, 585, mænegum 520.
mansceaða, wk.m. murderer of men? (or mānsceaða 'wicked revenger'?); ns. 37. (See Note.)
māra. See micel.
māðum, m. treasure, precious object; dp. māðmum 143; ap. mādmas 553.
*māðmhord, n. treasure; gp. māðmhorda 368.
meagollīce, adv. earnestly, emphatically; 570.
mearc, f. border; as. 160.
*mearchof, n. dwelling (court) in the borderland; np.? mearchofu 61. (See Note.)
mearcland, n. borderland, frontier country; dp. mearclandum 67.
*mearcþrēat, m. border-army; ds. mearcþrēate 173.
mearcweard, m. guardian of the borders, wolf; np. mearcweardas 168.
mearh, m. horse; gp. mēara 171. (Cf. MARE.)
mēce, mja. sword; ds. mēce 414, 495.

meltan, III. MELT; pret. 3 pl. multon 485.

menigeo, wk.f. multitude, crowd; ns. 521, mengeo 48, menio 334; as. menigeo 205.

*meorring, f. obstacle, hindrance; gp. meor[r]inga 62. (See Note.)

mēowle, f. maiden; ns. 547.

mere, mi. sea, (MERE) ; ns. 300, 459.

*meredēað, m. sea-DEATH; ns. 513; gp. meredēaða 465.

mereflōd, m. sea; gs. mereflōdes 504.

*merehwearf, m. seashore; ds. merehwearfe 559.

merestrēam, m. sea; ns. 210, 469; gs. merestrēames 489.

meretorht, adj. sea-bright; *346*.

*meretorr, m. sea-tower; np. meretorras 485.

mersc, m. MARSH; as. 333.

metan, v. measure, mark off, traverse; inf. 92, 104; pret. 3 pl. mǣton 171.

meteþegn, m. (MEAT-THANE), steward; np. meteþegnas 131.

Metod, m. God, the Lord; ns. 52, *414, 479*; gs. Metodes 102, 572.

meðel, n. (formal) speech; as. 255.

meðelstede, mi. meeting-place, place of assembly; ds. meðelstede 397, 585.

micel, adj. great, large, MUCH; nsm. 531; nsf. 521; nsn. 334; gsn. (adv.) miceles 'much' 143; asf. wk. miclan 275; comp. māra 'greater, MORE'; gsf. māran 426; gsn. 215; asm. 210; supl. mǣst 'greatest'; nsm. 349, 461, 465, 500, 522, 545, 583; nsn. 34, 85, 322, *557;* asn. 368, 395, 511; isn. mǣste 67.

mid, prep. with, together with, by means of; w. acc. 9, 416, 486; w. dat. or instr. 21, 56, 66, 86, 206, 245, 265, 275, 363, 407, 414, 420, 458, 502, 526.

middangeard, m. earth, world; as. 2, 48, 286, 583.

mid(d), adj. MID, middle of; dsf. middere 37; dpf. middum 168.

miht, fi. MIGHT, power; as. 9; dp. mihtum 517.

mihtig, adj. MIGHTY; nsm. 152, 205, 262, 292, 314, nsm.wk. mihtiga 485; comp. nsm. mihtigra 504.

*mihtmōd, n. strong feeling, passion; ns. 149.

milde, adj.ja. MILD, kind; supl. nsm. mildost 517.

mīlpæð, m. (MILE-PATH), road measured in miles; ap. mīlpaðas 171.

milts, fjo. kindness, mercy; as. miltse 292; gp. miltsa 572.

mīn, poss. pron. MY, MINE; d(i)sn. mīne 368; asf. mīne 262.

missenlīc, adj. of various kinds, of many kinds; comp. gpn.? missenlīcra (MS mismicelra) 373.

missēre, n. half-year; gp. missēra 49.

mōd, n. mind, spirit, heart; ns. 154, 245 ('courage'); gs. mōdes 98, 305; ds. mōde 226, 578; as.? mōd 'fury' 489; dp. mōdum 570. (MOOD)

mōder, fc. MOTHER; as. 371.

mōdgian, wk.2. behave proudly, rage; pret. 3 sg. mōdgade 331, mōdgode 459.

*mōdhēap, m. bold host; dp. mōdhēapum 242. (G-K *s.v.* mōdhæp 'reich an Mut'; but cf. mægenhēap.)

mōdhwæt, adj. brave, bold; npm. mōdhwate 124.

mōdig, adj. high-spirited, courageous; nsm. 55, 275, 469; gsm. mōdiges 255, 520; dsm. mōdgum 17; npm. mōdige 131, 327, 465; gpm. mōdigra 101, 300; apm. mōdge 480.

*mōdwǣg, m. wild or furious wave; gp. mōdwǣga *500*.

morgen, m. MORNing, MORROW; ns. 346; as. 98.

*mōrheald, adj. mountainous, in the MOORS?; np.? mōrheald 61. (See Note.)

morðor, n. MURDER, crime; as. 146.

mōtan, prp. be allowed, can, may; pres. 3 pl. mōton 264; pret. 3 pl. mōston 240; pret. (opt.?) 3 sg. mōste 510.

Moyses, m. (not declined) Moses; ns. 61, 101, 215, *559*, Moises 352; gs. 52, 152, 480; ds. 124; as. 2.

gemunan, prp. bear in mind, remember; pret. 3 pl. gemundon 220.

murnan, III. MOURN, be sad; pres. 3 pl. murnað 578.

*mūðhæl, n. safety or salutary words told by MOUTH; as. 520.

gemyntan, wk.1. determine, resolve; pp. gemynted 197.

nacud, adj. NAKED; nsm. 475.

nægan, wk.1. address, speak to; pret. 3 sg. nægde 23.

genægan, wk.1. approach (someone with something), bring; pret. 3 pl. genægdon 130.

nāgan. See āgan.

nalles, adv. NOt at ALL; 307.

nama, wk.m. NAME; as. naman 27, 381.

ne, adv. not (preceding vb.); 28, 82, 114, etc. (21✕); nē, conj. nor; 83, 238, 456.

nēah. near, NIGH; 1. adv. 1, 114, 381; comp. nēar 'NEARer'; 220, 308; 2. prep. 250.

nearo, nwa. difficulty, straits; np. nearwe 68.

nemnan, wk.1. name, call; pres. 3 pl. nemnað 561.

*genēopan, 11?. overwhelm?; pret. 3 sg. genēop (Nthb. for genēap?) 476. (See Note.) (Sievers-Brunner §384 An. 2: *genēopan, pret. genēop; cf. āhnēop *Guth.* 847.)

nēosan, wk.1. visit, seek, attack; inf. 475.

neowol, adj. prone, prostrate, deep; npm. neowle 114.

*nep, adj.? deprived of, lacking?; nsn.? 470. (Cf. ON hneppr, and Note.)

net, n. NET, network; ds. nette 74.

genēðan, wk.1. risk, venture; pret. 3 pl. genēðdon 538.

nigoða, adj. ninth; nsm. 378.

niht, fc. NIGHT; ds. niht 37; dp. nihtum 97, 168; ap. niht 63.

nihtlang, adj. NIGHT-LONG, lasting all night; asm. nihtlangne 208.

nihtscua, wk.m. NIGHT-shadow; np. nihtscuwan 114.

*nihtweard, m. NIGHT-guard; ns. 116.

geniman, IV. take, seize; pret. 3 sg. genam 406.

genīpan, I. grow dark, loom (over); pret. 3 sg. genāp 455.

nīwe, adj.ja. NEW; nsm. 'startling' 116; apm. nīwe 'unheard of, not existing before' 362; asm. wk. nīwan 381.

genīwian, wk.2. reNEW; pp. genīwad 35.

nō, adv. not at all, never; 399.

Nōe, m. Noah; ns. 362; ds. 378.

*norðweg, m. WAY to the NORTH; ap. norðwegas 68.

nū. 1. adv. NOW; 278, 525, 581; 2. conj. now that, since; 295, 421, 573.

nȳd, fi. necessity, compulsion; ds. nȳde 116 (or from nēod 'desire,' here meaning 'zealously, closely'—G-K).

genȳdan, wk.1. compel, force; pret. 3 pl. genȳddon 68. (See Note.)

*nȳdboda, m. messenger of force or distress; ns. 475.

*nȳdfara, m. one who travels from necessity, fugitive; ns. 208.

nymðe, conj. unless, except; 124, 439.

of, prep. w. dat. from; 155, 170, 269, 294, 417, 493, 538. (OF, OFF)

ofer, prep. 1. (w. dat.) OVER, above; 80, 110, 112, 117, 127, 163, 222, 239, 251, 320, 343, 345, 468; '(speak) to' 257; 2. (w. acc.) over, all over, across; 2, 48, 61, 286, 312, 318, 333, 362, 367, 403?, 437, 583.

oferbrǣdan, wk.1. OVERspread, cover over; pret. 3 sg. oferbrǣdde 73.

ofercuman, IV. OVERCOME, conquer; pret. 3 sg. ofercōm 21.

oferfaran, VI. pass OVER, traverse; pret. 3 sg. oferfōr 56.

ofergangan, rd. OVERrun, conquer; pres. 2 pl. ofergangað 529.

*oferholt, n. shield? (or spear?); ap. oferholt 157. (See Note.)

*oferteldan, III. cover OVER; pp. ofertolden 81.

ofest, f. haste, speed; ns. 293; ds. ofste 223; dp. ofstum 282.

oft, adv. OFTen; 191.

ōht, f. persecution, pursuit; ns. 136.

on, prep. 1. (w. dat.) ON, in; 8, 46, 106, etc. (45×); 2. (w. acc.) on, in, into; 32, 53, 59, 68, 98, 129, 135, 167, 186, 199, 216, 218, 229, 311, 319, 337, 350, 369, 375, 386, 534, 536, 554, 587.

on, adv. ON; 278, 313, 491.

onbrinnan, III. set fire to, kindle; pret. 3 sg. onbran 398.

oncyrran, wk.1. turn (back); pp. npm. oncyrde 452.

onettan, wk.1. hurry, hasten; pret. 3 sg. onette 313.

onfindan, III. FIND out, discover; pret. 3 sg. onfand 502.

ongangan, rd. go, move; inf. 156.

ongēn, prep. w. dat. AGAINst; 455.

onginnan, III. beGIN; pret. 3 pl. ongunnon 552.

ongitan, v. perceive, recognize, know; pret. 3 pl. ongēton 90, 453, 519.

onhrēran, wk.1. stir, arouse; pp. onhrēred 226, 483.

onlēon, I. give, grant, lend; pres. 3 sg. onlȳhð 572.

onlūcan, II. (UNLOCK), reveal; inf. 565.

*onnīed, f. compulsion? oppression?; as. 139. (Cf. ON ánauð.)

onriht, adj. proper, right, partaking of?; asn.? 358. (See Note.)

onsǣlan, wk.1. untie, loosen; pp. onsǣled 551.

onsēon, v. SEE; pret. 3 pl. onsēgon 178.

onþēon, I. be of service, thrive; inf. 241.

onþringan, III. press forward, press on; pret. 3 sg. onþrang 343.

onwist, f. being in a place, habitation; as. 18.

open, adj. OPEN; nsn. 580.

ōr, n. front, van; ds. ōre 326.

ortrȳwe, adj. hopeless, despairing; nsn. 154.

orþanc, m. skill, cunning; dp. orþancum 359.

orwēne, adj. w. gen. hopeless, despairing; npm. orwēnan 211.

oð. 1. prep. w. acc. up to, as far as; 298, 444; 2. conj. until; 215. (See also oðþæt.)

ōðer, adj. OTHER, one of two; nsn. 108; dsn. ōðrum 347, 544.

*oðfaran, VI. escape; pp. oðfaren 64.

oðlǣdan, wk.i. lead away, withdraw; pp. oðlǣded 537.

oðþæt, conj. until; 59, 127, 204, 479.

oððe, conj. OR; 210, 582.

*oðþicgan, v. take from, seize; pret. 3 sg. oðþah 338.

pað, m. PATH; as. 488. (See Note.)

rǣd, m. advice, counsel, what is of value; ns. 568; as. 6, 269; gp. rǣda 516; ap. rǣdas 558. (REDE)

rǣran, wk.i. REAR, raise; pret. 3 pl. rǣrdon 325.

rǣs, m. rush, onslaught; ns. 329.

ræst, fjo. REST, resting-place; ns. 134.

rǣswa, wk.m. leader, prince; np. rǣswan 234.

rand, m. shield; ap. randas 332, 554.

randburh, f. shield-wall (of the walls of water); np. randbyrig 464.

*randgebeorh, n. shield-wall, protection as of a shield (of the walls of water); as. 296.

randwiga, wk.m. (shield-)warrior; np. randwigan 126; gp. randwigena 134.

randwiggend, m. (shield-)warrior; gp. randwiggendra 436.

rēad, adj. RED; apm. rēade 296; dsm. wk. rēadan 134; dpm. wk. rēodan 413 (see Note).

rēaf, n. clothing; as.(p.?) rēaf 554 (or 'spoils'?); dp. rēafum 212.

reccan, wk.i. narrate, expound; pres. 3 pl. reccað 359.

gerecenian, wk.i. explain, solve; pp. gerecenod 568. (RECKON)

regnþēof, m. arch-THIEF; np. regnþēofas 581.

rēodan. See rēad.

*rēofan, II. break, rend; pp. npf. rofene 464.

reordigean, wk.2. speak, talk; inf. 256; pret. 3 sg. reordode 516.

rīce, nja. kingdom, rule; gs. rīces 256; as. rīce 524, 581.

rīdan, I. RIDE; pret. 3 sg. rād 173.

gerīdan, I. (RIDE), move; pret. 3 sg. [ge]rād 248.

riht, adj. (RIGHT), straight, direct; asf. rihte 126.

riht, n. RIGHT, duty, privilege; as. 186, 338, 352; on riht 'rightly' 554.

rīm, n. number, reckoning; ds. rīme 372; as. rīm 436. (RIME)

gerīman, wk.i. count, number; inf. 440.

*rincgetæl, n. number of warriors; as. 234.

rodor, m. sky, heaven; as. 464.

rōf, adj. strong, brave; np. rōfan 98; gp. rōfra 226.

Rūbēn, m. Reuben; gs. Rūbēnes 332.

rūn, f. mystery, secret; ns. 568. (RUNE)

rȳman, wk.i. clear away; pret. 3 sg. rȳmde 480.

gerȳman, wk.i. clear away, make room; pp. gerȳmed 284.

sǣ, m(f)i. SEA; ns. 473; ds. sǣ 134; dp. sǣm 443, 530.

sǣbeorg, m. SEA-hill, shore; gp. sǣbeorga 442.

*sǣcir, m. SEA-ebbing, retreat of water?; ns.? 291. (See Note.)

sǣd, n. SEED; gp. sǣda 374.

*sǣfæsten, n. SEA-FASTness, sea-stronghold; ns. 127.

sǣgrund, m. (SEA-bottom), sea-depth; ap. sǣgrundas 289.

sǣl, mfi. joy, happiness; dp. sǣlum 106, 532.

*sǣlāf, f. leavings of the SEA, spoils (or survivors of shipwreck?); ap. sǣlāfe 552.

sǣlan, wk.1. bind, tie; pp. apm. sǣlde 298.

gesǣlan, wk.1. befall, chance; pret. 3 sg. gesǣlde 316.

sǣleoda, m. SEAfarer, sailor; ns. 374.

sǣman, m. SEAMAN, sailor; np. sǣmen 105; gp. sǣmanna 479.

sǣstrēam, m. SEA-STREAM, sea, wave; dp. sǣstrēamum 250.

sǣweall, m. WALL formed by the SEA; ns. 302.

*sǣwīcing, m. SEA-viking, sailor; np. sǣwīcingas 333.

sanc. See sang.

sand, n. SAND, shore; ds. sande 220, 302; as.? sand 291; np. sand 471; ap. sand *442*.

sang, m. SONG, psalm, singing; gs. sances 309; as. sang 544.

sāwol, f. SOUL; dp. sāwlum 497; ap. sāwla 586.

sceacan, VI. SHAKE, move rapidly; pret. 3 sg. sceōc 176.

sceādan, rd. divide, separate; pret. 3 pl. sceō[don] 554.

gesceādan, rd. (divide), judge, decide; inf. 505.

scead, n. SHADE, shadow; np. sceado *113*.

sceaft, m. (SHAFT), spear; dp. sceaftum 344.

scēat, m. region, district; np. scēattas 429.

gescēon, wk.1. happen (to), befall, give; pp. gescēod 507.

scēotend, mc. (SHOOTer), warrior; dp. scēotendum 112.

gesceð ð an, VI. injure, harm; pret. 3 sg. gescēod 489.

scīnan, I. SHINE; inf. 110; pret. 3 sg. sceān 125; pret. 3 pl. scinon 113, 467.

scip, n. SHIP; gs. scipes 375.

scīr, adj. bright, gleaming; npm. scīre 112. (SHEER)

scīrwerod, adj. brightly clad; nsm. 125.

scræf, n. pit, cavern (of hell); ns. 580.

gescrīfan, I. decree, assign; pret. 3 sg. gescrāf 139.

scrīðan, I. glide, move, roam; pret. 3 sg. scrāð 39.

sculan, prp. SHALL, ought to; pres. 3 sg. sceal 423; SHOULD, had to, was to; pret. 3 sg. sceolde 116, 317.

scyld, m. SHIELD; np. scyldas 125.

gescyldan, wk.1. protect, guard; pret. 3 sg. gescylde 72.

scyldhrēoða, wk.m. shield-ornament; np. scyldhrēoðan *113*.

sē, sēo, þæt. 1. def. article and dem. pron. THE, THAT; nsm. se 141, 202, 273, 295, 380, 389, 393, 412, 485; nsf. sēo 48, 214, 304, 477; nsn. þæt (þ) 19, 310; gsm. þæs 508; gsn. þæs 315, 507; dsm. þām 122, 198, 224, 225, 321, 323, 397, 541?, 564, 585, ðām 153, 189; dsf. þǣre 275, 331; dsn. þām 170, 543; asm. þone 172, 364, 400, 406; asf. þā 83, ðā 205; ism. þÿ 21, ðÿ 496; isn. þÿ 56, þan 134; asn. þæt (þ) 150, 151, 186, 234; np. þā 297; dp. þām 197, 299, 532; ap. þā 82, 254, 513; 2. subst. that one, he she, that, it; nsn. þæt (þ) 233, 380; gsn. þæs 49, 144, 'so' 439; asm. þone 8; asn. þæt (þ) 359, 377, 406; isn. þan 245, þon 374, 381, 588 (see forðon), þÿ (before comp. 'THE, any') 259, 399; ap. þā 61;

3. rel. pron. that, who, which, what; nsm. sē 205, 274, 380, 522; nsn. þæt 185; asm. ðone 28; asn. þæt 525; isn. þȳ (læs) 'LEST' 117, þȳ 349; gp. þāra 95; ap. þā 285, 287, 540; 4. rel. w. particle þe. nsm. sē ðe 7, 54, 138, 476, 514; nsf. sēo þe 423; gsn. þæs þe (semi-conj. 'because') 51; np. þā þe 360; gp. þāra þe 189, 376, 395, þāra ðe 365, 563; ap. þā þe 235.

sealt, adj. SALT(y) ; asm. sealtne 333; dpf. sealtum 473; apf. sealte 442.

searo, nwa. armor, war-gear; as. searo 219; dp. searwum 471 (or 'cunningly, by tricks'?).

secgan, wk.3. SAY, tell; inf. 7, 510; pres. 3 pl. secgað 377, 573; pret. 3 sg. sægde 559.

gesecgan, wk.3. SAY, tell; pret. 3 sg. gesægde 24; ger. gesecgenne 438.

sefa, wk.m. mind, heart; ds. sefan 439.

segl, m. SAIL; ns. *105;* ds. segle *81;* np. seglas 89.

*seglrōd, f. (SAIL-rod), yardarm; as. seglrōde 83.

segn, mn. standard, banner; ds. segne 319; as. segn 127, 172; np. segnas 533; dp. segnum 552; ap. segnas 302.

segncyning, m. KING with banner?; ns. 172.

seledrēam, m. joy in the hall; np. seledrēamas 36.

sēlost. See gōd, adj.

seomian, wk.2. wait, lie in wait; pret. 3 pl. seomedon 209.

Sēon, f. Zion; gs. Sēone 386.

gesēon, V. SEE, perceive; inf. 83, 207; pret. 3 sg. geseah 88; pret. 3 pl. gesāwon 103, 126, 155, 387, 539, 550.

*setlrād, f. setting, sinking; as.? setlrāde 109. (See Note.)

gesettan, wk.I. SET, establish; pret. 3 sg. gesette 27.

sibgedriht, f. band of kinsmen; ns. 214.

sibgemāgas, m.pl. kinsmen; np. 386.

sīd, adj. large, broad, wide; apm. sīde 260; comp. apn. (asn.?) sīddra 428.

*sigebȳme, f. trumpet of victory; np. sigebȳman 533.

Sigelwaras (-e), m.pl. Ethiopians; gp. Sigelwara 69.

*sigerīce, n. realm of victory; as. 27, 530. (G-K, B-T: adj.).

*sigetīber, n. sacrifice for victory; ds. sigetībre 402.

sigor, m. victory; gp. sigora 16, 272, 434.

*sigorworc, n. deed of victory; gp. sigorworca 316.

Simeōn, m. Simeon; gs. Simeōnes 341.

sīn, pers. pron. his; asm. sīnne 412.

sinc, n. treasure, wealth; ds. since 36.

*sincald, adj. perpetually COLD; nsm. wk. sincalda 473.

singan, III. SING, sound; pret. 3 sg. sang 132; pret. 3 pl. sungon 159, 164, 533.

sittan, V. SIT; pret. 3 pl. sǣton 212.

gesittan, V. (SIT on), inhabit, occupy; pres. 2 pl. gesittað 530; pres. 3 pl. gesittað 443.

sīð, m. 1. journey, undertaking, expedition; ns. 207; gs. sīðes 53; ds. sīðe 105; as. sīð 97, 479, 510 ('fate'); 2. time, occasion; ns. 22.

*sīðboda, m. messenger or herald of the march; ns. 250.

sīðfæt, m. course, march, journey; ds. sīðfate 564; as. sīðfæt 81.

sīðian, wk.2. go, journey; pres. opt. 2 pl. sīðien 272.

sīðor, adv. later, following; 336.

siððan. 1. conj. (SINCE), when, after; 64, 86, 132, 144, 155, 224, 308, 316, 499, 503, 541; 2. adv. afterwards; 384.

slēan, VI. strike, SLAY; inf. 412; imper. 2 sg. sleh 419; pret. 3 sg. slōh 280, 485.

geslēan, VI. strike; pret. 3 sg. [g]eslōh 494. (See Note.)

slūpan, II. slip, glide; pret. 3 sg. slēap 491.

snelle, adv. quickly, promptly; 220.

snottor, adj. prudent, wise; nsm. 374, 439; nsm. wk. snottra 389.

somnigean, wk.2. assemble, collect; inf. 217.

somod, adv. together; 214.

sōð, adj. true; nsm. 479; dpm. sōðum 30; dpn. sōðum 438, 564. (SOOTH)

sōð, n. truth; ns. 420; as. 291.

sōðfæst, adj. righteous, upright; nsm. 9, 434; gpm. sōðfæstra 586.

*sōðwundor, n. true WONDER; gp. sōðwundra 24.

gespannan, rd. clasp, bind on; pret. 3 sg. gespēon 174.

spēd, fi. success, luck; as. spēde 153, spēd 514 (cf. Sievers-Brunner §269.1). (SPEED)

spel, n. tale, news; np. (as.?) spel 203. (See Note.) (SPELL)

spelboda, m. messenger; as. (p.?) spelbodan 514.

*spildsīð, m. destructive expedition; ds. spildsīðe 153.

spīwan, I. SPEW, spit out; pret. 3 sg. spāw 291?, 450.

sprǣc, f. SPEECH; ds. (as.?) sprǣce 560.

sprecan, V. SPEAK; pret. 3 sg. spræc 258, 277, 418, 520.

stæfn. See stefn.

stæð, n. shore, bank; ds. stæðe 548.

stān, m. STONE; ap. stānas 441.

standan, VI. STAND, stand out, arise, shine; inf. 539; pret. 3 pl. stōdon 111, 201, 460, 491, 533, stōdan 136.

gestandan, VI. STAND; pret. 3 sg. gestōd 303.

staðol, m. foundation, base; np. staðolas 285; ap. staðulas 474.

stefn, f. voice; ns. 417; ds. stefne 257, 276, 518; as. stefne 542; dp. stefnum 99, 546, stæfnum 463.

steorra, wk.m. STAR; ap. steorran 441.

gestēpan, wk.1. raise, support; pp. npm. gestēpte 297.

stīgan, I. go, climb (up or down); pret. 3 pl. stigon 319, 385.

gestīgan, I. climb (on), set foot on; pret. 3 sg. gestāh 503.

gestillan, wk.1. quiet, restrain, STILL; inf. 254.

stille, adv. STILL; 300, 518.

storm, m. STORM, tumult; ns. 460.

strǣt, f. STREET, highway; as. strǣte 126.

strēam, m. STREAM, water(s) of the sea; ns. 472; np. strēamas 460; ap. strēamas 296.

stȳran, wk.1. check, restrain; inf. 417.

sum, adj. (always written sū) SOMEone, one (w. gp.); nsm. 357; nsn. 345; asn. 279.

sund, n. sea; as. sund 319. (SOUND)

sunne, wk.f. SUN; gs. sunnan 81, 109.

sunu, mu. SON; ns. 389, 426; as. sunu 402, 420; np. sunu 332, 341; dp. sunum 18, 363.

sūðan, adv. (be sūðan) to the SOUTH; 69.

*sūðweg, m. (SOUTH-WAY), road(s) or region(s) to the south; dp. sūð-wegum 155.

*sūðwind, m. SOUTH-WIND; ns. 289.

swā, 1. adv. so, thus; 49, 143, 194, 314, 339, 377, 404, [514], 516, 562, 581; 2. conj. as; 82 ('so that'), 101, 352, 359, 388.

swǣs, adj. (one's) own, dear; asm. swǣsne 402.

swāpan, rd. drive, sweep, rush; pret. 3 sg. swēop 481.

swefan, v. sleep, be dead; pret. 3 pl. swǣfon 36, 496.

swēg, mi. sound, noise; ns. 309; as. 534.

*geswelgan, III. SWALLOW, devour; pret. 3 sg. geswealh 513.

sweltan, III. die; pret. 3 pl. swulton 465.

gesweorcan, III. grow dark; pret. 3 sg. geswearc 462.

sweord, n. SWORD; ds. sweorde 420.

*sweordwīgend, mc. (SWORD-)warrior; gp. sweordwīgendra 260.

swēot, n. band, troop; ns. 497; as. 220; dp. swēoton 127, swēotum 341.

swerian, VI. SWEAR; pres. 3 sg. swereð 432.

swipian, wk.2. scourge, lash; pret. 3 sg. swipode 464.

swīð, adj. strong; comp. nsf. swīðre 'right' 280.

swīðan, wk.1. strengthen; pp. swīðed 517.

geswīðan, wk.1. strengthen; pp. geswīðed 30.

swiðrian (sweðrian,) wk.2. retire, dwindle, subside; pret. 3 sg. swiðrade 242, swiðrode 309, 466; pret. 3 pl. swiðredon 113.

swōl, n. burning; as. 239 (MS swor).

sylf, intensive pron. SELF, own; nsm. sylfa 280, 584; gsm. sylfes 9, 27, 434.

gesyllan, wk.1. give, endow; inf. 400; pret. 3 sg. gesealde 16, 20.

syllīc, adj. strange, wonderful; nsn. 109.

synfull, adj. SINFUL; gpm. synfullra 497.

synn, fjo. SIN; dp. synnum 336.

tācen, n. TOKEN, symbol; ds. tācne 281.

tǣcan, wk.1. TEACH; inf. 570.

getellan, wk.1. count, number; pret. 3 pl. getealdon 224; pp. geteled 232, 372. (TELL)

tempel, n. TEMPLE; as. 391.

getēon, II. draw; pret. 3 sg. getēag 407.

tēonhete, mi. malicious hate; ds. tēonhete 224.

tīber, n. sacrifice, offering; as. 416.

[tīd, f. time; as. (288).]

getimbrian, wk.2. build; pret. 3 sg. getimbrede 391.

tīrēadig, adj. glorious, famous; gp. tīrēadigra 184, 232.

tīrfæst, adj. glorious; apm. tīrfæste 63.

tō, prep. w. dat. TO, towards, for, as; 88, 192, 197, etc. (19X).

tōsomne, adv. together; 207. (See Note.)

tredan, V. TREAD (on), traverse; inf. 160.

trēow, f. truth, faith, covenant; gs. trēowe 426; as. trēowe 423; dp. trēowum 149; ap. trēowa 366.

trum, adj. strong; nsm. 521.

trymian, wk.1. be arrayed; pret. 3 pl. trymedon 158.

tuddortēonde, adj. bearing offspring; gp. tuddortēondra 372.

getwǣfan, wk.2. take away, deprive; pret. 3 sg. getwǣf[d]e 119.

twēgen, m., twā fn., num. (TWAIN), TWO; nm. twēgen 94; af. twā 63; an. twā 184.

twelf, num. TWELVE; am. twelfe 225.

twēone, distrib. num. w. be. (two), BETWEEN; dp. twēonum 443, 530.

tȳn (tīen? tīn?), num. (written x) TEN; 232.

þā, 1. adv. then, thereupon; 30, 33, 63, 87, 98, 133, 142?, 154, 247, 249, 252, 310, 347, [411], 417, 547, ðā 22, 276; 2. conj. when; 48, 202, 277, 319, 406, 485, 537, ðā 404.

þǣr, 1. adv. THERE; 16, 24, 71, 89, 91, 172, 194, 206, 340, 347, 387, 389, 539, ðǣr 135, 456; 2. conj. where, wherever; 152, 272, 330, 458, 579, 588.

þæt, conj. (always written þ) THAT, so that; 23, 91, 123, 143, 206, 264, 270, 292, 294, 317, 336, 378, 409, 422, 435, 440, 496, 504, 529, 571.

þætte, conj. THAT; 151, 510.

þanon, adv. thence, thereupon; 558.

þe, rel. particle. See sē (þe), þēah (þe).

þēah, adv. nevertheless, however; (swā) þēah 339.

þēah, conj. THOUGH; 29; þēah þe 259; þēah ðe 209, 538; ðēah þe 141.

þeccan, wk.1. cover; pret. 3 pl. þeahton 288.

þegn, m. THANE, follower; np. þegnas 170.

þencan, wk.1. intend; pret. 3 pl. þōhton 51. (THINK)

þenden, conj. as long as, while; 255.

þengel, m. prince; ns. 173.

þēod, f. people, nation, army; as. 160; gp. ðēoda 326; ap. þēode 357, ðēode 487.

þēoden, m. lord, prince; ns. 363, 432.

þēodenhold, adj. loyal to (one's) lord; np. þēodenholde 182; ap. þēodenholde 87.

*þēodmægen, n. mighty host; ns. 342.

þēodscipe, m. law, authority; gs. þēodscipes 571.

geðēon, 1. prosper, flourish; pret. 3 sg. geðāh 143.

þes, þēos, þis, dem. pron. THIS; nsm. þis 273; nsf. þēos 280, 431, 521; nsn. þis 574; dsm. þissum 263; asm. þysne 577; asf. þās 25, ðās 274, 522.

geþicgan, v. receive, become entitled to; pret. 3 sg. geþah 354.

þider, adv. THITHER; 46, 196.

þīn, poss. pron. THY, (THINE); gsn. þīnes 435; asn. þīn 419; npm. þīne 445.

þolian, wk.2. suffer, endure; inf. 324. (THOLE)

þonne, conj. when(ever); 325; 586; THAN; 373, 410, 429.

þracu, f. attack, power, onrush; ns. þracu 326.

*þræcwīg, m. hard fighting; gs. þræcwīges 182.

þrī, num. THREE; dm. þrīm 363.

þridda, num. THIRD; nsn. þridda 87, þridde 342.

þrymfæst, adj. glorious, noble; nsm. 363.

þrȳð, fi. might, strength; dp. þrȳðum 340.

þū, pers. pron. THOU; ns. þū 419, 422; gs. þīn 421; as. þē 432; pl. gē 'YE'; 259, 270, 272, 278, 294, 528, 529; dp. ēow 266, 268, 271, 292.

þūf, m. military standard, banner; np. þūfas 342; ap. þūfas 160.

þunian, wk.2. stand out, be prominent; inf. 160. (THUNDer)
þurfan, prp. need; pres. 3 sg. þearf 426.
þurh, prep. w. acc. THROUGH; 262, 434, 480, 540.
þurstig, adj. THIRSTY; npm. þurstige 182.
þūsend, n. THOUSAND; ap. þūsendo 184.
þūsendmǣlum, adv. in or by THOUSANDS; 196.
þyncan, wk.1. seem, appear; pret. 3 pl. þūhton 540.

ūhttīd, f. time before daybreak; as. 216.
uncūð, adj. unknown, strange; asn. 58, 313?. (UNCOUTH)
under, prep. UNDER; 1. (w. dat.) 228, 236, 376, 579; 2. (w. acc.) 539.
unforht, adj. fearless, brave; nsm. 335; npm. unforhte 180, 328.
*ungrund, adj. bottomless, vast; gsm. ungrundes 509. (Cf. ungrynde, *Riming Poem* 49.)
*unhlēow, adj. offering no shelter, unfriendly; asm. unhlēowan 495.
unnan, prp. grant; pret. 1 sg. on 269.
unrīm, n. countless number; as. 261.
unswīciende, adj. unfailing, undeceiving; nsf. unswīciendo 425.
unweaxen, adj. not grown up, young; asm. unweaxenne 413.
up, adv. UP(wards), on high; 200, 248, 253, 282, 295, 411, 460, 462, 491.
uplang, adj. UPright; nsm. 303.
uprodor, m. sky, heaven; ns. 430; as. 4, 26, 76, 587.
ūt, adv. OUT; 187.

wāc, adj. weak, feeble; apm. wāc[e] 233.
wadan, VI. go, advance; pret. 3 sg. wōd 311. (WADE)
gewadan, VI. pervade; pret. 3 sg. gewōd 463.
wæccan, wk.1. WATCH, be awake; pres. ptc. nsf. wæccende 213.
wǣg, m. wave, sea; gs. wǣges (MS sæs) *467;* ds. wǣge 458; np. wǣgas 484.
wǣg, m. wall; as. 495.
wǣgfaru, f. passage through the waves; ns. 298.
wǣgstrēam, m. sea; as. 311.
*wælbenn, f. deadly wound; np. wælbenna 492. (See Note.)
*wælcēasega, wk.m. carrion-picker; ns. 164.
*wælfæðm, m. deadly embrace; dp. wælfæðmum 481.
*wælgryre, mi. deadly terror (or terror at death); np. (s.?) wælgryre 137.
wælhlence, f. coat of mail; as. wælhlencan *176.*
wælmist, m. death-MIST; ns. 451.
*wælnet, n. corselet; np. wælnet 202.
wælsliht, m. battle, carnage; np. (gs.?) wælslihtes 328. (See Note.)
wǣpen, n. WEAPON; gp. wǣpna 20, 328, 451.
wǣpnedcyn, n. male sex; gs. wǣpnedcynnes 188.
wǣr, f. covenant, treaty; gs. wǣre 140; as. wǣre 147, 387, 422.
wæstm, m. growth, size; dp. wæstmum 243.
wæter, n. WATER; ns. 283, 451; gp. wætera 539.
wǣðan, wk.1. hunt; pret. 3 sg. wǣðde 481.
wāfian, wk.2. be amazed, marvel; pret. 3 pl. wāfedon 78.
Waldend, mc. ruler, the Lord; ns. 16, 433; as. 422.

waðum, m. wave; gp. waðema 472.

wēa, wk.m. woe, misery; gs. wēan 213; as. (p.?) wēan 140.

wealdan, rd. control, have power over; pret. 3 sg. wēold 105.

wealhstōd, m. interpreter; ns. 565.

weall, m. WALL; ap. weallas 539.

weallan, rd. (WELL), gush; pret. 3 pl. wēollon 492.

weallfæsten, n. defending WALL, bulwark; as. wealfæsten 283; np. weall-
   fæsten 484.

weard, mf. guardian, keeper; ns. 487, 504, 566; np. weardas 221.

wēdan, wk.1. rage, be furious; pret. 3 sg. wēdde 490.

weder, n. WEATHER, storm; dp. wederum 118.

*wederwolcen, n. cloud; ns. 75.

weg, m. WAY, road; np. wegas 283, 458.

wegan, v. carry; inf. 157; pret. 3 pl. wǣgon 180 (intransitive? 'move'?), 540.
   (WEIGH)

wēn, fi. expectation; dp. wēnum 176, 213; wēnan 165.

weorðan, III. become; inf. 424; pres. opt. 3 sg. weorðe 439; pres. opt. 2 pl.
   weorðen 'escape' 294; pret. 3 sg. wearð 142, 154, 349, 455; pret. 3 pl.
   wurdon 144; aux. with pp.: pret. 3 sg. wearð 'was' 506.

geweorðan, III. happen, be; pret. opt. 3 sg. gewurde 365.

geweorðian, wk.2. honor, dignify; pres. opt. 2 pl. gewurðien 270; pp. asm.
   gewurðodne 31; pp. geweorðod 548; pret. 3 sg. gewyrðode 10, ge-
   weorðode 86.

wer, m. man; ns. 560; np. weras 539, 544; gp. wera 3, 149, 236, 515, 556.

*wērbēam, m. protecting pillar? gs.? wērbēamas 487. (See Note.)

wērig, adj. WEARY; npm. wērige 130.

werigean, wk.1. defend, protect; inf. 237; pres. 3 sg. wereð 274; pret. 3 pl.
   weredon 202.

werigend, mc. defender, protector; np. werigend 556.

werod, n. band, host; ns. 100, 221, 233, 299, 532, werud 204; gs. werodes 31,
   65, 230, 258; ds. werode 170; as. werod 123, 194, werud 535; gp. weroda
   8, 23, 92, 137, 590, wereda 433; dp. weredum 117.

werþēod, f. people, nation; np. werðēode 562; gp. werþēoda 383.

wesan. See eom.

wēsten, nja. desert, wilderness; ds. wēstenne 8, 123.

*wēstengryre, mi. terror of the wilderness; ns. 117.

wīc, n. camp, station; ns. 87, 133; dp. wīcum 200.

*wīcan, I. give way, yield; pret. 3 pl. wicon 484.

wīcian, wk.2. camp, dwell; inf. 117.

*wīcsteal, m. camping place; as. 92.

wīd, adj. WIDE, extended, spacious; dpm. wīdum 75; dsm. wk. wīdan 590;
   comp. apn. (asn.?) wīddra 428.

wīde, adv. WIDEly, far and wide; 39, 42, 481.

wīdeferð, mn. (as. as adv.) for a long time, forever; 51.

wīf, n. woman; np. wīf 544. (WIFE)

wīg, mn. war, fighting; gs. wīges 176.

wiga, wk.m. warrior; as. wigan 188; np. wigan 311.

*wīgblāc, adj. splendid in armor; nsn. 204.

wīgbord, n. battle-shield; np. 467.

wīgend, mc. warrior; np. 180, 328.

*wīgleoð, n. war-song; as. 221.

wīglīc, adj. warlike; nsn. 233.

wīgþrēat, m. war band; as. wīg[þrēat] 243.

willa, m. WILL; gs. willan 519.

willan, anv. WILL, wish, be about to; pres. 3 sg. wile 261, 525, 565, 570; pres. 2 pl. (imperative?) willað 266; pres. opt. 3 sg. wille 7; pret. 3 sg. wolde 256, 400, 412, 415, 505; pret. 3 pl. woldon 150, 323, 454; pret. opt. 3 sg. wolde 244.

windan, III. WIND, revolve; pret. 3 sg. wand 80; pret. 3 pl. wundon 342.

winnan, III. fight; pret. 3 pl. wunnon 515.

wīs, adj. WISE; npm. wīse 377; supl. nsm. wīsesta 393.

wīsa, wk.m. leader; ns. 13, 258.

wīsian, wk.2. guide, lead; pret. 3 sg. wīsode 348.

wīslic, adj. wise; apn. wīslīcu 569.

wist, fi. food, feast; ds. wiste 130.

witan, prp. know; pres. 1 sg. wāt 291; pres. 3 pl. witon 578; pret. 3 sg. wisse 409; pret. 3 pl. wiston 29, 69.

gewītan. I. depart, go; pret. 3 sg. gewāt 41, 346, 460.

wīte, n. punishment, torment; dp. wītum 33, 140.

wit(e)ga, m. prophet; gs. witgan 390.

witian, wk.2. pp. witod. appointed, ordained, certain; gsm. witodes 519; dsf. witodre 472.

wītig, adj. wise; nsm. 25, 80.

*wītrod (wīgtrod), n. path of an army, war-path; as. 492. (See Note.)

wið, prep. w. dat. or acc. against, WITH; 20, 72, 172, 224, 237, 303, 422, 515.

*wiðfaran, VI. escape; pret. 3 pl. wiðfōron 541.

wlanc, adj. proud, arrogant; npm. wlance 170; apm. wlance 204; apf. wlance 487.

wolcen, ma. cloud; (in pl.) heavens; ns. 93; gp. wolcna 298; dp. wolcnum 80, 350.

wōma, m. noise, uproar; ns. 202; as. wōman 100.

womm, m. stain, sin; dp. wommum 575.

wonn, adj. dark, black; nsm. 164. (WAN)

wōp, m. weeping, lamentation; ns. 42, 200.

word, n. WORD; as. 418, 428; dp. wordum 23, 299, 377, 438, 532, 564; ap. word 569.

wordriht, n. law in WORDS; ap. 3.

worn, m. large number, many; as. 56, 195.

woruld, f. WORLD; as. 25.

worulddrēam, m. earthly joy; gp. worulddrēama 42.

woruldrīce, nja. WORLD(-kingdom); ds. woruldrīce 365, 393.

wracu, f. suffering, exile; ds. wræce 383.

wræclīc, adj. strange, extraordinary; apn. wræclīco 3.

*wræcmon, m. fugitive, exile; ns. 137.

wrætlīc, adj. wonderful, splendid; nsf. wrætlīcu 298.

wrāð, adj. hostile, enemy; gpm. wrāðra 20. (WROTH)

wrecca, wk.m. wanderer, WRETCH; dp. wreccum 575.

wrōht, f. (slander), strife; as. 147.

wuldor, n. glory; gs. wuldres 100, 270, 418, 428, 535, 544; ds. wuldre 86;
   as. wuldor 387.

Wuldorcyning, m. glorious KING, God; as. 590.

wuldorfæst, adj. glorious; nsm. 390.

wuldorgesteald, n. glorious possessions; as. (p.?) 556.

wulf, m. WOLF; np. wulfas 164.

wundor, n. WONDER, miracle; ns. 108; as. 519; gp. wundra 10.

wurðmynd, fn.(m.)i. honor, dignity; dp. wurðmyndum 258.

wyrcan, wk.i. (WORK), make; pres. 3 sg. wyrceð 282; pret. 3 sg. worhte 25.

gewyrcan, wk.i. make, build; pret. 3 sg. geworhte 396.

wyrd, fi. fate, destiny; ns. 458; ds. wyrde *472;* gp. wyrda 433.

wyrm, mi. WORM, serpent; ns. 579.

wyrnan, wk.i. prevent; inf. 51.

wyrpan, wk.i. restore (oneself), recover; pret. 3 pl. wyrpton 130.

yfel, n. EVIL; gp. yfela 580.

ylde, mi.pl. men; np. yldo 437; gp. yldo 28.

yldo, wk.f. old age; ns. 582. (ELD)

ymb, prep. about, around, concerning; 63, 145, 180.

ymbhwyrft, m. circuit; ns. 430; as. 26.

*ymbwīcigean, wk.2. camp around, surround; inf. 65.

*ypping, f. mounting mass (of water)?; np. yppinge 499. (See Note.)

yrfelāf, f. heir; as. yrfelāfe 403.

yrfeweard, m. heir; ns.? 142.

yrmðu, f. misery, calamity; dp. yrmðum 265.

yrre, adj.ja. angry; nsm. 506.

ȳð, fjo. wave; ns. 282; np. ȳðe 288; gp. ȳða 456; dp. ȳðum 450, 473; ap.
   ȳða 442.

ȳðlāf, f. what is left by waves, shore; ds. ȳðlāfe 553.

YALE STUDIES IN ENGLISH

This volume is the one hundred and twenty-second of the Yale Studies in English, founded by Albert Stanburrough Cook in 1898 and edited by him until his death in 1927. Tucker Brooke succeeded him as editor, and served until 1941, when Benjamin C. Nangle succeeded him.

The following volumes are still in print. Orders should be addressed to YALE UNIVERSITY PRESS, New Haven, Connecticut.

117. KNIGHT, DOUGLAS, Pope and the Heroic Tradition. A Critical Study of His *Iliad*. $3.00.
118. BOWDEN, WILLIAM R., The English Dramatic Lyric, 1603–42. A Study in Stuart Dramatic Technique. $4.00.
119. DAVIS, MERRELL R., Melville's *Mardi*. A Chartless Voyage. $4.00.
120. WAITH, EUGENE M., The Pattern of Tragicomedy in Beaumont and Fletcher. $4.00.
121. MARSH, FLORENCE, Wordsworth's Imagery. A Study in Poetic Vision. $3.75.
122. IRVING, EDWARD BURROUGHS, JR. (Editor), The Old English *Exodus*. $5.00.